T0381794

THE EPISTEMOLOGY OF INDICATIVE CONDITIONALS

Conditionals are sentences of the form "If A, then B," and they play a central role in scientific, logical, and everyday reasoning. They have been in the philosophical limelight for centuries, and more recently, they have also been receiving attention from psychologists, linguists, and computer scientists. In spite of this, many key questions concerning conditionals remain unanswered. While most of the work on conditionals has addressed semantical questions – questions about the truth conditions of conditionals – this book focusses on the main epistemological questions that conditionals give rise to, such as: What are the probabilities of conditionals? When is a conditional acceptable or assertable? What do we learn when we receive new conditional information? In answering these questions, this book combines the formal tools of logic and probability theory with the experimental approach of cognitive psychology. It will be of interest to students and researchers in logic, epistemology, and the psychology of reasoning.

IGOR DOUVEN is Directeur de Recherche at Sciences, normes, décision, Université Paris-Sorbonne. He has published widely on topics in formal epistemology, social epistemology, the philosophy of language, metaphysics, and cognitive science.

THE EPISTEMOLOGY OF INDICATIVE CONDITIONALS

Formal and Empirical Approaches

IGOR DOUVEN

Sciences, normes, décision (CNRS)
Paris-Sorbonne University

CAMBRIDGE
UNIVERSITY PRESS

University Printing House, Cambridge CB2 8BS, United Kingdom

Cambridge University Press is part of the University of Cambridge.

It furthers the University's mission by disseminating knowledge in the pursuit of education, learning and research at the highest international levels of excellence.

www.cambridge.org
Information on this title: www.cambridge.org/9781107111455

© Igor Douven 2016

First published 2016

A catalogue record for this publication is available from the British Library

Library of Congress Cataloguing in Publication Data
Douven, Igor, author.
The epistemology of indicative conditionals : formal and empirical approaches : FINAL VERSION / Igor Douven.
pages cm
ISBN 978-1-107-11145-5 (hardback)
1. Grammar, Comparative and general – Conditionals.
2. Knowledge, Theory of. 3. Semantics (Philosophy) I. Title.
P292.5.D68 2015
415–dc23
2015016414

ISBN 978-1-107-11145-5 Hardback

Contents

List of Figures and Tables

Figures

Tables

Preface and Acknowledgments

The importance of the role that conditionals play in both everyday and scientific discourse and reasoning is hard to overestimate. Perhaps it is no surprise then that for quite some time, conditionals have been a central area of investigation not only in philosophy, but also in linguistics and psychology, and to some extent in computer science. What is surprising, however, is that despite the considerable expenditure of time and effort of many researchers from those fields, there is still little that one can say about conditionals that is not highly controversial. Even with regard to the most fundamental questions concerning conditionals, there is very little unanimity to be found. Those who have ever proposed a semantics of conditionals can consider themselves fortunate if the proposal won the approval of at least one colleague.

This book focusses on the distinctively epistemological questions that conditionals raise, such as questions concerning their acceptability conditions and probabilities. There is hardly more consensus on these epistemological questions than there is on the semantics of conditionals. And insofar as there *is* consensus, it is based on questionable assumptions. In this book, I aim to develop at least an outline of the epistemology of conditionals. I do so by relying on the combined use of formal and empirical methods.

While the use of formal and empirical methods in philosophy is viewed much more favorably now than it was when I was a graduate student twenty years ago – formal methods were then associated with logical empiricism, which was generally regarded as a deeply misguided research program, and empirical methods were considered to be perfectly fine, but just not as having a place in philosophy – I have in the course of working on this book met with considerable skepticism from friends and colleagues (some to be named in the following paragraphs) about the methodology of experimental psychology (which basically comprises the empirical methods I have relied on). The main complaint was invariably that this methodology fails to produce robust results: "Ask people a question in one way, and they'll give you one answer; ask the same question in a slightly different way, and you'll get a different answer."[1]

Probably the only real antidote to such worries is to engage in empirical research with experimental psychologists, who tend to operate in a much more careful and sophisticated manner than my skeptical friends and colleagues seem to suppose. The psychologists I have come to know and have worked with are all keenly aware of the possible sensitivity of their results to the way or ways these results have been elicited. Psychologists have devised refined methods for controlling for such sensitivity and for checking whether there are any artifacts in their data. Perhaps nothing is beyond *skeptical* doubt, but it is my firm conviction that many of the experimental results to be discussed in this book, on which the cogency of the conclusions to be reached will partly depend, are no more susceptible to *empirical* doubt than are the results from any experimental research.

Every day I benefit from what my teachers Jaap van Brakel and Dirk van Dalen taught me when I was a student at Utrecht University, and later at the University of Leuven. Dirk van Dalen introduced me to the use of formal methods, while Jaap van Brakel cautioned me against overenthusiastically using those methods for their own sake. I owe an equally great debt in this respect to Jos Uffink for many tutorials on Bayesian epistemology and probabilistic methods more generally. He was my unofficial teacher when we were both assistant professors at Utrecht University, Jos in the physics department while I was in the philosophy department. In those days, I also learned much from two other friends in the physics department, Henk de Regt and Fred Muller (later my colleague in Rotterdam), to both of whom I am grateful.

David Over and Sara Verbrugge introduced me to empirical approaches to conditionals. I am grateful to both for showing me the necessary ins and outs, and for opening up such a fascinating area of research for me. On various occasions, Shira Elqayam gave excellent advice on matters of experimental design, and I recollect with gratitude some practical SPSS tutorials that she gave. More recently, Henrik Singmann introduced me to R and often helped when I had got stuck. I thank Jean-François Bonnefon for instructing me on how to run online experiments.

---

[1] A related complaint from a (highly esteemed) colleague–philosopher: "If your participants' responses differ from my linguistic intuitions, there must be a design flaw somewhere in your experiment."

More or less for as long as I have been active in philosophy, I have been discussing philosophy and much else besides with Lieven Decock, Leon Horsten, and Mark van Atten. I have always enjoyed these discussions enormously, and have often been inspired by them. Even more than the discussions, I have enjoyed the friendship.

For the past five years, I have been able to spend most of my time on research, thanks to an Odysseus grant from the Government of the Flemish Community in Belgium, and to an endowment from the Board of Governors from the University of Groningen. The final stages of work on this book were completed after I had already been recruited by the CNRS as a senior research scientist and joined Sciences, Normes, décision at the Paris-Sorbonne University. I am profoundly grateful to all these institutions, and I am particularly grateful to Daniel Andler, the head of SND, and to the other members of the group for making me feel so welcome.

Vincenzo Crupi, Lieven Decock, David Over, Niels Skovgaard Olsen, Janneke van Wijnbergen-Huitink, and Christopher von Bülow read the whole manuscript. I am greatly indebted to them for pointing me toward shortcomings and providing me with many other valuable comments. I owe an equally great debt to Stefan Kaufmann and Philipp Koralus, who were the reviewers for Cambridge University Press and whose insightful reports led to numerous improvements of this work. Hilary Gaskin, my editor at the Press, also gave very valuable advice.

For comments on parts of the book, I thank Richard Bradley, Filip Buekens, Jake Chandler, Raf De Clercq, Kevin Demiddele, Richard Dietz, David Etlin, Jan Heylen, Leon Horsten, Hugh Mellor, Richard Pettigrew, and Sylvia Wenmackers. A synopsis of this book served as a basis for talks given at the universities of Bayreuth, Bochum, Lund, Milan, and Utrecht. The results reported in Chapter 5 were presented at the universities of Konstanz, Munich, and Tilburg, and in Joëlle Proust's research seminar at the Institut Jean Nicod. I thank the audiences present on the various occasions for their helpful comments and discussions.

I have learned much about conditionals from discussions with Jean Baratgin, Filip Buekens, Jake Chandler, Raf De Clercq, Nicole Cruz De Echeverria Loebell, Lieven Decock, Kevin Demiddele, Richard Dietz, Paul Égré, Shira Elqayam, David Etlin, Alan Hájek, Stephan Hartmann, Jan Heylen, Leon Horsten, Gernot Kleiter, Karolina Krzyżanowska, Hannes Leitgeb, David Over, Niki Pfeifer, Guy Politzer, Jan-Willem Romeijn, Hans Rott, Gerhard Schurz, Henrik Singmann, Wolfgang Spohn, Jan Sprenger, Paul Thorn, Jos Uffink, Matthias Unterhuber, Janneke van Wijnbergen-Huitink, and Sylvia Wenmackers. I was also helped by discussions that I had with students in Groningen who took the courses on conditionals that I taught in the past years.

For general good advice and encouragement over the years, I thank the late Jonathan Adler, Peter Brössel, Otávio Bueno, the late Werner Callebaut, Jake Chandler, Raf De Clercq, Lieven Decock, Helen De Cruz, Henk de Regt, Richard Dietz, Anna-Maria Eder, Paul Égré, Shira Elqayam, Pascal Engel, David Etlin, Branden Fitelson, Stephan Hartmann, Rainer Hegselmann, Frank Hindriks, Leon Horsten, Christoph Kelp, Karolina Krzyżanowska, Theo Kuipers, Gerd Lindenhovius, Uskali Mäki, Wouter Meijs, Fred Muller, Jennifer Nagel, Erik Olsson, David Over, Joëlle Proust, Stathis Psillos, Hans Rott, Jonah Schupbach, Sebastian Sequoiah-Grayson, Jos Uffink, Mark van Atten, René van Woudenberg, Jonathan Weisberg, and Timothy Williamson. I also owe a great debt of gratitude to Randa Dubnick and Christopher von Bülow, who painstakingly corrected my English and proofread the manuscript.

The book was written and typeset in WinEdt/LuaTEX. I thank Aleksander Simonic for developing WinEdt, and Hans Hagen, Hartmut Henkel, and Taco Hoekwater for developing LuaTEX. I thank Johannes Küster for providing technical support and advice on font-related matters.

My greatest debt is to my parents and to Jacqueline, my life companion for the past thirty-two years, for their steadfast love and support. I dedicate this book to my father, to Jacqueline, and to the memory of my mother, who passed away on the day I finished the manuscript.

Not all of the following is new. Chapter 2 uses material from the first section of "Indicative Conditionals," which appeared in Leon Horsten and Richard Pettigrew (eds.) *A Companion to Philosophical Logic*, London: Continuum Press, 2011, pp. 383–405. Chapter 3 makes use of parts of the second section of "The Epistemology of Conditionals," *Oxford Studies in Epistemology*, 2013, 4: 3–33. The final section of that chapter is based on "On Bradley's Preservation Condition for Conditionals," *Erkenntnis*, 2007, 67: 111–118. The second section of Chapter 4 is partly based on the third section of "The Epistemology of Conditionals"; the third and fourth section of that chapter use material from "The Evidential Support Theory of Conditionals," *Synthese*, 2008, 164: 19–44. Chapter 6 is a thinly rewritten version of "Learning Conditional Information," *Mind and Language*, 2012, 27: 239–263. The proof in Appendix A makes use of some results from "Reasoning about Evidence," *Journal of Applied Logic*, 2014, 12: 263–278.

CHAPTER I

Agenda

[T]he understanding of "if" is not a narrow academic concern, but a matter of central importance in the understanding of what makes human intelligence special and distinctive.

Jonathan Evans and David Over, *If* (p. 153)

Conditionals are sentences of the forms "If φ, [then] ψ" and "ψ if φ," such as

(1.1) a. If the village is flooded, then the dam must have broken.
      b. If Henry had come to the party, Sue would have come too.
      c. Paul would have bought the house if it hadn't been so expensive.

One may also classify as conditionals sentences that can be naturally put in the above forms, such as

(1.2) a. They will leave in an hour, unless John changes his mind.
      b. No guts, no glory.
      c. Give Louis a toy and he'll ruin it.

which can be rephrased as, respectively, (1.3a), (1.3b), and (1.3c):

(1.3) a. If John does not change his mind, they will leave in an hour.
      b. If a person lacks courage, there will be no glory for him or her.
      c. If one gives Louis a toy, he ruins it.

In "If φ, then ψ," φ is called the "antecedent" and ψ the "consequent."

Conditionals are *special*. They are special for a number of reasons, but probably most conspicuously for the heated controversy that they have generated, and continue to generate. Not that controversy is anything out of the ordinary in philosophy. But even in philosophy, controversies commonly take place against a shared background of basic assumptions. For instance, while there is ongoing controversy about the concept of knowledge, there is at the same time broad (if not universal) agreement on many core issues surrounding that concept. Few dispute that knowledge is factive; that it requires belief as well as justification; that justified true belief is not sufficient for knowledge, however; that coherence amongst one's beliefs is not enough to elevate these to the status of knowledge; that we can gain knowledge from testimony; and so on and so forth. Not so in the case of conditionals. For almost any claim about conditionals that is not downright trivial, it will be exceedingly hard to find a majority, or even a sizable minority, of philosophers who adhere to it. Nearly every interesting question about conditionals that one can think of must be considered to be still largely open. This is so in spite of centuries of hard work on the topic of conditionals by leading philosophers, and more recently also by linguists, psychologists, and (increasingly) computer scientists.

To get an impression of just how vastly theorists disagree on conditionals, consider a long-standing dispute about the semantics of conditionals. Some philosophers who have thought seriously about conditionals hold that conditionals like

(1.4)   If it continues to rain, the match will be canceled.

have the truth conditions of the corresponding material conditionals. That is to say, according to these philosophers, (1.4) and conditionals like it are false if their antecedent is true and their consequent false, and are true in all other cases, so that (1.4) would be logically equivalent to

(1.5)   Either it won't continue to rain or the match will be canceled (or both).

Some of the same philosophers hold that conditionals like

(1.6)   If it had continued to rain, the match would have been canceled.

are just loose talk and do not possess truth conditions at all. But then there are other philosophers who, having thought equally seriously about the matter, hold that conditionals like (1.4) *lack* truth conditions while conditionals like (1.6) do have truth conditions. (Most of these philosophers think the latter have the truth conditions attributed to them by Stalnaker's possible worlds semantics, to be encountered later on.) This is not a minor disagreement![1]

On the one hand, you will have suspected that conditionals are special even if you are a novice to this area of research. You may have found this book shouldering ones entitled *If* (Evans and Over [2004]), *Ifs* (Harper, Stalnaker, and Pearce [1981]), *A Philosophical Guide to Conditionals* (Bennett [2003]), and several books with the title *Conditionals* (e.g., Jackson [1987], Jackson (ed.) [1991], Crocco, Fariñas del Cerro, and Herzig (eds.) [1995], Woods [1997]), with no book called *And*, or *Ands*, or *A Philosophical Guide to Conjunctions*, or *Conjunctions* (or *Or*, etc.) in sight.[2]

On the other hand, however, it *is* surprising that conditionals are special. Conditionals may not be quite as common as conjunctions or disjunctions in daily parlance,[3] but they are common enough not to strike us as exotic beasts – not, at least, until we start viewing them from a theoretical perspective.

The question of why conditionals are special, of why there is all this disagreement about them, is not so easy to answer. In metaphysics, there is a lot of controversy about the notion of an object, even though, one would have supposed, we all know perfectly well what objects are, having been surrounded by them for all our lives. And yet it is a heavily debated question whether objects are three-dimensional or four-dimensional entities; and equally whether only the most elementary physical particles are really objects or whether, on the contrary, those particles do not deserve to be called "objects" in the first place; and whether objects are nothing over and above the properties they possess or whether there is some substratum to which those properties adhere;[4] and so on. But at least here it is reasonable to conjecture that much of the controversy has arisen in

[1] A prominent example of the first type of philosopher is Quine [1959]. Prominent examples of the second type are Gibbard [1981] and Bennett [2003].

[2] Though, admittedly, you may have come across *A Natural History of Negation* (Horn [1989]), *The Syntax of Negation* (Haegeman [2005]), and *The Genealogy of Disjunction* (Jennings [1994]).

[3] For what it is worth, comparisons of "if" with "and" and "or" on Google Fight (http://www.googlefight.com), which allows for a kind of poor man's version of corpus research, showed "if" to occur about three times more often on webpages and in documents accessible via the Internet than "and," although "if" apparently occurs only about half as often as "or." On the other hand, Google's Ngram Viewer (http://books.google.com/ngrams), when asked to search for the occurrence of "if," "and," and "or" in books that were published after 1800 and that are available online, gives a very different picture: then "and" comes out as being used much more frequently than "or," which is used somewhat more frequently than "if"; this outcome is stable over the whole period of time from 1800 onward. (These comparisons were made on January 29, 2013. Thanks to Sylvia Wenmackers for the pointer.)

[4] It is even debated whether there is any real difference between the bundle-of-properties view and the substratum view; see Benovsky [2008].

response to developments in physics, which has continued to reveal truths that tend to sit badly with our ordinary conception of objects (like, in the relatively recent history of physics, the idea that ordinary objects are mostly empty space). No such easy explanation is available for the controversy (or controversies) surrounding conditionals.

An observation made by experimental psychologists may go some way toward explaining why conditionals are special. It has been well documented that not only do young children have difficulty comprehending conditionals, but also that in adults, IQ is a good predictor of how well people comprehend conditionals. Specifically, young children and low-IQ adults tend to interpret conditionals as conjunctions (see Chapter 3). No such difficulties, or differences between cognitively more and less able people, have been found in the interpretation of conjunctions, for example. This suggests that interpreting conditionals is cognitively more demanding than interpreting most other types of sentences. Perhaps interpreting conditionals involves unique mechanisms that science is still to uncover.[5]

A further explanatory factor may be that conditional constructions are put to a great variety of uses (I say more about this below) and that philosophers, being naturally inclined to look for the most general theories, have tended to overgeneralize in the case of conditionals. The diversity of uses to which the word "if" is put is likely to cause trouble even if one resists the inclination. We may try the best we can to disentangle and keep separate the different uses, and yet the risk remains that intuitions related to one type of use contaminate our thinking about other types.

1.1 Key questions

As said, nearly *anything* about conditionals is controversial. This is so even with regard to the most fundamental questions concerning conditionals, which can be grouped into five clusters:

1. The first of these concerns *truth*. Specifically, what are the truth conditions of conditionals? Do conditionals have truth conditions at all? If so, should there be a uniform semantics for all conditionals, or may different types of conditionals have different truth conditions? Or may some types have truth conditions while others lack them?

---

[5] According to Récanati [2000:57 f], the cognitive complexity of conditionals is due to the fact that their evaluation requires us to go through a process of simulation. This idea is related to the Ramsey test, which we shall come across at various later points in this book.

We are strongly inclined (at least, I am) to think that (1.7a) is true and (1.7b) is false:

(1.7) a. If global warming continues unabated, various species will become extinct.
       b. If Lance Armstrong had admitted to doping earlier, he would not have been stripped of his seven Tour de France titles.

But however strong our inclinations, the failure of literally every extant truth-conditional semantics of conditionals to accommodate the various registered facts about conditionals – how we reason with conditionals, when we are willing to accept or assert them and when not, the probabilities we accord to them, and so on – constitutes something of an inductive argument against the idea that conditionals are true or false. It could be argued that, given the right division of labor between semantics and pragmatics, and possibly also given some pragmatic principles still to be discovered, some of our present semantics of conditionals will eventually get the relevant facts right. Even granting this, later on we shall come across considerations that appear to impinge more severely on the viability of truth-conditional semantics of conditionals.

So suppose, for now, that conditionals are not truth-conditional. Then what are we to make of the following apparent facts?

• We seem to believe many conditionals. But to believe something is to believe it to be true!
• We seem to know many conditionals. But knowledge requires truth!
• It seems that there can be evidence in favor of a conditional. But favoring evidence is understood as an indication of truth!
• Conditionals seem meaningful, and we seem to know their meanings. But according to the mainstream in semantics, the meaning of a sentence is given by its truth conditions, and knowing the meaning of a sentence is knowing its truth conditions!

This is merely scratching the surface, but it provides a sense of just how much is at stake in the debate concerning the semantics of conditionals.

2. The second cluster of questions concerns the *probabilities* of conditionals. What *are* these probabilities? Can we reasonably attribute probabilities to conditionals even if conditionals lack truth conditions? How much weight is to be given to actual data about people's judgments of the probabilities of conditionals? Might these judgments be systematically mistaken?

As will be seen, a number of the main semantics of conditionals make predictions about the probabilities of conditionals that not only clash with pretheoretic intuition but are also inconsistent with the outcomes of various recent experiments investigating people's probability assignments. What is more, one of the few issues about conditionals on which philosophers do agree is a claim concerning what these probabilities can *not* be: the probability of a conditional cannot, on formal grounds, be the conditional probability of the consequent given the antecedent, or so it is believed. Surprisingly, the aforementioned experiments appear to show that people do judge the probability of a conditional to be the corresponding conditional probability. According to mainstream thinking, these data are to be explained away, possibly as being due to some systematic bias in people's probability judgments, or to an error in the setup of the experiments, or to people's mistaking probability for something else. We shall see that it may be possible to take the data at face value after all.

3. Questions in the third cluster concern the *use conditions* – the acceptability and assertability conditions – of conditionals. What are these? That is, when are we warranted to accept a conditional, when to assert it? Is there a uniform account of use conditions for all types of conditionals? And what is the relation – if any – between the truth conditions of conditionals (if such there be) and their use conditions? What is the relation – if any – between the probabilities of conditionals and their use conditions?

Here again we find some agreement among philosophers. The agreement is on the degrees of acceptability of so-called simple conditionals, that is, conditionals whose antecedent and consequent are not themselves conditional in form. According to virtually all who have thought about the matter, a simple conditional is acceptable to the extent that its consequent is probable given its antecedent. But recent experimental results show this claim to be descriptively inadequate. That might just be another instance of people failing to obey a norm of rationality, on a par perhaps with the base rate fallacy (Kahneman and Tversky [1973]) and the conjunction fallacy (Tversky and Kahneman [1983]). That response to the data is hard to maintain, however, in the absence of any arguments to the effect that we *ought* to judge a conditional acceptable to the degree to which we believe its consequent, given its antecedent. There are also a fair number of philosophers who agree on the categorical acceptability conditions of conditionals: a conditional is categorically acceptable iff (if and only if) its consequent is highly probable given its antecedent. Again, it will be seen that this proposal is undermined by linguistic intuition as well as, probably more perniciously, experimental data. What are we to put in the place of these flawed proposals?

And what are we to say about the assertability of conditionals? Most philosophers nowadays hold that whether an assertion is warranted depends on the asserter's epistemic position vis-à-vis what he or she asserts. The main divide is over how strong that epistemic position must be: whether the asserter must know what he or she has asserted or whether something weaker, like rational acceptability, suffices.[6] Those holding that rational acceptability warrants assertion will have no further work to do concerning the assertability of conditionals once the (categorical) accept-ability conditions of conditionals have been specified. Insofar as specifying the conditions under which conditionals are known poses no difficulties over and above those associated with specifying their acceptability con-ditions, the same will be true for those who hold that assertion requires knowledge.

4. Then there are questions regarding the *logic* of conditionals. Which prin-ciples for conditional reasoning are valid? For instance, is "if" transitive, in the sense that "If φ, then χ" follows from "If φ, then ψ" and "If ψ, then χ"? Many instances of this schema strike us as embodying impeccable reasoning. For instance, the following argument is seemingly unassailable:

> If Jim passes the exam, his parents will buy him a car.
> If Jim's parents buy him a car, he will go to Italy on vacation this summer.
> ∴　If Jim passes the exam, he will go to Italy on vacation this summer.

However, philosophers have come up with counterexamples to the puta-tive transitivity of the conditional, like this one from Cooper [1978:183]:

> If Brown dies, Jones will win the election on Wednesday.
> If Jones wins the election on Wednesday, Brown will retire.
> ?? ∴　If Brown dies, Brown will retire.

Similar counterexamples have been discovered for quite a number of argument forms that have the same prima facie plausibility as the one considered here.

---

[6] For defenses of the claim that assertion requires knowledge, see, e.g., Williamson [1996], [2000], Ch. 11], Adler [2002], DeRose [2002], and Turri [2011]. For defenses of the claim that some-thing like rational acceptability suffices for assertion, see, e.g., Douven [2006], [2009], and Lackey [2007].

But for an even greater number of argument forms involving conditionals, no counterexamples are known to exist. Given, then, that certain inferences involving conditionals seem valid, do we have another argument against the view that conditionals do not have truth conditions? After all, logical validity is defined in terms of the preservation of *truth*. How can an inference involving one or more conditionals be said to preserve truth if conditionals are not truth-conditional? As Adams has shown, however, validity need not be defined in terms of truth-preservation but can be defined in terms of the preservation of some other property – like, in his own proposal, high probability: according to Adams, an argument is valid iff whenever its premises are highly probable so is its conclusion.[7] Later in this book, we look at conditional inferences and define validity in terms of acceptability-preservation.[8]

5. And finally there are questions related to *belief change*. How ought one respond doxastically to the acceptance of a conditional? That is, how ought one to revise one's beliefs, or degrees of belief, upon receiving conditional information? Specifically, are traditional mechanisms of belief change (such as Bayes' rule) also adequate for handling the receipt of conditional information, or does this kind of information require its own update rule or rules?

Unlike most of the previous questions, the questions in this cluster are not so much sources of continuing controversy among philosophers. Rather, they mark blind spots; they have been mostly overlooked, willingly or not. This cannot be because these questions appear not to be very pressing. No one will want to deny that we change our beliefs, or degrees of belief, upon receiving conditional information. For instance, upon being informed by a colleague that Millie will not pass the exam if she does not work harder, I may drop my earlier belief that Millie is among our brightest students, or lower considerably the degree to which I believe this. But however ordinary and natural such changes of belief appear, it will be seen that the familiar mechanisms of belief change have great difficulty handling conditional information.

---

[7] To be more precise, on his account an argument is valid iff the improbability of the conclusion (that is, 1 minus the probability of the conclusion) does not exceed the sum of the improbabilities of the premises. Adams [1966], [1975] proves that all arguments that are classically valid are also valid in his sense; see also Adams and Levine [1975].

[8] Field [2009] argues that it has been a mistake to think that logic is primarily concerned with identifying those argument forms that are truth-preserving. Rather, logic is concerned with identifying *good* arguments, where, on Field's notion of goodness, this brings logic close to being concerned with acceptability-preservation in our sense. I will not press this point in the following.

1.2 Scope of the book

Much time and effort has been spent trying to come up with a semantics of conditionals. This has led to an abundance of different proposals, a small number of which have at times enjoyed some popularity, or even widespread popularity, among the general philosophical or psychological readership. However, at least among specialists, there is currently no account of the truth conditions of conditionals that is favored by more than a tiny minority. Except for the question of the probabilities of conditionals – which, as will be seen, is intimately related to semantic questions – none of the epistemological questions concerning conditionals has received nearly as much attention as the cluster of questions concerning the truth conditions of conditionals. Perhaps this is just an oversight on the part of epistemologists. Or they may have thought that conditionals are unremarkable, epistemologically speaking. That thought would be understandable, for at least prima facie it seems that conditionals can be believed, asserted, known, disbelieved, doubted, and learned, in the same way that, for instance, conjunctions and disjunctions can be believed, asserted, and so on. The thought is wrong, however. For instance, as just mentioned, and as will be seen in detail later on, none of the known mechanisms for incorporating new information into one's belief system seems to yield materially adequate results when applied to conditionals.

Some epistemologists may also have thought it wiser to leave the epistemology of conditionals for a later date, when (it is hoped) we will have a firmer grip on their semantics. However, given that so little progress has been made with regard to stating a satisfactory such semantics, the time may be ripe for a sort of reverse-engineering approach, one that addresses the epistemological questions first and then, armed with new insights and data about the epistemology of conditionals, tackles the semantics with a fresh look, wholly or partly as a kind of optimization problem: which semantics does best in explaining why we assign to conditionals the probabilities we do, why we accept and assert certain conditionals but not others, why we change our beliefs in certain ways and not others upon the receipt of conditional information, and so on? There is no shortage of ideas as to what the truth conditions of conditionals might be. A clearer view of how conditionals function in our epistemic lives may help us choose among those ideas by asking which of them offers the best prospects for explaining the epistemic functioning of conditionals. At a minimum, it may enable us to eliminate some candidate semantics that otherwise (e.g., on grounds of simplicity) look theoretically appealing. Indeed, some of the clearest evidence against the already briefly mentioned material conditional account will be seen to come from work on the probabilities of conditionals.

This book deals primarily with the epistemology of conditionals. As intimated, some epistemologists may have refrained from considering epistemological questions concerning conditionals because it has seemed to them that these questions cannot be properly addressed without having a working semantics of conditionals at hand. That is not so, as I hope to show. Much can be said about the probabilities of conditionals, about their use conditions, as well as about updating on conditionals, that is independent of what the truth conditions of conditionals are, and independent even of whether conditionals have truth conditions to begin with. Moreover, while we cannot say anything about which inferential principles involving conditionals preserve truth without a semantics of conditionals, given an account of the acceptability conditions of conditionals, we *can* ask which inferential principles preserve acceptability. So, we may for instance ask whether "If φ, then ψ and χ" is acceptable if both "If φ, then ψ" and "If φ, then χ" are acceptable. In this sense, we can – and will – consider the logic of conditionals.

The scope of the book is actually still more specific: it will deal with the epistemology of *indicative* conditionals, and then mainly *normal* ones, and only *simple* ones. It was already stated in Section 1.1 that simple conditionals are conditionals whose antecedent and consequent are not themselves conditional in form. I will explain the other two terms.

It is common practice to group conditionals into two major types, *indicative* conditionals and *subjunctive* conditionals. I alluded to this distinction when, on page 2, I tried to give an impression of the kind of disagreement one finds in the literature on conditionals. We have also come across examples of both types; for instance, (1.1a), (1.4), and (1.7a) are indicative conditionals, and (1.1b), (1.6), and (1.7b) are subjunctive conditionals.

Indicative and subjunctive conditionals are usually distinguished on the basis of the grammatical mood of their antecedent. If the antecedent is in the indicative mood, the sentence is an indicative conditional; if the antecedent is in the subjunctive mood, the sentence is a subjunctive conditional.[9] Given that not all languages have a subjunctive mood,

---

[9] See, e.g., Bennett [2003:10]; see Gibbard [1981, Sect. 4] for a more precise grammatical characterization of the distinction. For recent evidence from neuroscience relating to the indicative–subjunctive distinction, see Kulakova et al. [2013].

this criterion is not fully general.[10] By way of alternative criterion, it has been suggested that the antecedents of subjunctive conditionals, but not those of indicative conditionals, are known to be false or at least strongly suspected to be false. This criterion is not unexceptionable either. For instance, one may reasonably suspect as false the antecedent of

(1.8) If I win the lottery, I will be rich.

which most would classify as an indicative conditional, yet reasonably suspect as true the antecedent of

(1.9) If I were to lose the lottery, I would need to get back to work on my job search.

which most would classify as a subjunctive conditional.[11] Be this as it may, I shall only be concerned with clear cases of indicative conditionals, so nothing to be said in the following depends on how and exactly where the line between indicative and subjunctive conditionals is to be drawn.

Among the main classes of conditionals that have been flagged as being somehow special or nonstandard in the literature are *biscuit conditionals*, also known as *speech act conditionals* or *relevance conditionals*, such as (1.10a) and (1.10b), and *non-interference conditionals*, such as (1.10c) and (1.10d):[12]

(1.10) a. If you're hungry, there are biscuits on the table.
        b. If you want a ride, I have to be heading home now.
        c. If we triple her salary, Bettie will leave the department.
        d. If hell freezes over, Jack won't marry Jill.

One main difference between the special and the normal conditionals resides in the fact that the latter, but not the former, report some kind of dependency of the truth of the consequent on that of the antecedent (where for present purposes the nature of this dependency may be left

---

[10] The criterion has been contested on other grounds as well. See, for instance, DeRose [2010], where it is argued that standard (what he calls) conditionals of deliberation, such as conditionals of the form "If I were to X, then I would Y," which are typically classified as subjunctive conditionals, are actually semantically indicative.

[11] See also Anderson [1951] and von Fintel [2012]. (Thanks to David Etlin here.)

[12] On biscuit conditionals, see, e.g., Austin [1956], DeRose and Grandy [1999], and Bennett [2003:125 f]; and on non-interference conditionals, see Bennett [2003:122 ff] and, in particular on classifying them as nonstandard, Burgess [2004:567]. Some authors (e.g., Jackson [1979], [1987:35 f], and Heylen and Horsten [2006]) also group so-called Dutchman conditionals – e.g., "If Kate passes the exam, I'm a Dutchman" – with the nonstandard conditionals.

open). For instance, an assertion of (1.10a) does not suggest that there being biscuits on the table somehow depends on whether you are hungry; rather, we infer from such an assertion that the biscuits are on the table either way. Similarly for (1.10b), which is most naturally interpreted as expressing that the speaker has to go home now and is offering the addressee a ride. In this type of conditional, it is not the *truth* of the consequent that depends on the truth of the antecedent – the consequent is outright asserted – but rather the *relevance* of the information given in the consequent that depends on the truth of the antecedent (see, e.g., Johnson-Laird [1986:69 f]). (Hence the name "relevance conditionals.") Non-interference conditionals assert their consequents as well. For instance, by asserting (1.10c) we are asserting that Bettie will leave the department, but in a way which suggests that that will happen whether or not we give her a raise. And by asserting (1.10d) we are asserting that Jack will not marry Jill, come what may. Non-interference conditionals seem meant to emphasize the inevitability or obviousness of the consequent, regardless of whether the antecedent obtains.[13]

Geis and Lycan [1993] list a number of other features that, according to them, normal conditionals have and special conditionals lack. Some of these are controversial at best, like the equivalence to the disjunction of the negation of the antecedent and the consequent, which they allege normal conditionals, but not special ones, to possess (see Chapter 2 on why this is controversial). But one strikes me as being clearly correct, namely, that nonstandard conditionals do not take the pronoun "then," or at least not without a change of meaning (see also Chisholm [1964]). For instance,

(1.11)   If you want a ride, then I have to be heading home now.

sounds a little puzzling; there will be few contexts in which this sentence can be naturally asserted. One imagines (with some difficulty) a context in which the addressee has expressed the wish to go home and the speaker (perhaps the addressee's over-friendly neighbor) seeing no one else around who might be able or willing to drive the addressee home. In any case,

---

[13] Some might see as yet another nonstandard use of "if" – one that is rarely mentioned in the philosophical literature and which seems to lack a separate label – the use exemplified by sentences like: "He asked if he could use the telephone" (Fillenbaum [1975:250]). Sentences of this type do seem easy to characterize, given that in them "if" appears to be a mere stylistic variant of "whether." In German and Dutch, these sentences do not allow the use of the standard translation of "if" ("wenn" in German, "als" in Dutch), but only the standard translation of "whether" ("ob" in German, "of" in Dutch). On the other hand, Koralus and Mascarenhas [2013] and Starr [2014] take precisely the "interrogative" use of "if" as a point of departure for developing their own theories of the indicative conditional.

there is no longer the suggestion that the speaker has to go home regardless of the addressee's (possible) wish to have a ride. Equally,

(1.12)   If we triple her salary, then Bettie will leave the department.

does *not* suggest that Bettie will leave the department whether or not we triple her salary, but rather that tripling her salary will *make* her leave the department. In some contexts, (1.12) could be perfectly assertable. For instance, imagine a context in which Bettie previously complained that tenured professors make too much money, given that they are compensated for their work in so many other (intellectual) ways, and that she asserted that she might not be able to reconcile a tripling of her salary with her moral standards. Note, incidentally, that these examples show that context matters in determining whether a conditional is normal or special.[14]

A final characteristic of non-interference conditionals to be mentioned here is that their assertability is not affected, or is hardly affected, by substituting in them "whether or not," or "regardless of whether," or sometimes also "even if," for "if" (and vice versa). That, at least, is true for all conditionals that I can think of as being relevantly similar to (1.10c) and (1.10d). The same is *not* true for biscuit conditionals. Substituting "whether or not" for "if" in (1.10a) or (1.10b) does appear to affect the assertability of these sentences. Whereas (1.10b) sounds like a friendly offer,

(1.13)   Whether or not you want a ride, I have to be heading home now.

sounds like a rather unfriendly expression of indifference.

To illustrate the importance of distinguishing between normal and special conditionals, note that if the material conditional account is correct, and thus the ordinary-language conditional-forming operator shares its semantics with the conditional-forming operator from classical logic, then Contraposition is a valid inferential principle, meaning that "If φ, then ψ" entails "If it is not the case that ψ, then it is not the case that φ" (every model of the language that makes the first true also makes the second true). But consider this sentence:

(1.14)   If your mother gets angry, she won't get furious.

---

[14]   If Dutchman conditionals qualify as nonstandard conditionals, as some maintain (see note 12), the same point pertains to them. For example, looking at my Dutch passport, I can honestly say, "If I'm not the victim of a massive conspiracy, I'm a Dutchman," which would be a perfectly normal conditional by any standards.

Applying Contraposition yields:

(1.15)   If your mother gets furious, she won't get angry.

which sounds self-contradictory. The material conditional account may well be untenable (as will be seen), but we should not reject it for the wrong reasons. And with respect to the above apparent problem, advocates of the material conditional account would be in the right to argue that (1.14) is really a non-interference conditional, saying that your mother will certainly not get furious (though she may get angry), and so (1.14) is not in the purview of the material conditional account, which aims to account for normal conditionals only.

This book is concerned with normal conditionals. For all I know, the epistemology of conditionals to be offered applies to various types of nonstandard conditionals as well. I just have not investigated whether that is so.

How bad would it be if the epistemology of conditionals presented here applied *only* to normal conditionals? Some philosophers hold that there must be a unified semantics for all conditional constructions; and those same philosophers, and perhaps some others as well, will probably also hold that there must be a unified *epistemology* for conditionals. I am not aware of any serious argument for believing that all conditional constructions must be treated on a par, whether semantically or epistemologically. According to Nolan [2003:215], it is desirable to have a unified semantic treatment of indicative and subjunctive conditionals because, "after all, 'if' means 'if'!" But that begs the question at issue, to wit, whether "if" has a uniform meaning in all its occurrences. Admittedly, everyone can see that it would be theoretically satisfying to have a grand unified theory of conditionals. But then again, it would be theoretically satisfying to have a grand unified theory of disease, which explains all ailments in terms of a limited number of key concepts, much in the way in which Hippocratic medicine tried to explain all phenomena in its domain in terms of four bodily fluids. In the latter case, the world has clearly refused to cooperate. There is no reason to expect data involving our use of the word "if" to be less recalcitrant to theoretical unification. Although these data are, in an obvious sense, of our own making, natural languages did not originate on the drawing boards of logicians.

On the contrary, indicative and subjunctive conditionals as well as normal and special conditionals strike me pretheoretically as being different enough, maybe not to *expect* them to have, but not to be surprised if they *turn out* to have, different semantics and epistemologies. Moreover, as stated earlier, that hardly any progress has been made in answering the questions summed up in Section 1.1 might be due to the fact that much of the research so far has proceeded under the implicit or explicit assumption that these questions must have *one* answer that holds for all conditionals alike.

Even if, in the end, all data involving our use of the word "if" must be accounted for by a single all-encompassing semantic and epistemological theory, I would estimate that a large part – probably the largest part – of those data concerns normal (indicative) conditionals. Given that all of the aforementioned key questions are wide open even when limited to normal conditionals, an adequate epistemology of this subclass of conditionals would constitute important theoretical progress. It would remain to be shown how that epistemology applies to special conditionals.

How much of a limitation is it that the book will only be concerned with *simple* conditionals? Not at all, if those are right who hold that all conditionals, insofar as we can make sense of them, are reducible to simple conditionals.[15] Below, it will be seen that this reducibility claim plays a key role in defending the view that conditionals lack truth conditions. It will also be seen, however, that the claim is probably wrong, or at any rate that presently it lacks a solid underpinning. If there are conditionals that are not reducible to simple conditionals, then a restriction to the epistemology of simple conditionals might be entirely harmless if there were reason to believe that simple and non-simple conditionals have different epistemologies. However, I do not see why that should be so, nor, for that matter, why they should have different semantics. So, I take the focus on simple conditionals to be a real restriction, and it is one that I regret. Nonetheless, the key questions are wide open *even* for simple normal indicative conditionals, and, as we shall see, the task of getting the epistemology of these conditionals right is a quite ambitious one.

There is evidence to suggest that even this more limited task is too ambitious still. Fillenbaum [1975] conducted studies in which participants were invited to rephrase conditionals in a way that avoids the use of "if." The materials used in these studies comprised conditional promises and threats, but also many sentences that pretheoretically would seem to be grouped most naturally with declarative sentences and that are clear instances of simple normal indicative conditionals. Among the latter sentences, Fillenbaum [1975:250] distinguishes between what he calls

---

[15] See, e.g., Jackson [1987:127–137] and Edgington [1995:282 ff].

"temporal-causal conditionals," which as the name suggests express a temporal or causal relationship between antecedent and consequent (one of his examples is "If he goes to Washington he will get drunk") and what he calls "contingent universals," by which he seems to mean instances of some sort of regularities (example: "If the truck is red it belongs to the Exxon Company"). The analysis revealed a significant and systematic difference in the way in which people rephrase these two subclasses of conditionals, the differences concerning the grammatical constructions that were used and the frequency with which particular words occurred. One of his conclusions is that "[i]nsofar as the meaning of a sentence is revealed by the sentences which are produced as its equivalents or paraphrases, there is some evidence that IF may have rather different meanings or uses in different contexts of the sort examined here" (p. 255). So, perhaps we need different semantics for different subtypes of the broader type of conditional considered in this book. That in turn *might* mean that we also need different epistemologies for those different subtypes. However this may be, I aim to show that some fairly general things can be said about the epistemology of simple normal indicative conditionals.

From here on out, the noun "conditional" is intended to refer to simple normal indicative conditionals, unless specified otherwise.

1.3 Methodology

Until very recently, psychologists and philosophers working on conditionals approached their subject of interest from rather different angles. Perhaps for that reason, there has been little interaction between the two research communities. For many years, psychologists took for granted the correctness of the material conditional account. They were mainly interested in whether ordinary people reason with conditionals in accordance with that account; and insofar as people were found not to do so, psychologists sought to explain these putative failures of rationality. In their research on conditionals, psychologists paid little attention to more recent developments in philosophy, which had increasingly come to cast doubt on the adequacy of the material conditional account. Conversely, philosophers have been concerned with devising semantics and pragmatics (theories stating use conditions), showing little to no interest in psychological findings that, as a matter of fact, would appear of immediate relevance to their endeavors.

Much of the research to be reported in this book reflects the firm conviction that the time has come for philosophers and psychologists to join forces on the problem of conditionals, and that combined research efforts from the two communities hold the key to important progress on all of the questions mentioned above. It is not just that psychologists could benefit from looking more closely at the formally precise work in semantics and pragmatics done by philosophers in the past twenty years or so, and that philosophers could benefit from the welter of empirical evidence about the use, understanding, and processing of conditionals already uncovered by experimental psychologists. Rather, it seems to me that in the study of conditionals (and not only there), much is to be gained from pursuing research questions by a combined formal-empirical approach. Instead of explaining here why I believe this to be so, I offer the work in Chapters 3 through 6 as making what I hope is a strong case for the claim.

The time for this interdisciplinary approach to conditionals has come for another reason as well, one which concerns the methodologies of the two research communities, which have steadily converged over the past ten years. That probabilities are fundamental to how people reason and make decisions is no longer contested by anyone in philosophy or psychology. Specifically with respect to conditionals, both philosophers and psychologists have taken their cue from work by Ramsey, de Finetti, and others, who sought to understand conditionals in probabilistic terms.[16] This is not to say that probability theory has replaced logic in psychology and philosophy. The tools available to psychologists and philosophers have rather been enriched by probability theory (as well as by logics that in many respects are more flexible and more powerful than classical logic; see Horsten and Douven [2008]).

Moreover, whereas reliance on linguistic intuitions has been standard practice in philosophy for much of its history, that approach has recently come somewhat under a cloud, and philosophers have started to give less weight to intuition and more to results from the sciences – not surprisingly, the main focus in the quarters of epistemologists and philosophers of language and mind has come to be on results from psychology and (to a lesser extent) neuroscience. What is more, some philosophers have turned to experimental methods themselves, often in collaborative projects

---

[16] See Ramsey [1926/1990], Ramsey [1929/1990], and de Finetti [1937/1964].

with experimental psychologists.[17] Parts of this book in effect rest on the outcomes of such projects.

Given that this dual methodology will play an important role in the following chapters, it is worth being more explicit about it and briefly tracing its origins. Probabilistic approaches are now quite common in epistemology. For much of the history of philosophy, however, probabilism – the view that probability theory is central to understanding epistemic rationality – has existed only as an "underground epistemology," as van Fraassen [1989:151] terms it. He locates the beginnings of probabilism in the seventeenth century, in the writings of Pascal and the logicians associated with the Jansenist Port-Royal Abbey. Yet even in 1989, van Fraassen's characterization seemed entirely appropriate, notwithstanding the important contributions to probabilism made by Ramsey and de Finetti at the beginning of the twentieth century, and by Carnap, Good, Jeffrey, and a few other philosophers and mathematicians some decades later.

In the 1990s, however, the underground epistemology turned almost overnight into a lively and high-profile research area, one that even started to dominate certain debates in epistemology. The first debate of which this was true was the debate about the nature and epistemic role of coherence. There had been a lot of talk in epistemology about how coherence amongst beliefs may determine the status of those beliefs *qua* being justified, but much of the discussion had been in terms too vague to allow any of the crucial questions – such as, most centrally, the question of whether coherence is truth-conducive – to be addressed with a real hope of finding a satisfactory answer. This changed radically when formal epistemologists started to formulate definitions of coherence, all in precise probabilistic terms, that enabled them to take important steps toward answering those questions, and even to settle some (see, e.g., Bovens and Hartmann [2003], Olsson [2005], and Douven and Meijs [2007]). Inspired by these successes, philosophers started using the same probabilistic machinery more generally in tackling questions concerning justification and evidence. The end of this development is not yet in sight.

The psychology of reasoning has witnessed a strikingly parallel development. Its practitioners have long conceived of classical logic as a

---

[17] As a purely practical point, which may be contributing to the growing enthusiasm among philosophers for experimental methods, it is to be mentioned that the availability of user-friendly software to create surveys and of crowdsourcing services like Amazon's Mechanical Turk and CrowdFlower makes it now easier than ever before to collect in a short time span large amounts of data. See Reips [2002], Oppenheimer, Meyvis, and Davidenko [2009], and Aust et al. [2013] for useful information on how to obtain high-quality responses via Internet-based experiments.

codification of the norms of rationality, in contrast to many of their colleagues working in the area of judgment and decision making, where probability theory and decision theory were regarded quite early on as providing the guiding principles of rationality. In the past one or two decades, this situation drastically changed, in that probability theory came to occupy a central role in the study of reasoning as well, giving rise to what has been dubbed "New Paradigm Psychology of Reasoning" (Over [2009]; see also Elqayam and Over [2013] and other papers in Elqayam, Bonnefon, and Over [2013]).

As remarked, the convergence of psychology and philosophy is also due to the fact that philosophers have started to give more weight to empirical results, and to some extent have even started to participate in experimental research. This change in the appreciation of empirical methods did not come about all of a sudden but has a history that starts more than half a century ago.

Speculation has always been a core activity of philosophers, but it is by no means unique to philosophy: science, too, involves a fair amount of speculation. However, whereas the results of scientific speculation ultimately must confront the data, and will be rejected in case of conflict with those data, philosophical speculation may more easily go uncontrolled and may thereby lead to results that cannot be regarded as constituting progress in any meaningful way. Twentieth-century philosophy has shown a growing awareness of this danger, although opinions have differed on how best to counteract it.

The logical empiricists urged philosophers to aim for the same rigor in their reasoning as mathematicians and logicians aim for in theirs. While this advice was well received and made the philosophical profession appear more scientific in various ways, it did little to ensure that philosophers were not really engaging in a kind of philosophical creative writing, however formally dressed up.

It was a step forward when, in the 1960s, post-positivist authors like Quine, Kuhn, Feyerabend, Hanson, and Laudan began to propagate the idea that, rather than trying (merely) to emulate the rigor of scientific inquiry, philosophers ought to start paying closer attention to science itself, both to its theories and to its practice. Quine [1969] famously argued that psychological findings about perception, memory, trust, and so on, are of immediate importance to epistemologists, and that if one's epistemology goes against the best scientific theories concerning any of these subjects, then that severely undermines one's epistemology (even if it does not refute it, given that our best scientific theories may still be false). At about the same time, Kuhn, Laudan, and other historically oriented philosophers of science advanced the idea that philosophical accounts of, for example, the evolution of science are to be tested against the historical track record of science, and are to be repudiated if they make the wrong predictions about what is to be found in that track record.[18]

Some have touted the recent emergence of experimental philosophy as a further step in the right direction. Philosophers are no longer just aiming to be as rigorous in their argumentation as scientists are, nor are they satisfied any longer with simply attending to the findings of science. Philosophers have now become scientists themselves! What this means, more in particular, is that philosophers have started to address what appear to be unmistakably philosophical questions – such as questions about moral responsibility and blameworthiness, about free will, and about the nature of knowledge and justification – with the help of unmistakably empirical research methods.

Whatever the virtues (or vices) of experimental philosophy, I should like to emphasize that, in my view at least, the empirical research on conditionals conducted so far – part of which is to be discussed in this book – does not belong to this new branch of philosophy. It is one thing to investigate empirically how the folk think about traditional philosophical concepts like knowledge, responsibility, and justice, and it is another to work out the empirical content of a philosophical account and then to see whether and to what extent this content matches reality. All empirical work on conditionals that I know of is of the latter sort: it does not try to elicit the intuitions of non-specialists about the philosophical notion of "conditionality," intuitions that are then perhaps hoped to be somehow pure, not being tainted by years of indoctrination by graduate school. The empirical work to be discussed typically proceeds by simply asking non-specialists how probable, or credible, or plausible, or acceptable, certain sentences (mostly, but not exclusively, conditionals) are, where these sentences themselves are generally devoid of any philosophically interesting content. Psychologists – whether concerned with conditionals or not – have been practicing this kind of research for decades.

To further clarify how I conceive of the relation between experimental philosophy and the empirical work on conditionals that will feature in many of the chapters of this book, consider some recent empirical work

---

[18] Callebaut [1993] gives an excellent overview of the naturalization program in philosophy up to the 1980s.

on word meaning. Semantic externalists famously hold that the meaning of a word is determined at least partly by worldly facts outside any speaker's head ("'meanings' just ain't in the head," as Putnam [1973:704] succinctly put the core tenet of the position). According to various stripes of externalists, the capacity to refer to an item by means of a given word does not require the capacity to recognize the item as falling into the word's extension. To give a well-known example, according to Putnam [1973] we can successfully refer to elms by using the word "elm" even if we are unable to tell elms from beeches. It might be of some interest to know how well (if at all) this claim accords with the folk's intuitions. Harry finds himself surrounded by elm trees, in clear daylight. Harry has 20/20 vision, is not mentally impaired, not high on anything, nor is any other factor present that could distort his vision or thinking. When asked whether he sees any nearby elm trees, Harry answers in the negative. Is Harry nevertheless able to refer to the trees around him by means of the word "elm"? This is a story plus question one could use to probe the consistency of externalism with the intuitions of ordinary people. Or one could go even further and use it to investigate the question of whether the answer depends on the cultural background of the respondents. That is basically what Machery et al. [2004] did in an influential study, using vignettes close to the foregoing example (though involving proper names rather than natural kind terms), and finding that intuitions about meaning and reference tend to be influenced by culture indeed.

Contrast this kind of empirical work on meaning with the work to be found in, for instance, Regier [1996], which studies the meanings of spatial relation terms (such as prepositions like "in," "outside," "between," and "next to") using computational methods; or contrast it with the work to be found in Regier, Kay, and Khetarpal [2007], which uses different computational methods to study the meanings of basic color terms. Or consider Gärdenfors' ([2000], [2014]) work on meaning, which brings together and extends various recent insights from formal semantics, cognitive psychology, psycholinguistics, and sociolinguistics to present a picture of meanings as regions in conceptual spaces and as emerging from complex social interactions; in this picture, if meanings are not in the head, they can still be in the *heads* of the language users (Gärdenfors [2014:18]). Or again, take the work of Tomasello (e.g., [2003], [2008]), which studies broadly semantic phenomena from the combined perspective of developmental psychology and evolutionary biology, and which grounds meanings in basic skills – like pointing, gesturing, and pantomiming – that humans share with non-human primates.[19] All this empirical work has potentially far-reaching implications for philosophical thinking about meaning and semantics more generally, even if it may not be informative about any person's semantic *intuitions*. Without wanting to deprecate the type of empirical research mainly concerned with people's semantic intuitions, I think of the empirical research on conditionals that much of what follows draws on as being more akin to the work on meaning cited in this paragraph than to the work cited in the previous paragraph.

It is not uncommon for psychologists to look at the philosophical literature for inspiration. So, we philosophers interested in and working on conditionals might as well lean back, hoping that psychologists will stumble upon our work and deem it interesting enough to take it as the starting point for new experiments. But why not try instead to actively *bring* our work – insofar as it has empirical content – to the attention of psychologists? Better yet, why not connect with them – if they are interested – and do joint empirical research? Where possible, that is the approach I have taken over the past years. Naturally, it can happen – and it has happened to me – that the kind of empirical research a given project calls for requires the use of experimental techniques that one's collaborators from the psychology department are insufficiently familiar with; or one may not always have the funding to conduct the requisite empirical research. But even in those cases one can still try to describe the kind of experiments that could be done to test one's account, which might then help those who do possess the right experimental skills (or have enough money). At a few places in the book, I have to resort to this second-best strategy.

To end this section, I would like to address two reasons that some philosophers might have for eschewing the more empirically oriented approach to conditionals that I am urging in this book, one being that such an approach will bring us nothing that cannot already be obtained by reflection from the armchair, the other being that the approach is not just needlessly involved but is even badly misguided in conflating normative issues with descriptive issues.

More specifically, the first reason is that, instead of asking other people to judge the truth values or probabilities (or whatever) of a given number of conditionals, we can simply ask ourselves how *we* judge those truth values, and so on, *given that we are normal, competent speakers of English*. For that reason, we can safely generalize from our own judgments to those of *all* normal speakers of English. Any judgments deviating from ours

---

[19] See in a similar vein Dessalles [2007].

can be dismissed out of hand as somehow exhibiting a crucial lack of understanding of the English language.

The second reason basically makes the accusation that experimental approaches to understanding conditionals are guilty of psychologism, that is, of conflating the laws of logic – which concern mathematical relationships (most notably, relations of entailment) among propositions – with those of psychology, which at best concern which propositions people *take* to be entailed by which propositions. Conditionals play a key role in our reasoning. As such, they are subject to rules of *proper* reasoning. Philosophers should be interested in discovering *those* rules, leaving to psychologists the study of how people *actually* reason with conditionals, as well as the conditions under which they *attribute* truth to a conditional, or *deem* a conditional acceptable, or probable (etc.). Asking people to fill out surveys may help with the latter project, but it will not help with the former. Studying laypeople's verdicts on the truth or probability (or what have you) of various conditionals, as well as studying how they reason with conditionals, will at best reveal the mistakes they make in judging and/or using conditionals. Somewhat ironically, many psychologists have been antipsychologists in this sense, in that – as previously mentioned – they took the standards for the correct usage of the conditional-forming operator, like the standards for the correct usage of other connectives, to be set by classical logic, and were then mainly or even exclusively interested in finding out if or to what extent people obey these standards, and whether some people are better in obeying these standards than others (Evans [2002]).

Neither of these reasons stands up to scrutiny. As to the former, it would seem that whether all speakers (even all normal speakers) interpret conditionals in the same way should be regarded as an empirical question itself. In fact, it was already noted that there is evidence suggesting that normal speakers do *not* all interpret conditionals in the same way (see p. 4; note that we certainly would not want to say that only high-IQ adults count as normal speakers).

A much more important consideration is that, in a way, we philosophers may *not* (or rather may no longer) be normal speakers. It is relatively common practice in psychological experiments on conditionals to ask participants whether they have any background in logic. Responses from participants who answer this question positively are then usually excluded from the analysis. This is because such participants may simply base their responses on their knowledge of the semantics of the conditional-forming operator in propositional logic that they were instructed on in some course they took. Including the responses of such participants might yield at least partial confirmation for the material conditional account, where this partial confirmation may then well be spurious, possibly only showing that some participants have satisfactorily memorized their lessons in logic. Obviously, philosophers would all fall into this category of participants to exclude in these experiments.

Equally important is the consideration that philosophers working on conditionals will not only have a background in logic; they will be familiar with all or almost all semantics for conditionals that have been proposed, among which they may have their favorite. There is no reason to believe that philosophers are less susceptible to confirmation bias than other people, which in the present context might amount to giving more weight to certain of one's intuitions than to others, or perhaps to reject as irrelevant all too easily those conditionals which one's preferred semantics does not adequately deal with.

As for the accusation of psychologism, it should be remembered that modern logic was devised to facilitate reasoning in mathematics, and the language of mathematics is in many respects unlike ordinary language. At a minimum, this makes it reasonable to treat as an open question at least initially whether the conditional that we know from propositional logic – the material conditional – captures the meaning of the natural-language "if . . . then . . ."-construction.[20] A still weightier consideration is that the evidence that the two are *not* the same is, by now, simply overwhelming – as will be seen at various junctures in the book. It is too much to believe that all or almost all of us are with great frequency mistaken about whether some conditional is true, or whether it is acceptable, or how probable it is. But *that*, as psychologists have shown, is precisely what must be concluded if the ordinary-language conditional is taken to coincide with the material conditional.

[20] There are general reasons for being doubtful about at least the radical form of antipsychologism that was famously propagated by Frege. If one wants one's logic to also pertain to the arguments encountered in everyday reasoning and cast in natural language, then surely one will want it to be descriptively adequate in the sense that people do not regularly violate the introduction and elimination rules associated with the various logical constants; if people in their reasoning frequently violate the introduction and/or elimination rules for (say) the conjunction operator, then that is a strong indication that those rules fail to capture the meaning of the natural-language expression "and." Note, however, that if this is granted, there may be no way to maintain the old ideal of logic as giving an account of purely form-based valid inference. For instance, experiments documented in Elqayam [2006] appear to show that whether people evaluate conjunctions with indeterminate conjuncts according to the weak Kleene table for the conjunction operator or according to the strong Kleene table depends on the *content* of the conjuncts (and possibly on the source of the indeterminacy).

This is not to suggest that there are no principles of correct reasoning governing the natural-language conditional; for all we know, such principles do exist. It is just that these cannot simply be taken to be provided by the introduction and elimination rules for the material conditional. And in trying to figure out just which logical principles the ordinary-language conditional does obey, we are more likely to be helped by having at hand a broad base of linguistic data, consisting of collections of judgments unbiased by formal training or a conscious or unconscious preference for this or that semantics, than by having as a basis only our own responses to a limited set of conditionals. To be clear on this, I am not urging that philosophers should stop caring about the norms of correct reasoning insofar as they involve conditionals, much less about normative issues in general. The point is merely that if we are interested in the norms that pertain to the natural-language conditional, then we cannot simply take for granted that this conditional's semantics is given by the truth table for the material conditional, or indeed by some other semantics arrived at purely on the basis of a priori reflection.

1.4 What is to come

While the emphasis of the book will be on epistemological questions pertaining to conditionals, Chapter 2 is devoted to semantic issues. Its main purpose is to give an overview of the best-known semantics of conditionals, as well as of their strengths and weaknesses. This will serve as background knowledge when we address the epistemological questions in the later chapters. The chapter will also cover some new ground, however, by drawing attention to a recent development in the semantics of conditionals that states truth conditions for conditionals in terms of the presence or absence of an inferential connection between a conditional's antecedent and its consequent.

The one epistemological question that *has* received much attention is the question of what the probability of a conditional is. As said, the work expended on this question so far has led to nearly universal agreement about what the probability of a conditional is *not*, namely, it is (allegedly) *not* the corresponding conditional probability. Meanwhile, data have accumulated which seem to indicate that people do evaluate the probability of a conditional as the corresponding conditional probability. Chapter 3 examines the formal arguments that have led theorists to believe that probabilities of conditionals are not conditional probabilities, as well as the experiments in the psychology of reasoning that suggest that people do judge a conditional to be probable to the extent to which they judge its consequent probable on the supposition of its antecedent. The chapter also canvasses some very recent experimental work on the probabilities of conditionals, arguing that this shows a way toward resolving the tension between the formal results and the earlier empirical data.

The aforementioned formal results have convinced many that conditional probabilities measure not the *probability* of conditionals, but rather their (degree of) *acceptability*. Chapter 4 discusses experimental work that discredits this claim. The relation between the degree to which people judge a conditional to be acceptable and their judgments of the corresponding conditional probability is much less straightforward than is generally believed. Also, it is not the same for all conditionals, not even as here understood (that is, as limited to simple normal indicative conditionals). But if we make the right kind of (further) distinctions between types of conditionals in this class, then some fairly precise and systematic claims *can* be made about how conditional probabilities and degrees of acceptability of the corresponding conditionals relate to each other.

Chapter 4 also looks at the categorical acceptability of conditionals, that is, the circumstances under which we deem a conditional acceptable and those under which we deem it unacceptable. On some influential accounts, whether a conditional is categorically acceptable depends on whether the corresponding conditional probability is "high enough." It has long been held that high conditional probability of a conditional's consequent given its antecedent is necessary and sufficient for the categorical acceptability of that conditional. I argue, on both theoretical and empirical grounds, that this is wrong and that the notion of evidential support plays a critical role in the acceptability of conditionals as well, alongside that of high conditional probability.

Granted the role of the notion of evidential support in the (categorical) acceptability of conditionals, which inferential principles are closure conditions for acceptability? That is to say, which inferential principles are such that whenever their premises are acceptable, so is their conclusion? Chapter 5 aims to answer this question. It will be seen that, given the acceptability conditions proposed in Chapter 4, only a limited number of inferential principles qualify as closure conditions for acceptability. In particular, some principles that pretheoretically appear plausible as closure conditions turn out not to preserve acceptability. The chapter explains away the clashing intuitions by introducing the notion of graded validity. With this notion at hand, it can be shown that, roughly, some principles that provably do not preserve acceptability are still such that in *almost* all models in which their premises are acceptable, their conclusion is acceptable too.

In Chapter 6, we look at how one should model belief updates due to the receipt of conditional information. In line with our general methodology, we address the question from a Bayesian perspective. There is no known answer to the question of how to model the accommodation of conditional information in a Bayesian framework. The chapter presents data suggesting that a strictly Bayesian account of updating on conditionals may not exist. As will be seen, the data appear to indicate that such updating proceeds at least sometimes on the basis of explanatory considerations, which are generally thought to have no place in Bayesian epistemology. The chapter proposes a model of updating on conditionals that is broadly Bayesian but that also explicitly factors in explanatory considerations. The model is shown to have clear empirical content and thus to be open to empirical testing; but that is yet to be undertaken.

1.5 Intended audience

This book was written with an audience of both philosophers and psychologists in mind. As noted in Section 1.3, I believe the time to be ripe for philosophers and psychologists interested in conditionals to team up and tackle the central questions concerning conditionals in collaborative work. Such joint work is more likely to be successful if each party has an understanding of what the other party has deemed important in past research. Some psychologists working on conditionals still seem to rely on assumptions in their work that philosophers have shown to be doubtful on a priori grounds. Some also appear to be unfamiliar with what in philosophy are more or less generally recognized distinctions between types of conditionals (like some of the distinctions highlighted in Section 1.2). Conversely, many philosophers working on conditionals are unaware of the level of methodological sophistication that characterizes much current experimental work on conditionals. That may be a reason why they feel justified to ignore the outcomes of that work, especially if these outcomes go against their favorite theory of conditionals. In fact, it is not uncommon to encounter philosophers holding that even the best experimental research on conditionals will only yield evidence of the many ways in which ordinary people are confused about conditionals (their truth conditions, their probabilities, how to reason with conditionals). But, as mentioned previously, if we are truly interested in becoming clearer about the semantics and epistemology of *natural-language* conditionals, then it is surely inappropriate to deem irrelevant how conditionals tend to be used and understood by those lacking a PhD in philosophy; then we should seek to make contact with how conditionals are being used and understood by the general public.

This book is meant to inform psychologists about what are the most recent ideas concerning conditionals launched by philosophers, and philosophers about recent empirical work on conditionals. This means that some parts may appear somewhat elementary from the perspective of a philosopher, while other parts may appear somewhat elementary from the perspective of a psychologist. It is hoped, however, that the bulk of the book has new things to say to both research communities and will help to foster the kind of collaborative work that, as mentioned, I believe to be presently called for and that also underlies some of the results to be reported in the following.

Conditionals have also been a long-time object of study in linguistics, and increasingly they are receiving attention from researchers working in Artificial Intelligence and from computer scientists more generally. In the field of Artificial Intelligence, researchers are trying to develop software that can help computers understand natural language, and so also natural-language conditionals. For that purpose, it is of the foremost importance that we acquire a better grip on how *humans* understand such conditionals. The present book aims to contribute to that understanding. As for linguists, it will be seen that at various junctures in the book reference will be made to a distinction between conditionals that originates in the linguistics literature, to wit, the distinction between inferential and content conditionals. Inferential conditionals in particular will play a key role in some of the empirical work to be reported. While linguists have proposed further typologies of conditionals based on the inferential/content divide, they seem to have missed a very natural and simple division of inferential conditionals in terms of the type of inference they embody (whether the inference is deductive, inductive, or abductive). This typology may deserve a place in linguistic research as well. Views about the acceptability of conditionals, to be discussed in Chapter 4, as well as about the semantics/pragmatics distinction insofar as it pertains to conditionals, which will come up at several places, should also be of interest to linguists.

CHAPTER 2

Semantics

Although many proposals have been made concerning the truth conditions of conditionals, three have been clearly dominant in the literature: the material conditional account, Stalnaker's possible worlds semantics, and the non-propositional view.

Of these three semantics, the first was once the orthodoxy in philosophy. That is no longer the case, even if it still seems to be regarded as the "default" position by philosophers *not* actively working on conditionals, and it still has its proponents among philosophers who presently work on conditionals.[1] Philosophers working on conditionals nowadays are more likely to favor a version of the non-propositional view, though most have their own specific semantics, which only they themselves adhere to, as a rule. (In this area of research, if one's semantics is not *completely* ignored by one's colleagues, it counts as a major achievement.)

In psychology, the situation is different in that relatively many psychologists working on conditionals, notably those working in the mental models tradition of Johnson-Laird [1983], are still inclined toward the material conditional account.[2] By contrast, those working within the New

---

[1] Most notably, Jackson [1979], [1987] and Rieger [2006], [2013]. Famous earlier proponents include Quine [1959], Lewis [1976], and Grice [1989a].

[2] In Johnson-Laird and Byrne's [2002] mental models account of conditionals, at least the "core" meaning of basic conditionals is given by the truth table for the material conditional, where basic conditionals are said to be "those with a neutral content that is as independent as possible from context and background knowledge, and which have an antecedent and consequent that are semantically independent apart from their occurrence in the same conditional" (p. 648). Johnson-Laird and Byrne [2002:657–660] argue that the core meaning of a conditional can be modulated, both by the meanings of the antecedent and consequent and by contextually salient background premises, in the sense that these factors can elicit connections between the antecedent and consequent which cannot be captured by a truth-functional account of conditionals. However, the examples they give in support of this claim fail to convince me. For instance, they claim that "If Vivien entered the elevator, then Evelyn left it one floor up" cannot be truth-functional because its truth depends on spatial and temporal relations between the events mentioned in the sentence, where they take these relations to be brought about by the use of the pronoun "it" in the consequent. But it seems that when we interpret this conditional, we automatically unpack it as something like: "If Vivien

Paradigm described in the previous chapter typically advocate some version of non-propositionalism. Stalnaker's semantics has never been popular as a semantics of *indicative* conditionals, either in philosophy or in psychology, but at least in philosophy many believe it to provide the best semantics of *subjunctive* conditionals.

In linguistics, again the situation is different. According to von Fintel [2011, Sects. 4, 5], there is hardly any support for non-propositionalism among linguists; instead, most linguists endorse the Lewis–Kratzer view.[3] In this view, there is no such thing as a conditional operator; rather, antecedent clauses attach to overt or covert operators, restricting the domain of quantification of those operators. The Lewis–Kratzer view has not received much attention from either philosophers or psychologists.[4]

All three main semantics of conditionals are known to have their virtues. However, all three also face severe problems. This chapter discusses these semantics and their virtues and problems.

2.1 The main semantics of conditionals

Among those who hold that conditionals have classical truth conditions – so are always either true or false – the main divide is over the question of whether these truth conditions are truth-functional, meaning that the truth value of a conditional depends on the truth values of its antecedent and consequent, and on nothing else. All agree that if the truth conditions of conditionals are truth-functional (and as long as we admit only two truth values), conditionals are equivalent to their material counterparts. Just consider the options for filling out the blanks in the following table:

φ	ψ	If φ, then ψ
T	T	?
T	F	?
F	T	?
F	F	?

entered the elevator, then Evelyn left the elevator one floor above and after Vivien entered the elevator." (This kind of unpacking is ubiquitous in interpretation and is well documented in the linguistics literature; see, e.g., Sperber and Wilson [1986] and Carston [2004].) Thus interpreted, the spatial and temporal relations are fully explicit in the consequent and thereby cannot pose an obstacle to a truth-functional analysis of the conditional. For a systematic critique of Johnson-Laird and Byrne's account of conditionals, see Evans, Over, and Handley [2005].

[3] See Lewis [1975] and Kratzer [1986].
[4] Though see Égré and Cozic [2011] for a recent discussion of the Lewis–Kratzer view from a philosophical perspective.

There are sixteen different ways of completing this table, but there appears to be at most one good candidate for stating the truth conditions of natural-language conditionals. Not *quite* all (see toward the end of this section), but *almost* all authors who hold that a conditional can have a truth value at all – regardless of whether it *always* has one – consider two cases as uncontroversial, to wit

φ	ψ	If φ, then ψ
T	T	T
T	F	F
F	T	?
F	F	?

If this is accepted, it leaves four options, which can then be reduced further. Filling the open places with Fs yields the truth table for the conjunction, and "If φ, then ψ" is certainly not equivalent to the conjunction of φ and ψ.[5] Similarly, entering an F on the third line and a T on the fourth yields the truth table for material equivalence, which is patently wrong as well: the truth of "If φ, then ψ" does not require φ to be a necessary condition for ψ;[6] intuitively, "If it starts raining, the match will be canceled" can be true even if the match will also be canceled in the event of snow. And entering a T on the third line and an F on the fourth would make a conditional equivalent to its consequent, which is again wrong: supposing "If this glass is dropped, it will break" can be true at all, it can be true even if the glass will never break. There is only one remaining option now:

φ	ψ	If φ, then ψ
T	T	T
T	F	F
F	T	T
F	F	T

This is the truth table for the material conditional. It may be rejectable, but at least it does not have the prima facie implausibility of the previous options. All who have considered the matter have taken this to convincingly show that *if* one thinks that conditionals have a truth-functional

---

[5] Although, as was mentioned on page 4, young children and cognitively less able adults are inclined to interpret conditionals this way.

[6] At least not typically; there *is* the phenomenon of conditional perfection, which some analyze in terms of material equivalence (see Geis and Zwicky [1971]).

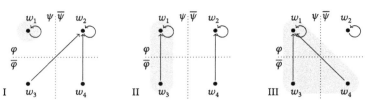

Figure 2.1 The Stalnaker conditional "If φ, then ψ" in different possible worlds models.

semantics, *then* one better think that their truth conditions are those of the corresponding material conditionals.[7]

The other main truth-conditional semantics of conditionals takes for granted the notion of a possible world, roughly understood as a way the world might be or might have been. On this position, a conditional is true iff its consequent is true in the "closest" possible world in which the conditional's antecedent is true, provided there *is* a world in which the antecedent is true, where "closest" means "most similar to the actual world."[8] Accordingly, the proposition expressed by a conditional "If φ, then ψ" corresponds to the set of those worlds whose closest φ-worlds (the worlds where φ holds) are also ψ-worlds. That is, more formally, where $f(w, \varphi)$ denotes the φ-world closest to w,[9] and $v(\varphi, w) = 1$ indicates that φ holds true in w, "If φ, then ψ" expresses the proposition $\{w \mid v(\psi, f(w, \varphi)) = 1\}$. Given that if φ is true at a world w, then w is its own closest φ-world, we can put the foregoing differently by saying that the proposition expressed by "If φ, then ψ" consists of the union of the set of φ- and ψ-worlds with the set of $\overline{\varphi}$-worlds whose closest φ-world is a ψ-world. (In formulas, I use overline notation to designate a proposition's negation.) Figure 2.1, in which arrows lead from given worlds to their closest φ-worlds and the gray areas indicate the propositions expressed by "If φ, then ψ," illustrates the semantics.

It might appear that because of its reference to the actual world in the truth condition, this proposal allows us to evaluate a conditional only if we know which world is actual (which we typically do not know). But that is not so. For instance, to be certain that "If φ, then ψ" is true, it is enough to be certain that each world we take to be a candidate for being the actual world has a closest φ-world that is also a ψ-world.

---

[7] See also Edgington [1995:242] for an elegant argument to the effect that the material conditional account is the only candidate for a truth-functional semantics of conditionals.

[8] See Lewis [1973a:91–95] for a thorough discussion of the notion of similarity between worlds.

[9] If φ holds in no world, $f(w, \varphi)$ is stipulated to denote the (unique) impossible world. This complication need not detain us here.

According to Stalnaker – its main proponent – the possible worlds account applies to both indicative and subjunctive conditionals.[10,11] However, in the case of indicative conditionals there is a pragmatic constraint on which worlds can count as "closest," to wit, that they must be among the ones that are not ruled out by anything that has been accepted or is presupposed in the context in which the conditional is asserted or evaluated.[12] As a result, in the possible worlds account, indicative conditionals have truth conditions only relative to contexts.

Restricted to indicative conditionals, the material conditional account and the possible worlds account partially agree: if a conditional's antecedent is true and its consequent false, then both assign the value "false" to the conditional; and if both the conditional's antecedent and its consequent are true, then both accounts assign it the value "true" – these are the cases on which virtually everyone agrees, as said above. In the remaining cases, however, the accounts may diverge in their truth value assignments. On the possible worlds account, it is not necessarily the case that a conditional is true if its antecedent is false; perhaps its consequent fails to hold in the closest world in which its antecedent is true. Differently put, it is not necessarily the case that the set of possible worlds in which either φ is false or ψ is true coincides with the set of worlds whose closest φ-worlds are ψ-worlds.

There is not a whole lot to explain about the standard version of the third main account, the non-propositional view, other than that it amounts to the negative claim that conditionals never have a truth value. There is more to say, however, about a less radical version of this view, according to which conditionals have the truth value of their consequent if their antecedent is true and are neither true nor false – and so, as some like to say, have a third "truth value"[13] – if their antecedent is false. For this view raises the question of what the truth value of a conditional is if its

---

[10] Lewis [1973a] independently developed a very similar possible worlds semantics, which, however, only applies to subjunctive conditionals in his view. (See Égré and Cozic [2014, Sect. 3] for a concise and clear comparison of Lewis' and Stalnaker's semantics.) Davis [1979] disagrees with both Lewis and Stalnaker in holding that the possible worlds account gives the right semantics for indicative conditionals and *only* for these conditionals.

[11] It will be noted that the material conditional account is not even a prima facie plausible candidate for giving the semantics of subjunctive conditionals. For it would have us evaluate as true all so-called counterfactual conditionals, that is, subjunctive conditionals with antecedents we take to be false; and we have no difficulty thinking of counterfactuals we deem to be false.

[12] See Stalnaker [1968:109 ff] for details. Subjunctive conditionals are obviously exempt from this constraint.

[13] Proponents of this version typically hasten to add that the third value stands for something like "uncertain" or "indeterminate" or "void," following suggestions made by Ramsey and de Finetti; see Politzer, Over, and Baratgin [2010] and Baratgin, Over, and Politzer [2014].

antecedent, or its consequent, or both, are neither true nor false. In other words, it raises the question of what to put in place of the question marks in the third column of this table:

φ	ψ	If φ, then ψ			
		?	de Finetti	Farrell	Cooper
T	T	T	T	T	T
T	U	?	U	U	U
T	F	F	F	F	F
U	T	?	U	U	T
U	U	?	U	U	U
U	F	?	U	F	F
F	T	U	U	U	U
F	U	U	U	U	U
F	F	U	U	U	U

While most of the $3^4 = 81$ ways of filling the gaps can be dismissed out of hand, the de Finetti, Farrell, and Cooper truth tables have some currency in the literature. However, non-radical non-propositionalists have not been able to provide convincing reasons why we should settle on one of these rather than on one of the others (supposing, that is, we grant the need for a third truth value).

In fact, once a third truth value is admitted, we also need new truth tables for the other connectives. We then want to know, for instance, what the truth value of a disjunction is if both disjuncts are indeterminate.[14] And as Farrell [1986], McDermott [1996], Gilio and Over [2012], and Baratgin, Over, and Politzer [2013] show, the task facing the non-radical non-propositionalist is still more daunting. Not only are there many different ways of extending the classical truth tables for conjunction, disjunction, and negation such that they incorporate the value of being

---

[14] At first, it might seem evident that the value of the disjunction should be indeterminate as well. But what if one disjunct is the negation of the other, so that the disjunction has the form of a tautology? The truth table for conjunction raises a similar problem, of course. Moreover, as already briefly mentioned in note 20, Elqayam [2006] presents empirical data suggesting that people may evaluate conjunctions with an indeterminate conjunct differently depending on the *source* of the indeterminacy. For example, her experiments show that people tend to evaluate conjunctions with a truth-teller sentence as a constituent according to the so-called Strong Kleene Schema for conjunctions (see Kleene [1952, Sect. 64]), whereas they are more likely to evaluate conjunctions with a liar sentence as a constituent according to the "collapsed table for conjunction," meaning that such conjunctions are evaluated as false (and not indeterminate) except when *both* conjuncts are liar sentences, in which case most people evaluate the conjunction as indeterminate. While Elqayam's work shows that conjunctions with an indeterminate conjunct are sometimes evaluated as false and sometimes as indeterminate, McDermott [1996:8] argues that such conjunctions can also sometimes be true.

neither true nor false, for any given choice of extending those truth tables there are further choices to be made with respect to the accompanying notion of validity. Is this to be taken as preservation of truth – every valuation that makes the premises come out true makes the conclusion come out true – or rather as preservation of non-falsity – every valuation that makes each premise come out not false makes the conclusion come out not false – or as both, or as something else altogether? Among proponents of the present view, there is no unanimity on any of these questions.[15],[16]

These are just the *main* semantics of conditionals. A host of other semantics have been proposed, which I will not try to catalogue here. I do, however, want to briefly draw attention to an old idea that has recently been revived and that appears promising to me.

2.2 Inferentialism

When I introduced the distinction between normal and special or non-standard conditionals (on p. 12), I mentioned that, in contrast to special conditionals, normal conditionals seem to suggest the existence of some kind of dependency relation between antecedent and consequent. At various junctures in the history of theorizing about conditionals, the idea has surfaced that the suggested dependency is part of the semantic content of the conditional (and so is not, for instance, conventionally or conversationally implicated, as some Griceans might have it). Specifically, conditionals have been said to require for their truth the presence of a "connection" linking their antecedent and consequent.[17]

---

[15] See McDermott [1996], Milne [1997], Cantwell [2008], and van Wijnbergen-Huitink [2008, Ch. 5] for different views on this matter.

[16] It is worth remarking that Stalnaker and Jeffrey [1994] in effect present an interesting, infinite-valued variant of the non-radical non-propositionalist approach. In their account, a conditional has the semantic value of its consequent if its antecedent is true, and has as its semantic value the mathematical expectation of its consequent conditional on the antecedent if the antecedent is false (which can be any value in the interval $[0, 1]$).

[17] Stalnaker [1968:100 f] also considers the idea that the truth of a conditional requires the presence of some connection between antecedent and consequent. He dismisses that idea, however, because he thinks that there are true conditionals whose antecedent and consequent manifestly lack a connection. To buttress this point, he gives as an example the conditional "If the Chinese enter the Vietnam conflict, the United States will use nuclear weapons," and he considers it from the perspective of someone (viewing the matter in the late 1960s) who believes that the United States is going to use nuclear weapons in the Vietnam war in any case, and that it will not make much of a difference whether the Chinese enter the war as well. That person, Stalnaker thinks, will still judge the conditional to be true. Note, however, that here distinguishing between normal and special conditionals pays off. For we are presented a clear example of a non-interference conditional, which also passes the litmus test with flying colors, given that replacing "if" by "whether or not" in the conditional has, from the sketched perspective, no noticeable impact on the assertability of the

Proposals in this vein immediately raise the question of what the nature of the supposed connection could be. Candidate answers abound: it could be logical, statistical, causal, explanatory, metaphysical, epistemic; or the "connector" could be a second-order functional property, notably, the property that there is some first-order property or other that links antecedent and consequent, much in the way in which some have argued that truth is a second-order functional property, instantiated by correspondence to the facts in some domains of discourse, by assertability or verifiability in other domains, and by yet some other first-order property in yet other domains.[18]

According to the best-known accounts in this class, the requisite connection is *inferential*. More exactly, according to these accounts a conditional is true iff there is a valid argument with the conditional's antecedent plus, possibly, contextually indicated background assumptions as its premises and the conditional's consequent as its conclusion. This idea dates back to ancient times and has been defended by many philosophers since (see Kneale and Kneale [1962, Ch. 3] and Sanford [1989, Chs. 1, 2]). For example, in Mill's *System of Logic* we find the following passage:

> When we say, If the Koran comes from God, Mahomet is the prophet of God, we do not intend to affirm either that the Koran does come from God, or that Mahomet is really his prophet. Neither of these simple propositions may be true, and yet the truth of the [conditional] may be indisputable. What is asserted is not the truth of either of the propositions, but the inferribility of the one from the other. (Mill [1843/1872:91])

Ramsey [1929/1990:156] seems to agree when he says that "[i]n general we can say with Mill that 'If *p*, then *q*' means that *q* is inferrible from *p*, that is, of course, from *p* together with certain facts and laws not stated but in some way indicated by the context."[19] And Mackie [1973:67] states something like this view under the heading of "the consequentialist account."[20] Récanati [2000, Ch. 4] in passing arrives at a semantics of conditionals that also falls into the category at issue.

conditional. Jackson [2006, Sect. 4] also invokes what appear to be non-interference conditionals to argue against semantics that require some kind of support relation between antecedent and consequent.

[18] See, e.g., Wright [1994] and Lynch [2009].

[19] Woods [1997:20] suggests that this passage pertains only to counterfactuals. There is no textual evidence to support this view, however. To the contrary, commenting on the passage Ramsey uses an indicative conditional ("If I open my eyes I shall see red") for purposes of illustration.

[20] Mackie, at least in his 1973 paper, endorses a different account of conditionals, which he dubs "the condensed argument account." According to this account, a conditional is itself an argument in truncated form. The view is only superficially related to the consequentialist account, for given that an argument is neither true nor false, the condensed argument account is really a non-propositional semantics of conditionals.

In the psychological literature, this view has been defended by Braine [1978]; see also Braine and O'Brien [1991]. As Braine [1978:8] puts the core idea, "the logical function of if–then is taken to be the same as that of the inference line, that is, if–then and the inference line are different notations for indicating the same relation between two propositions." The treatment of conditionals favored by linguists, which is due to Kratzer [1986], [1991], [2012] (who takes her cue from Lewis [1975]), also seems to be in this vein, especially when cast in the form of what Lewis [1981] calls a "premise semantics." On this account, conditionals involve (often implicit) modal expressions like "must." According to Kratzer [2012:9], "[t]he meaning of must is related to logical consequence: a proposition is necessary with respect to a premise set if it follows from it." Then a conditional is said to be true just in case its consequent follows from the premise set joined with the antecedent.

Krzyżanowska [2012], [2015] notes that if this type of semantics – dubbed "inferentialism" in Douven et al. [2015] – enjoys little popularity today, then that may be because so far its champions have tended to unpack the notion of a consequent following from an antecedent strictly in terms of (classical) deductive inference. For it is not difficult to conceive of conditionals that pretheoretically appear true, yet whose consequent does not follow deductively from their antecedent. Consider, for instance,

(2.1)   If Millie misses her bus, she will be late for the movies.

It is easy enough to imagine a context in which we would pretheoretically regard (2.1) as being true, even though we can never rule out that, through some freak quantum event (say), Millie is transported from her present location to the cinema before the beginning of the movie – that is, even though we are not licensed to infer the conditional's consequent from its antecedent.[21]

As Krzyżanowska also notes, however, this problem can be avoided by doing justice to the fact that a consequent following from an antecedent

---

[21] To state the problem with greater precision and generality, identify a context with the background premises accepted in it, and let $\vdash$ stand for the classical consequence relation and $\supset$ for the material conditional operator. Then, according to the proposal we are considering, a conditional "If φ, then ψ" is true in a given context Γ if and only if $\Gamma, \varphi \vdash \psi$, which, in virtue of the deduction theorem for classical logic, means that $\Gamma \vdash \varphi \supset \psi$, which, in virtue of the compactness theorem for classical logic, means that there is a finite $\Gamma^* = \{\gamma_1, \ldots, \gamma_n\} \subseteq \Gamma$ such that $\Gamma^* \vdash \varphi \supset \psi$, which, finally, again by the deduction theorem, means that $\vdash (\gamma_1 \wedge \cdots \wedge \gamma_n \wedge \varphi) \supset \psi$. In words, on this account, whenever a conditional is true in a context, there are background premises in that context such that conjoining them to the antecedent of the conditional and interpreting the conditional materially yields a theorem of classical logic. This may hold for some true conditionals, but it certainly does not hold for all.

may be understood in terms of a number of different inferential connections, including (but not limited to) deductive inference.[22] Krzyżanowska, Wenmackers, and Douven [2014], elaborating on these observations, propose a contextualist semantics for the specific type of conditionals – so-called inferential conditionals, to be properly introduced and discussed in Section 4.1 – with which they are concerned in their paper. Sticking to their basic idea but generalizing to other types of conditionals, the proposal amounts to the claim that a conditional is true iff there is a valid argument from antecedent to consequent, where – importantly – the notion of validity is understood by reference not just to deductive logic but also to inductive and abductive logic, so that an argument can be valid even if its conclusion does not follow deductively from its premises. More exactly, the proposal is that a conditional is true in a given context iff the consequent follows via a number of inferential steps from the antecedent, possibly in conjunction with contextually given background knowledge, where, first, the steps are all valid in a deductive, inductive, or abductive sense; second, the consequent does not follow (in the same generalized sense) from the background knowledge alone; and third, the antecedent is (deductively) consistent with the background knowledge.[23,24]

---

[22] According to most commentators, the Stoics, or at least some Stoic philosophers, understood the conditional as requiring for its truth a *deductive* connection between antecedent and consequent; see, e.g., Mates [1953:42] and Kneale and Kneale [1962:161]. That also seems to hold for Ramsey, who continues the passage cited in the main text by saying, without further comment, that "[t]his means that $p \supset q$ follows from these facts and laws" (where $\supset$ again symbolizes the material conditional). The equivalence plainly holds – in virtue of the deduction theorem – if the notion of inference assumed is that of deductive inference. It is by no means obvious that it holds if a broader notion of inference is assumed. Braine [1978] and Braine and O'Brien [1991] also explicitly commit to a deductive notion of inference; in fact, the notion of inference countenanced by Braine and O'Brien is even a bit weaker than the one defined by standard deductive logic, inasmuch as they banish the Ex Falso rule, which allows one to infer anything from a contradiction (Braine and O'Brien [1991:184 f]). In his description of the consequentialist account, Mackie [1973:67] requires that there be *some* consequence relation between antecedent and consequent, where this relation may be a different one for different types of conditionals. However, in his critical discussion of the view, Mackie [1973:82 ff] makes it clear that any consequence relation must at least be such as to *ensure* the truth of the consequent on the basis of the truth of the antecedent (plus the truth of possible background assumptions). That requirement still seems too demanding. Whether Mill thought a deductive link is required is unclear; see on this Skorupski [1989:73 f].

[23] Without the second clause, the proposal would still fail to capture the intuitive requirement of a connection between antecedent and consequent. Together, the second and third clause are also meant to block the paradoxes of strict implication: without the second, conditionals with a logically true consequent would count as true, and without the third, conditionals with a logically false antecedent would count as true.

[24] The same semantics could be considered for subjunctive conditionals, given that an argument can be valid even if its premise or premises are false, or believed to be false. As such, the semantics could be thought of as a distant cousin of Goodman's [1955, Ch. 1] "cotenability" theory, according to which a subjunctive conditional is true iff its antecedent in conjunction with some law or laws of

Both the aforementioned paper and Krzyżanowska, Wenmackers, and Douven [2013] provide (admittedly modest) empirical evidence in support of their version of inferentialism. In particular, these papers report some success with this semantics in predicting the effect that so-called evidential markers (notably, "probably," "must," and "should" in English, and "waarschijnlijk," "zou moeten," and "moet" in Dutch) have on the assertability of different types of inferential conditionals.

Stronger empirical support for inferentialism was recently obtained in a study reported in Douven et al. [2015]. In this study, participants were presented with a soritical color series of fourteen patches, ranging from clearly green to clearly blue. They were then asked to evaluate conditionals pertaining to these patches. Specifically, they were asked to judge as true, false, or neither true nor false conditionals of the form "If patch number i is X, then so is patch number j," where, depending on the test condition, X was either "green" or "blue" and, depending on a further test condition, either $j \in \{i-2, i-1, i+1, i+2\}$ or $j \in \{i-3, i-1, i+1, i+3\}$. In this paper, Douven and coauthors derive, for all the main semantics as well as for the above version of inferentialism, predictions about which factors will influence the participants' answers. For instance, according to non-propositionalism, nothing matters except the fact that all sentences to be evaluated by the participants are conditionals: that predicts that all answers will be in the "neither true nor false" category. To give another example, the material conditional account predicts that only the ranks in the soritical series of the patches referred to in the antecedent and consequent matter (given that these ranks determine the truth values of the conditional's parts). Douven and coauthors derive similar predictions for Stalnaker's semantics as well as for the three-valued semantics discussed at the end of the previous section. As for the version of inferentialism at issue, they show that it implies that participants' answers will be determined by three factors, to wit, (i) the position of the consequent patch relative to the antecedent patch (is the consequent patch located to the left or to the right of the antecedent patch in the soritical series?), (ii) the

---

nature and possibly also with some auxiliary assumptions that are compatible with the antecedent (classically) entails the conditional's consequent. This inferentialist semantics would be more liberal than Goodman's in a number of ways, most notably by not requiring that the entailment be classical, but also by not requiring that there be a law of nature cited among the premises (which has been found to be problematic; see, e.g., Edgington [1995:249]). Naturally, for the present proposal to apply to counterfactuals, there must be an acceptable account of explanation (which the account of abduction that will go into the definition of entailment can build on) that does not itself rely on a prior theory of subjunctive conditionals; but such accounts exist (see, e.g., de Regt and Dieks [2005]). I leave it as a question for future research whether the proposal to apply the inferentialist semantics to subjunctive conditionals faces other problems.

number of patches lying in between the antecedent patch and consequent patch, and (iii) the absolute location of the consequent patch in
the series of fourteen patches; together these factors determine whether
there is a strong argument from antecedent to consequent, for the conditionals in the materials of the experiment. Douven et al.'s [2015] analysis
of the data shows that inferentialism provides the best model by far of
those data.[25]

To be sure, Douven et al.'s [2015] study uses an experimental paradigm
of a very specific type and with very specific materials. However, it is not
difficult to conceive of further and rather different experiments that can
help us decide between the various semantics for conditionals that are currently on offer. A main distinguishing feature of inferentialism is that it
does not validate the inferential principle – commonly called "Centering,"
or CS – that allows us to infer the conditional "If φ, then ψ" from the
conjunction of φ and ψ, a principle that *is* valid given *any* of the main
semantics for conditionals discussed in Section 2.1. So, for instance, given
that Obama is the president of the United States and the 2018 Winter
Olympics will be held in South Korea, Centering allows us to infer that
if Obama is the president of the United States, then the 2018 Winter
Olympics will be held in South Korea, as well as that if the 2018 Winter Olympics will be held in South Korea, Obama is the president of the

---

[25] In Douven et al. [2015], the semantics of Krzyżanowska, Wenmackers, and Douven [2013] is glossed
as follows: a conditional is true iff there is a strong enough argument leading from its antecedent
plus background knowledge to its consequent. As noted in Douven et al. [2015], what counts as
strong enough may be different for different people and it may also be a vague matter. As also noted
there, however, people sharing the same background knowledge may differ in their assessment of
the truth value of a conditional; indeed, Douven et al.'s study provides ample empirical evidence for
this claim. Moreover, it can be vague whether a given conditional is true or not (Edgington [1992],
[1997a]). In the absence of worked-out accounts of induction and abduction, there is little reason
to prefer the definition in Krzyżanowska, Wenmackers, and Douven [2013] over the seemingly
more informal gloss in Douven et al. [2015]. In fact, what Krzyżanowska, Wenmackers, and Douven tried to capture in their 2013 paper is exactly the intuition that the antecedent should provide
strong grounds for believing the consequent. In view of this, as well as in the light of arguments
given in Nelkin [2000] to the effect that purely statistical arguments fail to give strong grounds
for belief, I would now say that an argument connecting antecedent (plus background knowledge)
and consequent that consists strictly of inductive steps is not enough for the truth of the given
conditional. A more definite and precise statement of the semantics will have to await the development of better formal accounts of inductive and abductive inference. (See Cialdea Mayer and Pirri
[1993], [1995], Kyburg and Teng [2001], and Gabbay and Woods [2005] for some first attempts to
formulate such accounts. One reason why in particular abductive inference has received relatively
little attention from logicians may be that various philosophers have dismissed this type of inference as leading to irrational belief changes (e.g., van Fraassen [1989, Ch. 6]). See Douven [2011b]
for a general overview of the debate concerning abduction, and see Psillos [1999, Ch. 4], Douven
[1999], [2013a], [2016a] and Douven and Wenmackers [2015] for some arguments in defense of
abduction.)

United States. My guess is that few people will want to endorse either of these conditionals. Obviously, however, there is no need to go by my guesses, for it should be easy enough to subject the claim to experimental testing.

Although the basic idea of inferentialism dates back to antiquity, as noted earlier, in its present form the position is still in its infancy. For that reason alone, it is not surprising that inferentialism calls not only for further empirical work, but for attention to some outstanding theoretical issues. I mention four in particular.

First, in their experiment, Douven and coauthors found only a relatively small percentage of "neither true nor false" responses (around 10 percent). In other experimental work, however, such responses were seen to be more prevalent (see, e.g., Barrouillet, Gauffroy, and Lecas [2008], Politzer, Over, and Baratgin [2010], and Baratgin, Over, and Politzer [2013]). More specifically, it was seen in previous experiments that, at least for particular types of materials, people tend to evaluate conditionals with false or indeterminate (neither true nor false) antecedents as indeterminate. (These data are often collectively referred to as "the defective truth table data.") As it currently stands, inferentialism recognizes only the classical semantical values. If it is to be both a general semantics for conditionals and empirically adequate, then inferentialism will have to accommodate the defective truth table data, and so will have to be extended to incorporate indeterminacy as well.

Second, as will be seen in more detail in the next chapter, there is now a large body of data on how people evaluate the probabilities of conditionals supporting the hypothesis that people tend to evaluate those probabilities in line with what has come to be known as "Stalnaker's Hypothesis," according to which the probability of a conditional should equal the corresponding conditional probability (i.e., the probability of the consequent given the antecedent; see Section 2.6 and, especially, Chapter 3). It is currently unclear what inferentialism predicts about the probabilities of conditionals, and, accordingly, it is currently unclear how the designated data bear on inferentialism.

Third, more work is needed on the notions of inductive and abductive inference, on which the version of inferentialism considered here relies. The accounts of these forms of inference that are available today are simply not precise enough to make the empirical content of this semantics fully transparent. Once better accounts are available, there will be new opportunities for subjecting inferentialism to empirical testing.

Finally, it was mentioned above that mainstream thinking has it that *if* conditionals have truth values under at least some circumstances, then they have the truth value of their consequent if their antecedent is true. On the present account, this manifestly fails.[26] A conditional may have a true antecedent and a true consequent without there being a valid argument connecting the two, and thus without the conditional being true. This is a feature, not a bug: it is precisely the failure of Centering, and this failure is intended. After all, the whole point of the proposal is to capture the idea that the existence of a connection between antecedent and consequent is necessary for the truth of a conditional, and that connection is not ensured to exist by the antecedent and the consequent merely both being true.

But the other case – true antecedent, false consequent – raises a stickier issue. Because inductive and abductive inference are both ampliative and so not guaranteed to preserve truth, there may be a valid argument (in the present sense) connecting a true antecedent and a false consequent. If that is the case for a given conditional, should that conditional really count as true, as it does on this proposal? What then remains of the intuition that conditionals obey the rule of Modus Ponens, according to which we can infer ψ from φ and "If φ, then ψ"? If a conditional and its antecedent can both be true while its consequent is false, Modus Ponens is clearly not valid for conditionals in the classical sense of guaranteeing truth-preservation. McGee [1985] and Lycan [2001, Ch. 5] have argued against the validity (in this sense) of Modus Ponens on grounds unrelated to the present matter, but it is fair to say that their arguments have found little acclaim. As will be seen in Chapter 5, however, there may be a way to explain why Modus Ponens appears (classically) valid even if it is not. Particularly, it will be seen that the claim that Modus Ponens is (classically) invalid may sound more dramatic than it is; the rule could still be nearly (classically) valid, in the sense that its conclusion virtually always holds if its premises hold. To repeat, however: this book has no aim to defend any specific semantics of conditionals. I mentioned inferentialism here because I believe that, in the above version, it is a promising approach to the semantics of conditionals. I am not currently prepared to bet a significant sum of money on its truth, and it will not be assumed as

---

[26] It also fails on Lycan's [2001] semantics, which analyses conditionals as contextually restricted quantifiers over events. Roughly, "If φ, then ψ" is true in this semantics iff ψ is true in any contextually envisaged event in which φ is true. Because the domain of contextually envisaged events may fail to include any actual events, it can happen that a conditional and its antecedent are both true while its consequent is not.

a background semantic theory in any of the later chapters concerned with epistemology.

2.3 Why believe that conditionals have truth conditions?

There are some general reasons why one might favor truth-conditional semantics of conditionals over non-truth-conditional semantics. There are also some reasons in favor of specific truth-conditional semantics of conditionals. This section starts by looking at the general reasons and then considers specific reasons favoring the material conditional account and possible worlds semantics, respectively.

Students are typically surprised to learn that there is a controversy about the truth conditions of conditionals; it is not as though there were any disagreement over the truth conditions of conjunctions or disjunctions, after all. They are then even more surprised that there is a genuine dispute about the question of whether conditionals have truth conditions to begin with. Of course, not all sentences have truth conditions; commands and questions do not, for instance. But conditionals are not commands or questions; as previously noted, they seem to be declarative sentences, at least prima facie. It thus might already be a point in favor of truth-conditional accounts of conditionals that they do not make conditionals appear oddballs among the declarative sentences. However, those who hold that conditionals lack truth conditions will note that conditionals are special anyway, as we also remarked immediately at the outset. Thus, the "oddness claim" is unlikely to convince many that conditionals must have truth conditions.

The advocates of the truth-conditional accounts of conditionals have advanced more compelling arguments in favor of their commitment to truth conditions than simply the contention that non-truth-conditional views make conditionals appear too special. One such argument starts by noting that, on the known conceptions of propositions, sentences count as expressing propositions only if they have truth conditions. But if conditionals do not express propositions, then it should be puzzling how we can make sense of Boolean embeddings of such sentences, such as

(2.2)   a. Joan won't come, but if Henry comes, he will bring Sue.
      b. It is not the case that if she fails the exam, she will be allowed to resit.
      c. Either he will change his mind if he hears my arguments or he will leave the department.

After all, the Boolean connectives are *propositional* connectives. Clearly, though, we have no difficulty comprehending these sentences.[27]

Those who deny that conditionals have truth conditions may argue that in ordinary language, grammar does not always transparently reveal logical form, and that for instance (2.2a) is not really a conjunction but is to be thought of as consisting of two sentences, as follows:

(2.3)   Joan won't come. If Henry comes, he will bring Sue.

For pragmatic or stylistic reasons we may concatenate these sentences using "but," which, however, does not function as a propositional operator in that case.

Similarly, it may be suggested that the conditional in (2.2b) is only apparently in the scope of the negation operator, and that the sentence can plausibly be rephrased as

(2.4)   If she fails, then she won't be allowed to resit.

As Edgington [1995:283] argues more generally, "A is to $\neg A$ as 'If A, B' is to 'If A, $\neg B$' [and] 'It's not the case that if A, B' has no clear established sense distinguishable from ['If A, $\neg B$']."[28],[29]

The third example, (2.2c), requires more explaining. It may, to begin with, be paraphrased as

---

[27] See Lewis' [1976:141 f] for an objection along these lines. It might be objected that we *can* make sense of, for instance, disjunctions whose disjuncts do not have truth conditions. For instance, we have no difficulty making sense of "Will climate change dominate the summit or will the ailing economy dominate?" As noted, questions do not have truth conditions and yet it is perfectly natural to concatenate questions by means of a propositional operator ("or," in the example). However, since Frege it is customary to recognize a theory of force next to theories of sense and reference, where this theory of force identifies both the speech act performed by an utterance – whether it is an assertion, a question, a command, and so on – and the declarative statement that is the content of that act. So, for our example, the theory of force identifies it as a question with content "Climate change will dominate the summit or the ailing economy will dominate the summit." The role of the disjunction operator in the question is to be understood via its role in the corresponding declarative statement. Unfortunately, for all anyone has shown, there is no similar story to be told for pretheoretically meaningful compounded sentences with conditionals as constituents, at least not for all of them.

[28] See, in the same vein, Ramsey [1929/1990:147 f]. The claim was already defended by Boethius; see Kneale and Kneale [1962:191].

[29] This general claim may appear too strong, for it seems that sometimes we deny a conditional "If φ, then ψ" to indicate that ψ might be false even if φ holds true (cf. Grice [1989a:81]). Note, however, that in such a case the denial would be more properly expressed by asserting something like "It might well not be" or "I wouldn't be so sure" rather than by "It's not the case that if φ, then ψ."

(2.5) If he hears my arguments, then if he does not change his mind, he will leave the department.

which is a right-nested conditional, that is, a conditional of the form "If φ, then if ψ, then χ." It has been argued – convincingly, most think – that such conditionals can be reduced to simple conditionals via the following principle:[30]

> IMPORT–EXPORT (IE) "If φ, then if ψ, then χ" and "If φ and ψ, then χ" are logically equivalent.

In the present case, this principle indisputably yields the right result, for (2.2c) can be naturally understood as meaning

(2.6) If he hears my arguments and does not change his mind, he will leave the department.

However, those favoring a non-truth-conditional view on conditionals will have to show that *all* embedded conditionals that we can intuitively make sense of are somehow reducible to simple conditionals or that they can be otherwise reformulated to avoid the embedding. That this can be accomplished is far from obvious. Left- *and* right-nested conditionals, like the following sentences, appear especially recalcitrant to reformulation:

(2.7) a. If the match is canceled if it starts raining, then the match is canceled if it starts snowing.
   b. If your mother gets angry if you come home with a B, she'll get furious if you come home with a C.
   c. If Paul gets a bonus if he sells more than 1,000 subscriptions, he'll get a double bonus if he sells more than 5,000 subscriptions.

It is hopeless to try to apply IE to these sentences. Consider (2.7a). One might first make a right-nested conditional out of it, yielding

(2.8) If it starts raining, then if the match is canceled and it starts snowing, the match is canceled.

---

[30] It is true that the literature contains no instances of this principle that strike one as clear counterexamples to it (at least not for indicative conditionals; see Etlin [2009] for a discussion of IE in relation to subjunctive conditionals). However, in the next chapter it will be seen that people's probability judgments are at variance with what one would expect if people heeded IE.

and then apply IE to obtain

(2.9) If it starts raining and the match is canceled and it starts snowing,
       then the match is canceled.

But this sounds trivial and nonsensical at the same time, and in any event
(2.9) is not an adequate rephrasing of (2.7a). It cannot be excluded that,
with enough ingenuity, sentences like (2.7a)–(2.7c) *can* be rephrased as
simple conditionals, or even as non-conditional sentences. Still, the proponents of the non-truth-conditional view on conditionals have not shown
us how to do it.[31,32]

Note that if, by contrast, conditionals do express propositions, then the
conditionals (2.7a)–(2.7c) should pose no special interpretational difficulties – which is in accordance with how we intuitively assess these sentences,
to wit, as being readily interpretable.

A second reason for thinking that conditionals have truth conditions
was already hinted at earlier, namely, that conditionals appear to be bona
fide candidates for belief. For example, many of us believe the following:

(2.10) If no measures are taken to reduce the emission of greenhouse gases,
        then sea levels will keep rising.

But how else can we make sense of believing something than as believing
the thing to be true? And how can we believe a conditional to be true if it
does not have truth conditions? The same can be asked for any of the other
propositional attitudes that one can seemingly have toward conditionals.

It was remarked that some philosophers who hold that conditionals do
not have truth conditions in the ordinary sense think there are conditions

---

[31] As mentioned earlier, some of the proponents of the less radical version of this view – according to
which conditionals can be true or false, but are neither if their antecedent is false – have taken on
the ambitious project of developing a partial logic for handling truth value gaps. As also mentioned,
however, this project has thus far remained rather unsatisfactory, insofar as its proponents have been
unable to come to an agreement even among themselves on a number of pressing questions raised
by the admission of a third truth value into the semantics.

[32] Following Gibbard [1981:237 f], one might try to rephrase left-nested and left- and right-nested
conditionals in terms of dispositions or other "factual bases" (Gibbard's term) in order to reduce
them to simple conditionals. For example, (2.7b) might be rephrased as: "If your mother is disposed
to get angry upon your coming home with a B, she is disposed to get furious upon your coming
home with a C." First, however, one would think that (2.7b) can also be understood by a person
who lacks the concept of a disposition. Second, the ease and especially speed with which we are able
to process conditionals like (2.7a)–(2.7c) makes it doubtful that we understand these sentences by
rephrasing them in the manner of Gibbard: one can ascertain for oneself that a plausible rephrasing
of such sentences does not always come easily, let alone automatically, to mind.

under which conditionals are true – namely, when the antecedent and the consequent are both true – and also conditions under which they are false, namely, when the antecedent is true and the consequent false. But this does not help with the present issue: we may believe (doubt, fear, etc.) that (2.10) is true regardless of whether measures will be taken to reduce the emission of greenhouse gases.

A seemingly more effective reply is to claim that we do not really believe (doubt, fear, etc.) conditionals to be true but still have the intuition that sometimes we do, because we are prone to mistake (2.11a) for (2.11b):

(2.11) a. {It is true that sea levels will keep rising} if no measures are taken to reduce the emission of greenhouse gases.
       b. It is true that {sea levels will keep rising if no measures are taken to reduce the emission of greenhouse gases}.

Because we are insufficiently sensitive to this scope ambiguity of the truth predicate, we may take ourselves to have a belief (doubt, fear, etc.) expressed by (2.11b), while what we actually have is the *conditional* belief (doubt, fear, etc.) that we could express by (2.11a): we believe (doubt, fear, etc.) something to be true, or better perhaps, we are prepared to believe (doubt, fear, etc.) something to be true (to wit, that sea levels will keep rising), on the condition that something else is true (that no measures are taken to reduce the emission of greenhouse gases).[33] Still, one may not find this reply very satisfactory, given that it assumes people to be massively mistaken about the correct interpretation of a sizeable portion of their beliefs as well as other propositional attitudes.

As one might expect, next to the foregoing general reasons for favoring truth-conditional semantics of conditionals over non-truth-conditional semantics, the advocates of truth-conditional accounts have also advanced reasons for specifically favoring their own account.

The material conditional account has been claimed to be particularly attractive because the logic of the material conditional is simple and well understood: it comes packaged with classical propositional logic, familiar from introductory logic courses. Another reason that has been given in support of the material conditional account is that it is provably the *only* semantics of conditionals that validates the so-called Or-to-if principle, which licenses the inference of "If it is not the case that φ, then

---

[33] See Leitgeb [2007]. This point about believing conditionals parallels von Wright's [1957:131] view that in asserting a conditional, one conditionally asserts a proposition rather than asserts a conditional proposition.

ψ" from "Either φ or ψ (or both)," an inference that strikes many as intuitively compelling. Rieger [2013] catalogues some further advantages of the
material conditional account. For instance, he notes that if the material
conditional account is correct, then Williamson's [2009] "collapse argument" is completely unsurprising. According to this argument, it follows
from reasonable constraints on the actuality operator in conjunction with
some seemingly plausible assumptions concerning the logical properties
of the conditional that the conditional is extensionally equivalent to the
material conditional.[34]

Arguments for Stalnaker's semantics typically compare it with the material conditional account and then aim to show that the comparison turns
out in favor of Stalnaker's semantics. Among other alleged advantages,
Stalnaker's semantics has been claimed to accord better than the material
conditional account with our intuitions concerning which inferences are
valid and which are not. (As will be seen shortly, the material conditional
account licenses some inferences that are pretheoretically clearly invalid.)
Stalnaker's semantics has also been said to be phenomenologically plausible in that it seems a kind of formalization of the process we go through
when we evaluate a conditional: we imagine how the world would be on
the supposition that the antecedent holds – where, in doing so, we stay as
close to the actual world as the supposition permits – and then we ask ourselves whether the consequent holds in the imagined world; if the answer
is positive, we judge the conditional true; if not, we judge it false. Stalnaker [1968:102] explicitly mentions this intuitive idea as motivating his
semantics.[35] The idea is based strictly on evidence from introspection; to
date, there is no more solid evidence suggesting that this is indeed how we
go about evaluating a conditional.[36]

It is not as though proponents of the view that conditionals lack truth
conditions are blind to the attractions of the material conditional account
or of the possible worlds semantics, nor are they unaware of the problems
for their view that were described above. For instance, Adams [1998:273],
one of the major proponents of the non-truth-conditional view, admits

[34] It is to be noted that Williamson's argument is not watertight. It relies on the assumption that the conjunction of "If φ, then ψ" and "If φ, then χ" is logically equivalent to "If φ, then ψ and χ." And some results to be looked at in Chapter 5 suggest an explanation of how this assumption may be false while at the same time appearing plausible.

[35] Stalnaker [1968: 102] notes that the idea was inspired by (what is now generally called) the Ramsey test, which refers to belief states instead of worlds; see Chapter 4 for more on this.

[36] Krzyżanowska [2013] cites some evidence from psychology suggesting that something akin to the Ramsey test plays a role in the practice of belief ascription. She does not discuss its role in the assessment of conditionals.

that "'the problem of iterated conditionals' [i.e., the problem of how to account for conditionals such as (2.7a)–(2.7c)] is still very much an open one." Nevertheless, they see serious problems for the opposition as well and believe that, on balance, their own view does best. Some of their arguments are specifically directed against the truth-conditional accounts that were summarized above. But they have also leveled some arguments against truth-conditional accounts generally. The next three sections review the most cogent specific arguments. Section 2.7 and Chapter 3 discuss the general arguments.

2.4 Arguments against the material conditional account

It is a common complaint about the material conditional account that, while it validates many inferential principles that we deem pretheoretically valid, it at the same time overgenerates "validities" in that some inferential principles that are intuitively *rejectable* come out as valid on this account. The best-known examples of this phenomenon are the two so-called paradoxes of material implication, which are often discussed in introductory logic courses. One paradox is due to the fact that, on the material conditional account, a conditional is true whenever its antecedent is false. Yet we do not think that the falsity of

(2.12) Jim has retired.

entails

(2.13) If Jim has retired, then he will teach next year's epistemology course.

The other paradox derives from the fact that a material conditional is true whenever its consequent is true. But we do not think that the truth of

(2.14) Bill Gates is a billionaire.

entails

(2.15) If Bill Gates just lost all his money, he is a billionaire.

In defense of the material conditional account, several attempts have been made to explain away along pragmatic lines the counterintuitiveness of the above and other seemingly problematic inferences. It has been argued, for instance, that while the falsity of (2.12) does entail (2.13), we still have the intuition that the inference from the falsity of (2.12) to (2.13) is invalid because, typically, when the negation of (2.12) is assertable, (2.13) is *not*: by asserting the latter when one is in a position to deny the former one would say less than one could, with more words, thus violating a fundamental principle of conversational practice.[37] The details of these attempts vary somewhat, for not all authors taking this line of defense agree on the question of which conditions make a conditional assertable. A very general objection that has been raised against pragmatic defenses of the material conditional account is that we think that, for instance, (2.12) is an insufficient basis not only for *asserting* (2.13) but also for *accepting* that sentence, and pragmatics concerns only assertion and not acceptance (see, e.g., Edgington [1995:245]).[38] Moreover, the material conditional account validates other problematic inferences, whose counter intuitiveness is not so easily explained in pragmatic terms. For instance, this holds for the Transitivity schema – from "If φ, then ψ" and "If ψ, then χ," infer "If φ, then χ" – that is valid according to the material conditional account but to which there exist counterexamples, as we saw in Section 1.1 (p. 7). The same is true for the schema of Strengthening the Antecedent – from "If φ, then ψ," infer "If φ and χ, then ψ" – which equally has counterintuitive instances, like this one from Harper [1981:6]:

> If I put sugar in this cup of tea, it will taste fine.

?? ∴ If I put sugar and diesel oil in this cup of tea, it will taste fine.

Earlier we saw that embedded conditionals have been adduced to argue in favor of a truth-conditional semantics of conditionals. However, embedded conditionals have also been adduced *against* the material conditional account.[39] Gibbard [1981:235] invites us to consider this conditional:

(2.16) If the cup broke if dropped, then it was fragile.

---

[37] See Grice [1989b].

[38] Though the latter claim is dubitable. See Douven [2010], where it is argued that much the same pragmatic principles as apply to assertion also apply to acceptance.

[39] In fact, they have been adduced against truth-conditional semantics for conditionals generally, the claim being that of some embedded conditionals we cannot make sense, which is then alleged to be puzzling if conditionals have truth conditions. First, however, it takes little effort to construct syntactically very complex non-conditional declarative sentences that we cannot make sense of. Second, even if they express propositions, conditionals may be harder to process mentally than non-conditional sentences, as we saw earlier (p. 4). So, there may be a natural explanation – namely, in terms of limitations on people's processing capacities – of why we cannot make sense of all embedded conditionals.

As he points out, (2.16) is assertable even if we deem it unlikely that the cup was dropped or that it is fragile. This is a problem for the material conditional account, Gibbard claims, for if the cup was not dropped and is not fragile, then, on the material conditional account, (2.16) is false. As a result, (2.16) would be assertable even if one thinks it unlikely to be true. According to Gibbard [1981:236], invoking pragmatic principles of conversation will not help one out here, for (he contends) such principles explain only why a believed truth may be unassertable, not why a sentence one believes to be false may be nonetheless assertable.

First off, the claim about pragmatic principles is contestable. The following sentences may be perfectly assertable:

(2.17)   a. It's two hours by train from Brussels to London.
      b. The Eiffel Tower is 324 meters tall.
      c. There is no more beer.
      d. There ain't no sunshine when she's gone.

even though they are false: it takes (currently) *slightly* over two hours to get from Brussels to London by train; the given height of the Eiffel Tower will (we may be sure) not be accurate to the nearest millimeter; there will be beer somewhere on earth even if there is no more beer in the refridgerator (which is what, we may suppose, (2.17c) is meant to convey); and for sure there will be sunshine (somewhere, at least) no matter who is or is not gone. Authors have suggested various pragmatic explanations of the phenomenon at issue here. Already Grice [1989b:34] was very outspoken about the role of pragmatic principles in understanding irony and metaphor, which often involve the assertion of manifest falsehoods.

But grant that, at least in the case of (2.16), pragmatic principles will not help to explain why it is assertable if false. Then it still holds that (2.16) poses a threat to the material conditional account only if it must further be granted that, on this account, (2.16) is false if the cup was not dropped and is not fragile. And why should that be so? Gibbard's argument supposes that (2.16) is to be analyzed as a left-nested conditional, that is, as

(2.18)   If {the cup broke if it was dropped}, then [it was fragile].

where the part between curly braces is (2.18)'s antecedent and the part between square brackets its consequent. In this analysis, (2.18) is false indeed if the cup was not dropped – so that the antecedent is true – and the cup is not fragile, so that the consequent is false. But (2.16) does not carry its logical form on its sleeve, and there is room for disputing that the sentence is to be analyzed as (2.18) and for claiming that (2.16) is properly analyzed as follows:

(2.19) If {the cup was dropped}, then [if it broke, it was fragile].

At a minimum, it is far from evident that (2.19) misconstrues (2.16). For Gibbard's argument to go through, however, (2.19) must be ruled out as a reasonable interpretation of (2.16), because read as a right-nested conditional, (2.16) comes out *true* on the material conditional account if, as Gibbard supposes, the cup was not dropped. Even if Gibbard could argue that (2.16) *cannot* properly be read as (2.19), those in favor of the material conditional account might still point to the fact that, pretheoretically, it seems all right to read (2.16) as (2.19), and that this (then mistaken) reading may fuel our intuition that (2.16) is assertable under the circumstances Gibbard assumes, even if, under those circumstances, it comes out false – which, from the perspective of the material conditional account, it does if (2.18) is the only legitimate analysis of (2.16).

2.5 Arguments against the possible worlds account

It is a clear point in favor of the possible worlds account that it validates neither the paradoxes of material implication nor Transitivity or Strengthening the Antecedent. For instance, that φ is false in the actual world makes no predictions about what holds or does not hold in the closest word in which φ is true; so, "If φ, then ψ" may be just as well true as false. That blocks the first paradox of material implication. One similarly checks that the other paradox is blocked and that Transitivity and Strengthening the Antecedent fail in the possible worlds account.

However, if the material conditional account overgenerates inferences, critics of the possible worlds account have argued that this account undergenerates, in that it fails to validate inferential principles that intuitively do appear valid. A case in point is the Or-to-if principle, which, as we said, is validated *only* by the material conditional account. To see why Or-to-if does not hold on the possible worlds account, note that if φ is true in the actual world, then so is φ or ψ. However, nothing follows from this about any $\overline{\varphi}$-world, so in particular it does not follow that ψ holds in the $\overline{\varphi}$-world that is closest to the actual world.

In reply to this objection, Stalnaker [1975] first observes that a semantics cannot both block the paradoxes of material implication and validate the Or-to-if principle. After all, given that ψ entails $\overline{\varphi} \vee \psi$, by the Or-to-if principle and (we may assume) the transitivity of the entailment relation, ψ would entail "If φ, then ψ," which is the paradox we illustrated by means of (2.14) and (2.15). So one will either have to explain away this paradox or explain how Or-to-if can appear plausible even if it is invalid.

Stalnaker [1975] takes the second route, arguing that although the Or-to-if principle is not valid on his preferred semantics of conditionals, it nevertheless embodies (what he calls) a reasonable inference, where an inference from given premises to a given conclusion is reasonable precisely if, in any context in which the premises are assertable or can be presupposed, one cannot accept them without being committed to the conclusion. And, according to Stalnaker, in every context in which "Either not φ or ψ (or both)" is assertable, one cannot accept that disjunction without being committed to "If φ, then ψ." The argument for this claim relies on the pragmatic constraint – which in Stalnaker's account governs the use of indicative conditionals – that the closest antecedent worlds must be consistent with what is presupposed in the given conversational context. For broadly Gricean reasons, Stalnaker takes a disjunction to be assertable only in contexts which allow either disjunct to be true without the other. In terms of possible worlds, "Either not φ or ψ (or both)" is assertable in a context only if neither all $\varphi \wedge \psi$-worlds (where ψ is true without $\overline{\varphi}$) nor all $\overline{\varphi} \wedge \overline{\psi}$-worlds (where $\overline{\varphi}$ is true without ψ) are ruled out by contextual background assumptions. If all but $\overline{\varphi} \wedge \psi$-worlds are ruled out in advance, an assertion of "Either not φ or ψ (or both)" would violate the Gricean maxim of Quantity, given that one could just as easily be more informative (namely, by asserting "Not-φ and ψ"). Now, accepting "Either not φ or ψ (or both)" rules out any $\varphi \wedge \overline{\psi}$-world that might still have been consistent with contextual background assumptions. But then all remaining φ-worlds must be $\varphi \wedge \psi$-worlds. Hence, the closest φ-world is necessarily a ψ-world. And so, finally, "If φ, then ψ" must be true in this context. In Stalnaker's view, this is what creates the illusion that the Or-to-if principle is valid.

According to some, it is more troubling for the possible worlds account that it does not validate IE. This principle, recall, postulates the equivalence of "If φ, then if ψ, then χ" and "If φ and ψ, then χ." Given the possible worlds account, however, there is nothing to guarantee that the equivalence holds: for all that the defenders of the account have said, the ψ-world that is closest to the φ-world that is closest to the actual world need not be identical to the φ-and-ψ-world that is closest to the actual world. And if the two are distinct, then the one might be a χ-world while the other is a $\overline{\chi}$-world. On the present account, this would yield a counterexample to IE.[40] As mentioned earlier, there are no known counterexamples to IE as restricted to indicative conditionals – which, as was also briefly mentioned (in note 30), is not to say that there is no evidence against the principle (see p. 77).

What many consider to be the most serious threat to the possible worlds account is that it appears to make the propositional content of a conditional much more sensitive to context than one would reasonably expect it to be. The point was most forcefully made in Gibbard's [1981]. Gibbard starts by observing that the possible worlds account entails the principle of Conditional Non-Contradiction (CNC), according to which "If φ, then ψ" is inconsistent with "If φ, then not ψ," provided φ is consistent: the φ-world closest to the actual world cannot be both a ψ-world and a $\overline{\psi}$-world. He then asks us to consider the following story:

> Sly Pete and Mr. Stone are playing poker on a Mississippi riverboat. It is now up to Pete to call or fold. My henchman Zack sees Stone's hand, which is quite good, and signals its content to Pete. My henchman Jack sees both hands, and sees that Pete's hand is rather low, so that Stone's is the winning hand. At this point, the room is cleared. A few minutes later, Zack slips me a note which says "If Pete called, he won," and Jack slips me a note which says "If Pete called, he lost." I know that these notes both come from my trusted henchmen, but do not know which of them sent which note. I conclude that Pete folded. (Gibbard [1981:231])

Gibbard then argues that if

(2.20) If Pete called, he won.

and

(2.21) If Pete called, he lost.

express propositions, they must both express *true* propositions: Zack and Jack are both warranted in their assertions, and their warrants do not rest on any false beliefs about relevant matters of fact. If so, however,

---

[40] In fairness, though, it is to be noted that McGee [1985:469 f], [1989, Sect. 7] proposes a modified version of Stalnaker's semantics of conditionals that does validate IE. At the same time, McGee's semantics may not quite have the intuitive plausibility of Stalnaker's proposal.

then this creates a problem for the possible worlds account, for it would seem that, by CNC, these conditionals are jointly inconsistent. The only escape route that Gibbard sees for the proponent of the possible worlds account is to claim that (2.20) does not express the same proposition when it is uttered by Zack as when uttered by Jack, so that we would equivocate by taking CNC to apply to the pair of (2.20) and (2.21). But according to Gibbard, that route leads to a rather extreme form of context-sensitivity that is difficult to uphold, given that, in the setting of the above story, we would be able to interpret Zack's and Jack's notes, even if – like the first-person narrator of the story – we are ignorant of the epistemic states that the authors of these notes were in at the time of their writing.[41]

The proponent of the possible worlds account is by no means committed to Gibbard's claim that if one of (2.20) and (2.21) is true, then so is the other. Even if neither Jack's nor Zack's assertion rests on a mistaken belief, Lycan [2001:169] is right to remark that Zack, in contrast to Jack, lacks knowledge of a seemingly highly relevant matter of fact, to wit, what cards Pete is holding. While Zack may not have any *mistaken* beliefs about these cards, his ignorance might still lead him to assert something false – even warrantedly so, given the quality of the evidence that *is* in his possession. However, this asymmetry in the protagonists' epistemic positions may be an inessential feature of Gibbard's story; see, for instance, Bennett [2003:85] for a defense of this claim.

Even granting that (2.20) and (2.21) must both be true if one of them is, Gibbard's appraisal of the escape route he mentions seems dubitable. Why should it be more objectionable to claim that a conditional can express different propositions in the mouths of different speakers than to claim that, for instance,

(2.22)   I am the owner of this house.

expresses different propositions in the mouths of different speakers, and may be true when uttered by one speaker and false when uttered by another? According to Gibbard, these cases are not analogous because we

---

[41] It is worth remarking that Gibbard's argument does not directly jeopardize the material conditional account, given that CNC is no consequence of this account. In fact, on that account, CNC is false, given that, on the material reading of the conditional, "If φ, then ψ" and "If φ, then not ψ" are both true if φ is false. However, some (e.g., Bennett [2003:84]) see the failure to validate CNC as being itself a reason for doubting the material conditional account.

can rely on fairly straightforward rules for detecting the relevant contextual information necessary to interpret sentences like (2.22) – " 'I' refers to the speaker, 'this' to whatever the speaker points at" – but there do not seem to exist similarly straightforward rules for interpreting putatively context-sensitive conditionals.

This seems wrong, however. As argued in Krzyżanowska, Wenmackers, and Douven [2013], interpreting context-sensitive conditionals is not fundamentally different from interpreting sentences containing indexicals. Suppose one finds a note of unknown origin with (2.22) written on it. Then while one cannot *fully* interpret (2.22), one still gets *something* from the note; one gets from it that whoever wrote the message claims to be the owner of whichever house "this house" is meant to refer to. In some contexts, one may even be able to go beyond this and guess with some confidence who the author is and to which house he or she is referring.

In Krzyżanowska et al.'s view, much the same holds for (2.20) and (2.21). Having been given the notes with (2.20) and (2.21) on them, but not knowing who supplied which note and what the persons' epistemic states are or were, one can still get *something* out of those messages even if the conditionals have a hidden indexical parameter referring to the authors' epistemic states at the time of writing the notes. On Krzyżanowska et al.'s version of the inferential semantics, one gets from the note with (2.20) on it that, according to its author at the time of writing, there is a valid argument from the premise that Pete called, possibly in conjunction with background assumptions deemed acceptable by the author, to the conclusion that Pete won, and *mutatis mutandis* for the note with (2.21) on it. Naturally, one gets *more* out of the messages if one does know by whom one was handed which note, and what the relevant beliefs of the authors were at the time they wrote their respective notes. But that is as with the note with (2.22) on it: one gets more out of that if one knows the intended referents of "I" and "this house" than if one does not.

Krzyżanowska et al.'s general point – which is independent of their preferred semantics, and which it seems open for the possible worlds theorist to embrace – is that interpretation is not an all or nothing affair. Sometimes we completely get what the speaker means and sometimes we completely miss it. But in between these extremes, there are many shades of partial understanding, and sometimes we just understand to some degree what a given speaker means. By reading the henchmen's notes, the first-person narrator in Gibbard's story does not get everything, but he gets a lot – enough, at any rate, to warrant saying that he can make sense of the notes.[42]

2.6 The probabilities of conditionals: further considerations against the material conditional account and the possible worlds account

There are a number of well-known probabilistic arguments that are meant to generally undermine truth-conditional semantics of conditionals. These arguments require a bit of stage-setting and will be canvassed in the next chapter. In this section, we look at some more readily appreciable probabilistic considerations that cast doubt specifically on the material conditional account and the possible worlds account.

Given that I believe φ to a degree of x, to what degree should I believe the negation of φ? Any epistemology that respects probability theory – perhaps in view of some Dutch book argument (e.g., de Finetti [1937]) or some accuracy domination argument (e.g., Joyce [1998]) – will answer that I ought to believe that negation to a degree of $1 - x$. Here is an equally legitimate and seemingly equally simple question: Given that I believe φ to a degree of x, and ψ to a degree of y, to what degree should I believe "If φ, then ψ"? Or, if my degrees of belief for just φ and ψ are not enough to answer that question, given as many of my other degrees of belief (conditional or unconditional) as you like, what should my degree of belief for "If φ, then ψ" be?

Of the better-known semantics of conditionals, only the material conditional account makes the probability of a conditional come out as a function of other probabilities: on this account, $\Pr(\text{If } \varphi, \text{ then } \psi) = \Pr(\overline{\varphi} \vee \psi) = 1 - \Pr(\varphi \wedge \overline{\psi}) = 1 - \Pr(\varphi) \Pr(\overline{\psi} \mid \varphi)$. But, as is easy to see, this account renders any conditional with a highly improbable antecedent highly probable – which is implausible.

For one, it is commonly held that high probability is at least close to being sufficient for acceptability. To be more precise, most hold that high probability cannot be *quite* sufficient in view of Kyburg's [1961] Lottery Paradox (more on this later), but that, barring the kind of propositions that figure in Kyburg's paradox, high probability *is* sufficient for acceptability. But consider this sentence:

---

[42] Williams [2008] offers a different response to Gibbard's argument from the perspective of the possible worlds theorist. Williams' response also allows (2.20) and (2.21) to both come out true at the same time.

(2.23)   If Manchester United finishes at the bottom of this year's Premier
         League, they will give their manager a raise.

Although it is exceedingly unlikely that Manchester United will finish at
the bottom of this year's Premier League, we do not find (2.23) acceptable; to the contrary, it strikes us as being highly unacceptable! Because
(2.23) is unrelated to the kind of propositions that give rise to the Lottery
Paradox, it appears that – assuming the material conditional account –
high probability is not even nearly enough for the acceptability of a conditional. Arguably, the deeper problem here is that the assignment of a high
probability to (2.23) is wrong to begin with. If the point needs further
underscoring, contrast (2.23) with

(2.24)   If West Ham United wins next year's Premier League, the players
         will receive a bonus on their salaries.

The antecedents of (2.23) and (2.24) both seem extremely unlikely. Thus,
supposing the material conditional account, both conditionals would have
to be highly likely. But that is not at all how it appears. Whereas (2.24)
will strike most as very probably true indeed, (2.23) will strike most as
probably false.

   Proponents of the material conditional account are aware that they
have to explain away our intuitions about the probabilities of conditionals like (2.23). What they tend to do, is claim that these intuitions are
grounded in our mistaking probability for some other, putatively closely
related, property that conditionals have, like their degree of assertability
or their degree of acceptability. As such, the move would seem to be on
a par with the attempt to explain the earlier-cited conjunction fallacy, by
arguing that people are inclined to misinterpret questions about probability as questions about, for instance, coherence (e.g., Bovens and Hartmann
[2003:85–88]) or inductive confirmation (e.g., Crupi, Fitelson, and Tentori
[2008] and Tentori, Crupi, and Russo [2013]). On further and more careful consideration, however, the parallel appears to be not quite so close. For
empirical research has shown that people are much less likely to commit
the conjunction fallacy once it has been brought to their attention that
a conjunction can never be more likely than its conjuncts (Moutier and
Houdé [2003]), or even when the questions about the probabilities of the
conjunction and the conjuncts are phrased in terms of relative frequencies
(Hertwig and Gigerenzer [1999]). By contrast, even if I attend carefully
to the distinction between probability and assertability (or acceptability),

I still deem (2.24) to be much more *probable* than (2.23). To be sure, I also deem (2.24) to be much more *assertable*, and also much more *acceptable*, than (2.23), but for all I can introspect, that is at least in the present case mainly or even solely due to the fact that the former is more probable than the latter. It thus seems that explaining our intuitions about the probabilities of conditionals will be even harder than explaining why people sometimes assign a higher probability to a conjunction than to its conjuncts.[43]

At first glance, Stalnaker's possible worlds semantics might seem to do justice to our intuitions about the probabilities of both (2.23) and (2.24). For is it not much more probable that we inhabit a world whose closest West-Ham-finishes-on-top world is a West-Ham-players-get-bonus world than that we inhabit a world whose closest Manchester-finishes-at-bottom world is a Manchester-manager-gets-raise world? Well, yes, but note that this is simply to *rephrase*, using the terminology of Stalnaker's semantics, our intuition that (2.24) is much more likely than (2.23). In particular, it gives no indication how to compute the probabilities of these conditionals on the basis of the probabilities we assign to other propositions expressible in our language and so does not suggest anything like the rules for calculating the probabilities of negations, conjunctions, and disjunctions that probability theory offers us.

In a sense, Stalnaker himself presented a rule for calculating probabilities of conditionals of precisely that kind when in his [1970] he proposed the following as an adequacy criterion for any semantics of conditionals:

STALNAKER'S HYPOTHESIS (SH)   For all probability functions Pr such that $\Pr(\varphi) > 0$, $\Pr(\text{If } \varphi, \text{ then } \psi) = \Pr(\psi \mid \varphi)$.[44]

While this hypothesis has undeniable intuitive attraction, it is easy to see that at least Stalnaker's semantics does *not* validate it. Recall that, in this semantics, the proposition expressed by a conditional may be thought of as corresponding to the set of worlds whose closest antecedent worlds (i.e., worlds in which the antecedent holds) are consequent worlds. Then consider again Figure 2.1 (p. 32). If we set $\Pr(\{w_i\}) = p_i > 0$ for all $i \in \{1, \ldots, 4\}$ in models I–III in that figure, then the probabilities of "If φ, then ψ" in these models are, respectively, p_1, $p_1 + p_3$, and $p_1 + p_3 + p_4$. On the other hand, the conditional probability of ψ given φ is $p_1/(p_1 + p_2)$ in

---

43 In this connection, it is not encouraging that almost thirty years after the discovery of the conjunction fallacy there is still no consensus on what underlies it.

44 This thesis also goes by the names "the Equation" (e.g., Edgington [1995:271]) and "the conditional probability hypothesis" (e.g., Gilio and Over [2012:119]).

all three models. That is, in these models, $\Pr(\text{If } \varphi, \text{ then } \psi) \neq \Pr(\psi \mid \varphi)$, in violation of SH.[45]

It is also worth briefly mentioning here Nolan's [2003] variant of Stalnaker's semantics of conditionals, according to which a conditional is true (false) precisely if its consequent is true (false) in all closest antecedent worlds (plural, where Stalnaker has singular), given that, toward the end of his paper, Nolan explicitly considers the issue of the probability of a conditional. Most of his discussion centers around the following concrete example:

(2.25)   If the coin was flipped, it came up heads.

which is supposed to be asserted of a coin we know to be fair. Where we deem it only 20 percent likely that the coin was indeed flipped, the probability of (2.25), according to Nolan, is 10 percent, namely, the probability that the coin was flipped multiplied with the conditional probability that the coin came up heads given that it was flipped. Nolan stops short of suggesting this as a fully general rule for computing the probability of a conditional. Nor is there any indication that he would be opposed to this rule, even though, as a general rule, it would seem pretty hopeless. For, suppose I have been informed that there is a current on the fence. That makes it highly likely to me that

(2.26)   If I touch the fence, I will get an electric shock.

At the same time, the information makes it highly *un*likely to me that I shall touch the fence. Reasonable though these two probability judgments seem, if Nolan's proposal were meant to hold generally, they cannot both be correct, for then a conditional cannot be more probable than its antecedent. However, even if the proposal is only meant to apply to (2.25) and sentences that are somehow more similar to it than (2.26) is, it is at

---

[45] Figure 2.1 in effect illustrates a theorem proved in Lewis' [1976:147 f], to wit, that the probability of a Stalnaker conditional "If φ, then ψ" is the probability of ψ after *imaging* on φ (again provided there is a world in which φ holds), where imaging on φ consists of transferring the probability of any $\overline{\varphi}$-world to its closest φ-world. (See Gärdenfors [1982] for a strengthening of Lewis' result.) The picture makes it easy to see why this must hold. After imaging ψ on φ, the ψ-worlds come to carry all the probability mass that, before the operation, was carried by the worlds that have a $\varphi \wedge \psi$-world as their closest φ-world, which are the worlds that have an arrow going to a $\varphi \wedge \psi$-world, and which are precisely the worlds in the gray areas. As a result, the sum of the probabilities assigned to the ψ-worlds after imaging on φ – which is the probability of ψ after imaging on φ – cannot but equal the sum of the probabilities assigned to the worlds in the gray area before the imaging operation, which is the probability of the Stalnaker conditional "If φ, then ψ."

odds with how people actually evaluate the probabilities of conditionals, as will be seen further on.

2.7 Edgington against truth-conditionality

Bennett is a champion of the non-propositional view, in its less radical variant. In his overall excellent 2003 book, he lists four arguments for the general conclusion that conditions do not have truth conditions (pp. 102–105). The first is basically Gibbard's riverboat argument looked at earlier, the idea being that, given that (2.20) and (2.21) would appear to be both true if conditionals have truth conditions, and given that they cannot both be true, conditionals do not have truth conditions. As we saw, however, there is more than one reason to dismiss this argument. Most notably, it was seen that (2.20) and (2.21) may well both be true, yet that we would equivocate by applying CNC to them.

The third and fourth argument on Bennett's list are the various so-called triviality results that have been leveled against SH and, respectively, a recent argument presented in Bradley [2000]. These arguments will be discussed in the next chapter.

The second general argument on the list is a pointed argument from Edgington. According to Edgington [1995:279], no truth-conditional semantics of conditionals can satisfy both (2.27a) and (2.27b):

(2.27) a. Minimal certainty that $\overline{\varphi} \vee \psi$ (ruling out just $\varphi \wedge \overline{\psi}$) is enough for certainty that if φ, then ψ.
   b. It is not necessarily irrational to disbelieve φ yet disbelieve that if φ, then ψ.

For – Edgington claims – the material conditional account satisfies (2.27a) but not (2.27b); and whereas accounts that attribute stronger truth conditions may satisfy (2.27b), they cannot satisfy (2.27a). Granting (for now) that (2.27a) and (2.27b) are "desirable properties of indicative conditional judgements" (*ibid.*), it follows that conditionals do not have truth conditions.[46]

---

[46] She supposes that accounts which attribute truth conditions weaker than the material conditional account – in the sense that according to these accounts a conditional can be true even if the corresponding material conditional is false – are not worth considering. As we saw in Section 2.2 (p. 42), not all agree with Edgington on this point.

Why is it that, according to Edgington, the material conditional account fails to satisfy (2.27b)? This is her argument (the symbol ⊃ designates the material conditional operator):

> Someone who believes $\overline{\varphi}$ but disbelieves "If φ, ψ" is [on the material conditional account] making an Incredibly Gross Logical Error. For to disbelieve $\varphi \supset \psi$, i.e. $\varphi \wedge \overline{\psi}$, is to believe its negation, $\varphi \wedge \overline{\psi}$. How can anyone be so stupid as to believe $\varphi \wedge \overline{\psi}$ yet disbelieve φ, i.e. believe $\overline{\varphi}$? (p. 244; notation altered for uniformity of reading)

There may seem little to contest here. The underlying assumption that for the material conditional account loyalist to disbelieve that if φ, then ψ is to disbelieve $\varphi \supset \psi$ may seem particularly unassailable. On closer inspection, however, this assumption appears doubtful.

To see why, first note that to disbelieve something, at least in the presently relevant sense, is to believe the thing to be false, or equivalently, to believe that it is not the case.[47] If we further grant Edgington's claim, cited in Section 2.3, that "It is not the case that if φ, then ψ" has no clear established sense distinguishable from "If φ, then not ψ," it would seem that the natural interpretation of "disbelieving that if φ, then ψ" is this: "believing that if φ, then not ψ." And believing that if φ, then not ψ is quite evidently not the same as believing $\varphi \supset \psi$ not to be the case, that is, as believing $\varphi \wedge \overline{\psi}$.

If the advocates of the material conditional account can go along with this, they have a perfectly good reply to the charge that their account fails to satisfy (2.27b). For they can then claim that, since to disbelieve that if φ, then ψ is to believe that if φ, then not ψ, the former does not amount to believing $\varphi \wedge \overline{\psi}$ but rather to believing $\varphi \supset \overline{\psi}$; and surely it can be rational to believe both $\overline{\varphi}$ and $\varphi \supset \overline{\psi}$.

To undermine Edgington's argument, it thus suffices to notice that there is no reason why the advocates of the material conditional account could not go along with the suggested natural interpretation of "disbelieving that if φ, then ψ." It is not the exclusive privilege of those who, like Edgington, think that conditionals do not have truth conditions to hold that surface grammar does not always reflect logical form. In particular, those advocating the material conditional account can consistently maintain that, to reveal the logical form of sentences containing the expression "disbelieves

---

[47] According to Webster's Dictionary, "disbelieve" can mean both "deem false" and "refuse to believe." Given the latter, less common and in the present context obviously unintended, interpretation, it is straightforward that the material conditional account does satisfy (2.27b): surely it can be rational to be agnostic both about a conditional and about the conditional's antecedent.

that if φ, then ψ," this expression is to be replaced by "believes $\varphi \supset \overline{\psi}$" (and similarly for similar expressions).[48]

Thus, the material conditional account satisfies not only (2.27a); on the natural interpretation of the phrase "to disbelieve that if φ, then ψ," the material conditional account satisfies (2.27b) as well. That gives the lie to Edgington's contention that no truth-conditional semantics of conditionals satisfies (2.27a) and (2.27b).

Given all the evidence against the material conditional account, Edgington's argument could still be said to be effective if it sank all other truth-conditional accounts. But it does not do so. To see how a response from a Stalnakerian perspective could go, recall that we granted Edgington (2.27a) and (2.27b) as desiderata for semantics of conditionals. However, thereby we may have been granting her too much. For note that in particular (2.27a) may appear as plausible as it does for pragmatic rather than semantic reasons. Indeed, what else than our reliance on the Or-to-if principle inclines us toward agreeing with (2.27a)? And, as Stalnaker has argued (see Section 2.5), the seeming plausibility of the Or-to-if principle can be explained along pragmatic lines, given his possible worlds semantics. I will not go on to consider how the advocates of other truth-conditional accounts of conditionals might respond to Edgington's argument. It is damaging enough for that argument that the two main truth-conditional semantics of conditionals survive it without a scratch.

---

[48] More generally, they can maintain that the truth conditions of "It's not the case that if φ, then ψ" are those of $\varphi \supset \overline{\psi}$. Edgington also seems to miss this when in her [1995:281] work she alleges the advocates of the material conditional account to be committed to the following ontological argument: "If God does not exist, then it's not the case that if I pray my prayers will be answered. I do not pray. Therefore God exists." Here, Edgington is clearly assuming the (nested) conditional to have the logical form: $\overline{G \supset (P \supset A)}$ (where G stands for "God exists," and so on), which is equivalent to $G \vee \overline{(\overline{P} \vee A)}$, or $G \vee (P \wedge \overline{A})$. Thus read, the conditional together with $\overline{P}$ does entail G. As explained, however, advocates of the material conditional account can maintain that the conditional has instead the logical form $\overline{G} \supset (P \supset A)$, or $G \vee \overline{P} \vee A$, which does not entail G in the face of $\overline{P}$.

Furthermore, she relies on the same uncharitable view of how the advocate of the material conditional account must read negated conditionals in her [2001:393] work, where she presents what she thinks of as yet another problem for the material conditional account: "$\overline{(\varphi \supset \psi)}$ is equivalent to $\varphi \wedge \overline{\psi}$. Intuitively, one may safely say, of an unseen figure, 'It's not the case that if it's a pentagon, it has six sides.' But by [the lights of the proponents of the material conditional account], one may well be wrong; for it may not be a pentagon" (notation altered for uniformity of reading). Patently, this has as a hidden premise that the proponents of the material conditional account ought to accept that "It's not the case that if it is a pentagon, it has six sides" is of the logical form $\overline{(\varphi \supset \psi)}$, a premise which – again – appears to be false; they can insist that the sentence is naturally interpreted as saying that if the figure is a pentagon, then it does *not* have six sides, and thus is of the logical form $\varphi \supset \overline{\psi}$.

CHAPTER 3

Probability

Much work has been expended on trying to answer the question of what the probabilities of conditionals are. Yet no attempt so far has led to a clearly correct answer. We saw that the material conditional account gives a clear, but also clearly wrong answer, while Stalnaker's possible worlds semantics has nothing much informative to say about the probabilities of conditionals. What about Stalnaker's Hypothesis (SH), according to which the probability of any conditional equals the probability of its consequent conditional on its antecedent (provided the latter is defined)? While there is no known argument for this thesis showing that it has any normative force, to many the proposal does ring true, at least prima facie. However, not long after Stalnaker had proposed SH, Lewis [1976] presented two so-called triviality results seemingly showing that, loosely stated, SH cannot hold generally, and in effect can hold only for very special, "trivial" probability functions, which have various features that make them unrealistic as representations of people's states of graded belief.

3.1 Triviality

Where Pr denotes an arbitrary probability function that obeys SH, and φ and ψ are such that both $\Pr(\varphi \wedge \psi) > 0$ and $\Pr(\varphi \wedge \overline{\psi}) > 0$, Lewis' [1976:136 f] first triviality result observes that, by the law of total probability,

(3.1) $\Pr(\text{If } \varphi, \text{ then } \psi) = \Pr(\text{If } \varphi, \text{ then } \psi \mid \psi)\Pr(\psi) + \Pr(\text{If } \varphi, \text{ then } \psi \mid \overline{\psi})\Pr(\overline{\psi}),$

which, using SH, can be rewritten as

(3.2) $\Pr(\text{If } \varphi, \text{ then } \psi) = \Pr(\psi \mid \varphi \wedge \psi)\Pr(\psi) + \Pr(\psi \mid \varphi \wedge \overline{\psi})\Pr(\overline{\psi}),$

which further simplifies to

(3.3) $\Pr(\text{If } \varphi, \text{ then } \psi) = 1 \times \Pr(\psi) + 0 \times \Pr(\overline{\psi})$.

That is to say, for all Pr, φ, and ψ that satisfy the aforementioned conditions, it holds that $\Pr(\text{If } \varphi, \text{ then } \psi) = \Pr(\psi)$. This can hardly be true for every real person's belief state. Subsequently, Lewis and other authors have published a great number of further triviality results, all seemingly showing (in often just slightly different ways) the untenability of SH.

These triviality arguments have had, and continue to have, a great impact in philosophy. For some philosophers – including Bennett, as we said – they are one of the main routes to a non-propositional view of conditionals, the thought being that if conditionals do not express propositions, then neither of the conditional probabilities in (3.1) is well defined. After all, by probability theory it should hold that $\Pr(\text{If } \varphi, \text{ then } \psi \mid \psi) = \Pr\big((\text{If } \varphi, \text{ then } \psi) \wedge \psi\big) \div \Pr(\psi)$, and similarly for the other conditional probability. And, as mentioned in Section 2.3, conditionals can occur as conjuncts only if they are propositions.

As was also seen, however, abandoning the view that conditionals have truth conditions has dire consequences. For one, it then becomes unclear how conditionals combine with the rest of our language. For another, it becomes difficult to account for nestings of conditionals. And for a third, and most relevantly in the present context, if conditionals cannot be true or false, then strictly speaking they do not have probabilities, at least not if by "probability" we mean "probability of truth," as would be in line with common parlance. So, although the non-propositional view might seem to allow for keeping the true-ringing SH on board, insofar as this thesis is concerned with probabilities of truth, it is actually incompatible with the non-propositional view.

So, with respect to the question of what the probabilities of conditionals are, what philosophers have to offer is quite disappointing. Some philosophers will tell you – or should tell you, if they want to be true to their non-propositional view of conditionals – that conditionals do not have probabilities. But it is not as though the others had an answer to offer that was any more informative, at least not an answer that is not blatantly false (like the answer given by the material conditional account). It may be time to take a different approach to the question of the probabilities of conditionals.

In line with our general methodology, a natural idea is to attend to what probabilities people do actually assign to conditionals and see whether there is any pattern to be discerned in those assignments. If there is a pattern, then that could point the way toward answering the question under scrutiny. As it turns out, over the past ten years or so, psychologists have conducted a great many experiments concerned with the probabilities of conditionals. In Section 3.2, we look at the results of these experiments. It will be seen that there is a clear tension between these results and the triviality arguments. However, in Section 3.3 it will be argued that very recent empirical work also suggests a way to resolve the tension, though in a way that will cast doubt on the relevance of the triviality arguments to the question of whether natural-language conditionals have truth conditions. Section 3.5 considers, and finds fault with, a different probabilistic argument that equally targets the view that conditionals have truth conditions.

3.2 Probabilities of conditionals: the empirical turn

Conditionals have been the subject of psychological studies for many decades. For instance, numerous studies have been conducted in an effort to determine why people untrained in logic are prone to infer φ from "If φ, then ψ" and ψ (a pattern that is known as "Affirming the Consequent"), or to infer $\overline{\psi}$ from the same conditional with the additional premise $\overline{\varphi}$ (a pattern known as "Denying the Antecedent"). However, in all these studies, it was simply assumed that the semantics of the conditional is given by the material conditional account. The goal of the studies was to discover whether people reason in accordance with this semantics, and, if not, whether there is any system in the "mistakes" they make.

As mentioned, it has only been some ten years since psychologists also turned to the question of the probabilities of conditionals. Pioneering work in this regard has been done by Evans and Over, whose earliest results were gathered in their [2004].[1] In view of the triviality arguments, the unarguably most surprising of these results is that people do generally judge the probability of a conditional to be equal to the corresponding conditional probability. What is more, this result was later replicated several times over, in experiments conducted both by Evans and Over and by other experimentalists.[2] A few of these studies found the conditional probability only as the *modal* evaluation (i.e., the response that occurred most frequently

---

[1] For some relevant earlier papers, see Hadjichristidis et al. [2001], Evans, Handley, and Over [2003], and Over and Evans [2003].

[2] See, e.g., Oaksford and Chater [2003], Oberauer and Wilhelm [2003], Weidenfeld, Oberauer, and Horning [2005], Evans et al. [2007], Oberauer, Weidenfeld, and Fischer [2007], Over et al. [2007], Gauffroy and Barrouillet [2009], Douven and Verbrugge [2010], [2013], Pfeifer and Kleiter [2010], Politzer, Over, and Baratgin [2010], and Fugard et al. [2011].

in the data sets) of the probability of a conditional; a minority of their participants evaluated the probability of a conditional as the probability of the conjunction of antecedent and consequent. Evans et al. [2007] found that this "conjunction response" was more prevalent among those of lower cognitive ability, and Barrouillet and Lecas [1999] and Lecas and Barrouillet [1999] found the response to be predominant even in young children. Importantly, however, there was no evidence for the conjunction response in studies that used "real world conditionals" – conditionals pertaining to events that have actually occurred or might still occur and about which participants may be expected to hold prior beliefs – or conditionals about fictional but ordinary situations.[3]

When taken at face value, and in view of the triviality arguments, the data obtained in these experiments would seem to leave *no* semantics on the table. The semantics cannot be truth-conditional, for then the degrees-of-belief functions of the various participants ought to have had features that, we can be sure, they did not have (leaving aside some exceptional cases, perhaps). On the other hand, the data also seem to give the lie to the view that conditionals do not express propositions, for apparently people do assign probabilities of truth to conditionals.

That is how things *seem* to be, and how they seem to be *if* the data are taken at face value. But surely conditionals either do or do not express propositions. So, things can hardly be as they seem to be. Perhaps the experiments pertaining to SH are methodologically flawed, or their results are to be discounted for some other reason. In fact, it would seem that something *must* be wrong with them, for the triviality arguments simply do not permit interpreting the experimental results as showing what they appear to show, namely, that people's probabilities of conditionals equal their corresponding conditional probabilities, in accordance with SH.

As to methodology, three points are worth making. First, it is to be emphasized that in none of the experiments apparently supporting SH were participants simply asked whether they deem SH intuitively plausible. These studies did not ask participants *about* SH at all. Instead, they asked participants to rate the probabilities of conditionals as well as the corresponding conditional probabilities. To be more exact, in one type of experiments – what psychologists call "within-participants experiments" – the same participants who were asked to rate the probabilities of a number of conditionals were also asked to rate the corresponding conditional probabilities; in another type – called "between-participants

---

[3] See Over et al. [2007] and Douven and Verbrugge [2010], [2013].

experiments" – one group of participants was asked to rate the probabilities of conditionals while another group of participants was asked to rate the corresponding conditional probabilities. Despite the difference in design, in both types of experiments the same close match between probabilities of conditionals and conditional probabilities was found to exist.

Second, there were also differences between the various studies on SH as regards the types of stimuli used. Some studies used as stimuli so-called causal conditionals (conditionals stating a causal connection between antecedent and consequent); others used various types of inferential conditionals (see p. 96). Some studies used conditionals concerning actual matters of fact about which participants could be expected to have opinions; others offered fictional vignettes and asked for the equally fictional probabilities of conditionals pertaining to those stories. In addition, different methods of eliciting conditional probabilities were deployed in the various studies: while some studies determined conditional probabilities via Kolmogorov's well-known ratio definition, other studies relied on the procedure suggested to that end by Ramsey (see p. 92), that is, they asked participants to judge the probability of the consequent on the supposition that the antecedent holds true.[4] Nevertheless, each time the results were in favor of SH.[5]

Third, Johnson-Laird and co-authors have criticized the experimental work on SH because of how these studies elicited probabilities of conditionals.[6] Specifically, they have claimed that there is a general tendency for people to interpret operators as having narrow scope in conditionals, and further that this supposed tendency makes the finding that $\Pr(\text{If } \varphi, \text{ then } \psi) = \Pr(\psi \mid \varphi)$ in people's responses trivial and theoretically uninformative. After all – they reason – if the probability operator takes narrow scope under conditionals, then people naturally understand the phrase "the probability that $\{$if φ, then $\psi\}$ equals x" as meaning "if φ, then $\{$the probability of ψ equals $x\}$." As a result, when asked how probable "If φ, then ψ" is, people hear this as a mere stylistic variant of a question asking for the probability of that conditional's consequent given its antecedent. And so – the critics conclude – we should not be surprised

---

[4] According to some theorists, this procedure provides the best definition of conditional probability. See, for instance, Bennett [2003:53]: "The best definition [of conditional probability] we have is the one provided by the Ramsey test." Edgington [1995:266 f], [1997b:108 f], Oaksford and Chater [2007:109], and Zhao, Shah, and Osherson [2009] express similar views.

[5] Which is not to say that each time the results were the same. As noted, in some studies it was only the modal response that accorded with SH.

[6] See Johnson-Laird and Byrne [2002], Girotto and Johnson-Laird [2004], [2010], Byrne and Johnson-Laird [2010], and Khemlani, Orenes, and Johnson-Laird [2012].

to find a close match between what are supposed to be the probabilities of conditionals and the corresponding conditional probabilities: we have been asking for the same value twice over, just in slightly different words.

Support for their claim concerning the scope of the probability operator is to come by analogy, so to speak, from considering how certain other operators behave in the face of conditionals. For instance, as Johnson-Laird and his co-workers point out, and as was admitted in Section 2.7, the negation operator normally takes narrow scope under conditionals.

However, Politzer, Over, and Baratgin [2010] are surely right to protest that Johnson-Laird and his co-authors are much too quick to take this as evidence for their claim that the probability operator has narrow scope in the face of a conditional. As they note, it would, for instance, be absurd to suggest that the necessity operator takes narrow scope under conditionals: "Necessarily, if φ, then φ" appears nothing more than a truism, whatever one's exact view of the semantics of conditionals; but "If φ, then necessarily φ" seems plainly false, apparently claiming that whatever obtains, obtains of necessity.

While this response is well taken, it does not settle the question of whether the probability operator is to be grouped with the operators that take narrow scope under conditionals or with those that take wide scope over conditionals. To make progress on this question, Over, Douven, and Verbrugge [2013] conducted a number of experiments investigating scope ambiguities of the probability operator and closely related epistemic operators. The results of these experiments consistently indicate that the probability operator takes *wide* scope over conditionals.

For example, one experiment investigated whether asking for the acceptability/credibility/plausibility of a conditional yielded the same value as asking for the acceptability (etc.) of the conditional's consequent on the supposition of its antecedent. The method used in this experiment was designed to parallel one used in experiments supporting SH. Specifically, Over et al., in their experiment, extended Ramsey's procedure for determining conditional probabilities – which, as mentioned, assesses participants' judgments of the probability of ψ conditional on φ by inviting them to suppose φ and then to judge the probability of ψ under this supposition – to the acceptability, credibility, and plausibility operators. Using this generalized method, they checked whether $\Pr(\text{If } \varphi, \text{ then } \psi) = \Pr(\psi \mid \varphi)$, for all conditionals in their materials, but also, for each $X \in \{\text{acceptable, credible, plausible}\}$, whether $X(\text{If } \varphi, \text{ then } \psi) = X(\psi \mid \varphi)$, where $X(\psi \mid \varphi)$ stands for the degree of acceptability, credibility, or plausibility of ψ under the supposition that φ.

While the four operators Over et al. focussed on in their experiment do not have the same meaning, they are syntactically the same and are in the same broad semantic category of epistemic modals. Moreover, acceptability, credibility, and plausibility are, like probability, all naturally conceived as permitting of very fine-grained, even continuum-many, distinctions, and as having maxima and minima; for instance, clearly recognizable tautologies would seem at least as credible as any other proposition, and clearly recognizable contradictions would seem at least as incredible as any other proposition. These operators are also conceptually close to probability. Credibility may not be entirely a matter of probability, but, for instance, few hold that something can be highly credible if it is highly improbable. And Halpern [2003:50] explicitly takes plausibility to be a generalization of probability. Furthermore, as will be seen in Chapter 4, Adams took the probability operator as applied to conditionals to actually measure not probability but acceptability. Finally, while all four operators in Over et al.'s experiment are *graded* operators, each has a categorical counterpart; just as we sometimes say that it is *probable* that such-and-such (as opposed to: that such-and-such has a probability of *x*), we sometimes say that such-and-such is *acceptable*, or *credible*, or *plausible*.

Asking for the probability of a conditional and asking for the corresponding conditional probability tend to yield the same values, as work on SH has amply shown. If Johnson-Laird's grounds for dismissing that work hold, one would expect the same to happen for the other operators; that is to say, one would expect that asking for the acceptability of a conditional and asking for the corresponding conditional acceptability yield the same values, and similarly for the credibility and plausibility operators. However, Over et al. found that neither for acceptability nor for credibility did the values match, not even approximately (for plausibility, the values did match). This is strong evidence for the claim that the acceptability and credibility operators take wide scope over conditionals. As Over et al. argue, the evidence extends, by analogy, to the probability and plausibility operators, given that in view of the aforementioned reasons one would expect the four operators to behave the same in terms of the scope they take over expressions.

Naturally, falsifiers of SH might still be lurking in types of stimuli that have not been considered so far. Most notably perhaps, all experiments that have been hitherto conducted were limited to simple conditionals. But even if SH were to hold only in the form limited to simple conditionals, that would not really diminish the tension between the empirical findings and the triviality results. After all, the latter seem to show that SH cannot even hold true for simple conditionals.[7]

In another attempt to resolve the tension with the triviality arguments, one might note that the data obtained in the experiments are bound to be noisy to some extent, so that all they can be taken to show is that people's probabilities of conditionals *approximately* match the corresponding conditional probabilities. Thus, perhaps we should replace SH with an approximate version of it, with $\approx$ replacing $=$. Unfortunately, this will not fly. It can easily be shown that from an approximate version of SH, a variant of (for instance) Lewis' first triviality argument can be obtained that has as a conclusion that, for all φ, ψ such that $\varphi \wedge \psi$ and $\varphi \wedge \overline{\psi}$ have both positive probability, the conditional probability of ψ given φ is close in value to the unconditional probability of ψ.[8] This is no harder to refute than the contention that conditional probabilities are always strictly equal to unconditional probabilities.

A more radical way to neutralize the empirical data is to interpret them as manifesting people's limited capabilities when it comes to probabilistic reasoning; perhaps the experiments concerning the probabilities of conditionals should be regarded as having unearthed something akin to the previously mentioned conjunction fallacy. However, before attributing massive error to people, we should consider whether there is not a more charitable interpretation of the data. The most charitable proposal is, of course, to take the data as showing that people's bona fide judgments of the probabilities of conditionals are indeed equal to their bona fide judgments of the corresponding conditional probabilities indeed, and then to explain how this is consistent with the triviality arguments. That may seem well-nigh impossible to accomplish, but, I want to argue, the triviality arguments do not as unimpeachably discredit SH as they are commonly held to do.

3.3 Triviality undone

A first crucial observation to be made is that the triviality arguments rely on more than just SH and standard probability theory. Look again at Lewis' first triviality argument as presented earlier, and notice that in substituting $\Pr(\psi \mid \varphi \wedge \psi)$ and $\Pr(\psi \mid \varphi \wedge \overline{\psi})$ for, respectively,

---

7 Moreover, as noted in Douven [2016b], no experiments on SH have considered so-called missing-link conditionals, that is, conditionals patently without a connection (inferential or otherwise) between their antecedent and consequent. Thus, whether people's probability assignments to such conditionals are in accordance with SH is unknown.

8 See Douven and Dietz [2011:35]; also Hájek and Hall [1994:102–105].

$\Pr(\text{If } \varphi, \psi \mid \psi)$ and $\Pr(\text{If } \varphi, \psi \mid \overline{\psi})$, when we go from (3.1) to (3.2), we are really relying on the following generalization of SH:

> GENERALIZED STALNAKER'S HYPOTHESIS (GSH) $\Pr(\text{If } \varphi, \text{ then } \psi \mid \chi) = \Pr(\psi \mid \varphi \wedge \chi)$, provided $\Pr(\varphi \wedge \chi) > 0$.

From this, we obtain SH as a special instance by letting χ be an arbitrary tautology.

GSH is not a basic assumption of Lewis' argument. Rather, Lewis derives GSH from SH in conjunction with what *is* a basic assumption of the argument, namely, that the class of probability functions for which SH holds is closed under conditionalization, meaning that for any probability function Pr in the class and any proposition φ such that $\Pr(\varphi) \neq 0$, the probability function $\Pr_\varphi$ that results from conditionalizing Pr on φ is in the class as well.[9]

With this extra premise, Lewis derives GSH as follows: Let Pr be an arbitrary probability function in an arbitrary class $\mathscr{P}$ of probability functions such that (i) $\mathscr{P}$ is closed under conditionalization and (ii) SH holds for all probability functions in $\mathscr{P}$. Then, by (i), where $\Pr(\chi) \neq 0$, $\Pr_\chi$ is in $\mathscr{P}$. Thus, by (ii), for any φ and ψ such that $\Pr_\chi(\varphi) \neq 0$, $\Pr_\chi(\text{If } \varphi, \text{ then } \psi) = \Pr_\chi(\psi \mid \varphi)$. And so, given that by the definition of conditionalization $\Pr_\chi(\text{If } \varphi, \text{ then } \psi) = \Pr(\text{If } \varphi, \text{ then } \psi \mid \chi)$ and $\Pr_\chi(\psi \mid \varphi) = \Pr(\psi \mid \varphi \wedge \chi)$, it follows that GSH holds for Pr. Because Pr was an arbitrary element of $\mathscr{P}$, GSH holds for all probability functions in $\mathscr{P}$. Finally, because $\mathscr{P}$ was chosen arbitrarily, GSH holds for all probability functions in any class of such functions for which (i) and (ii) hold.

I should note at once that it is fairly innocuous to assume that the class of probability functions for which SH holds is closed under conditionalization, even if this assumption is not *entirely* uncontentious. For we are interested in SH only insofar as it might pertain to probability functions that could represent rational degrees-of-belief functions; if *irrational* people violate SH, then surely that should not be held against the thesis. So then the assumption is that conditionalization preserves rationality of degrees of belief. It is to be emphasized that the assumption is *not* that *only* conditionalization will take one from one rational degrees-of-belief function to another; rather it is that, possibly along with several other update rules, conditionalization will do so. Indeed, the closure assumption is perfectly consistent with the supposition that rational people sometimes just give up their probability function (throw away their priors, as it is also called) and arbitrarily pick another one. And even those philosophers who

---

[9] That $\Pr_\varphi$ results from conditionalizing Pr on φ is to say that, for all propositions ψ, $\Pr_\varphi(\psi) = \Pr(\psi \mid \varphi)$.

do not buy into dynamic Dutch book arguments (as presented in, e.g., Teller [1973]) or accuracy domination arguments (as presented in, e.g., Rosenkrantz [1992]) – which implore us to believe that conditionalization is the *only* rational update rule – typically have no difficulty accepting conditionalization as *a* rational update rule.[10]

If I think, nonetheless, that the triviality arguments are not as airtight as they have appeared to be, where is the rub? There is yet another assumption underlying Lewis' derivation of GSH, one that is easily overlooked, namely, the assumption that the conditional-forming operator has an interpretation that is independent of belief states. For suppose the interpretation of "if" were allowed to vary with a person's belief state so that, in effect, for each Pr we might have a different, tacitly indexed, conditional-forming operator. Thus, let "if" denote the conditional corresponding to the probability function Pr and let "if$_\chi$" denote the conditional corresponding to the probability function Pr_χ that comes from Pr by conditionalizing on χ. Then from the assumption that SH holds for each pair consisting of a probability function and a corresponding conditional, we get that $\text{Pr}_\chi(\text{If}_\chi \, \varphi, \text{then } \psi) = \text{Pr}_\chi(\psi \mid \varphi)$. By the definition of conditionalization, we have both $\text{Pr}_\chi(\psi \mid \varphi) = \text{Pr}(\psi \mid \varphi \wedge \chi)$ and $\text{Pr}_\chi(\text{If}_\chi \, \varphi, \text{then } \psi) = \text{Pr}(\text{If}_\chi \, \varphi, \text{then } \psi \mid \chi)$. But this only gives us GSH if we can assume that $\text{Pr}(\text{If}_\chi \, \varphi, \text{then } \psi \mid \chi) = \text{Pr}(\text{If } \varphi, \text{then } \psi \mid \chi)$, which we can *not* assume if the interpretation of conditionals may vary across belief states.

We have so far considered only one triviality argument. As mentioned, however, after the publication of Lewis' triviality arguments in his [1976] paper, many more triviality arguments have appeared, not all of which rely on GSH.[11] But whatever the details of these further arguments, it is known, due to a result by van Fraassen, that *all* of them – as well as any possible future such arguments – are committed to the assumption that the conditional-forming operator has a fixed interpretation across belief

---

[10] Appiah [1985:94 ff] may be one of the few who deny conditionalization even that status. According to him, rationality mandates that one assign probability 1 only to tautologies. Because conditionalization always results in assigning probability 1 to a contingent proposition, it is, in Appiah's view, not a rational update rule. Clearly, though, if rationality were really to require that we reserve probability 1 for tautologies, then very few of us, if any, would qualify as rational.

[11] However, a number of these arguments do rely on GSH, or even on the Import–Export (IE) principle encountered earlier (e.g., the triviality arguments offered in Blackburn [1986], Jeffrey [2004:15 f], and Douven [2011a:394]). Recall that according to this principle, "If φ, then if ψ, then χ" is logically equivalent to "If φ and ψ, then χ," which in the face of SH is an even stronger assumption than GSH. After all, from IE and the fact that probability theory respects logic, it follows that $\text{Pr}(\text{If } \varphi, \text{then if } \psi, \text{then } \chi) = \text{Pr}(\text{If } \varphi \text{ and } \psi, \text{then } \chi)$. Applying SH to both sides of this equation yields $\text{Pr}(\text{If } \psi, \text{then } \chi \mid \varphi) = \text{Pr}(\chi \mid \varphi \wedge \psi)$, which is GSH. The triviality arguments that rely neither on GSH nor on IE include the ones to be found in Stalnaker [1976], Hájek [1989], [1994], Hall [1994], and Etlin [2009]. (Hájek's 1989 argument will be discussed at length further on; for some comments on his 1994 argument, see note 21.)

states (unless one is willing to impose certain restrictions on the probability functions representing those belief states; more on this below). More specifically, van Fraassen [1976] proves not only that SH is tenable provided that the interpretation of "if" may depend on a person's belief state, but also that this remains the case if, in each interpretation, "if" is required to satisfy certain logical principles generally agreed to be characteristic for conditionals.[12]

In short, all triviality arguments have as a premise not only SH but also the fixedness of the interpretation of the conditional (with the proviso still to be discussed), and these premises, when conjoined with the assumption that the class of probability functions we are considering is closed under conditionalization, entail GSH. The hypothesis that rational people's probability functions validate GSH should be testable in much the same way in which SH has been tested. Yet, whereas much experimental work has been devoted to testing the empirical adequacy of SH, the question of the empirical adequacy of GSH has been largely neglected. In fact, GSH has only very recently been subjected to empirical testing in experiments reported in Douven and Verbrugge [2013].

The main experiment in Douven and Verbrugge's paper is a between-participants experiment in which one group of participants was asked to rate the *conditional* probabilities of a number of conditionals and another group was asked to rate the corresponding "doubly" conditional probabilities. The experimental setup is made clearer by the example of a question that was presented to the first group:

Suppose that the global economic situation stabilizes in the next year.

Then how probable is the following sentence?

If the British government is unsuccessful in creating more jobs, there will be more riots in the UK like the ones we saw a few months ago.

Highly improbable   1   2   3   4   5   6   7   Highly probable[13]

[12] To be still more exact, van Fraassen's paper shows that the result holds good if "if" satisfies the principles of the conditional logic CE. It further shows that if SH is restricted to simple conditionals, simple left-nested conditionals (i.e., conditionals whose antecedent is a simple conditional and whose consequent is a factive sentence), and simple right-nested conditionals (conditionals whose consequent is a simple conditional and whose antecedent is a factive sentence), then "if" will even satisfy the stronger conditional logic C2. The latter result is particularly noteworthy, given that, as mentioned, the empirical data so far only support the hypothesis that people judge the probabilities of simple conditionals in accordance with SH.

[13] The numbers 2–6 were also labeled, in the obvious way (2 = Improbable, 3 = Somewhat improbable, etc.).

The corresponding question posed to the participants in the second group was this:

Suppose that both of the following sentences are true:

1. The global economic situation stabilizes in the next year.
2. The British government is unsuccessful in creating more jobs.

Then how probable is the following sentence?

There will be more riots in the UK like the ones we saw a few months ago.

Highly improbable   1   2   3   4   5   6   7   Highly probable

---

In this study, Douven and Verbrugge found a significant difference between people's judgments of the probability of a conditional, conditional on a given proposition, and their judgments of the probability of the conditional's consequent, conditional on the same given proposition in conjunction with the conditional's antecedent. Thus, their study presents clear evidence against GSH.

Given that GSH follows from *three* premises – SH, the closure-under-conditionalization assumption, and the fixedness of the conditional – we seem to be confronted with a veritable case of underdetermination (cf. Douven [2008a]). How are we to identify the culprit?

Note that the statuses of these premises were not equal to begin with. We saw that during the past decade, a long list of studies have reported what appears to be strong empirical evidence for SH. And, as intimated, the second premise should be largely uncontroversial, given that we are throughout concerned with the class of rational probability functions only. As to the third premise, Lewis [1976:138] thought that denying it would be tantamount to denying that there could be any genuine disagreements about conditionals, given that, being in different belief states, people ostensibly disagreeing about a conditional would in effect be talking past each other. But, as critics have pointed out, that was rash: meaningful disagreement does not require that parties have *exactly* the same proposition in mind, and, as far as van Fraassen's result goes, differences between the propositions expressed by a conditional relative to different belief states may be exceedingly small.[14]

---

[14] See Hájek and Hall [1994:96] and Douven and Dietz [2011:32]. Hájek and Hall [1994:99] think that van Fraassen still owes us an explanation of what it is for two propositions to be close to each other in the relevant sense. Here, van Fraassen could usefully appeal to work done in the area of truth approximation, where some authors have developed general accounts of one theory being

It is not just that there is nothing much to say on behalf of the third premise. The opposite is the case, in that the idea that the interpretation of conditionals is sensitive to belief states has some independent plausibility. It will certainly appear that way to anyone who is attracted to something along the lines of Stalnaker's semantics and holds that similarity relations between possible worlds are involved in the truth conditions of conditionals, given that similarity judgments are known to be sensitive to background beliefs.[15] The belief-sensitivity of conditionals is also implied by the inferential semantics of conditionals that was summarized in Section 2.2, given that that semantics refers to acceptable background premises, and given that which premises count as acceptable will depend on the speaker's or evaluator's belief states. Lindström [1996] reaches the conclusion that conditionals are belief-sensitive via again a different route, notably, by considering how accepting new factual (i.e., non-conditional) information may alter our attitude toward conditionals we have previously accepted.[16] Finally, and equally important, theorists have of late been proposing general semantics that make the interpretation of many more types of sentences than only conditionals relative to belief states.[17] This makes arguing for the belief-sensitivity of conditionals appear less outlandish than it otherwise might.

Thus, taking everything into consideration, the best explanation of why GSH is empirically inadequate is that the third premise involved in its derivation – the assumption that conditionals have a fixed interpretation across belief states – is false.

It is presumably fair to say that most theorists working on conditionals find van Fraassen's tenability result technically impressive but otherwise of academic interest at most. At least that would explain

close to another (see Kuipers [2000] and Oddie [2007]). Another problem that van Fraassen's result faces, according to Hájek and Hall (*ibid.*), is that it fails to specify a rule that governs the change from one interpretation of a conditional to another as we move from one belief state to another. It is true that neither van Fraassen nor anyone else has been able to specify such a rule. But, as will be seen in Chapter 6, we at most know some rules for updating on conditionals under special circumstances. For a broad class of circumstances, we do not know how we update on conditionals. Yet, we do update on conditionals even in such circumstances, and we also have clear intuitions about when such updates go right and when they go wrong. If the absence of explicit rules for updating on conditionals is no impediment to such updating, nor to discriminating between such updates that are intuitively correct and such that are intuitively incorrect, then why should the absence of explicit rules for going from one interpretation of the conditional to another be an impediment to carrying out such transitions, or for doing so in an intuitively correct way?

[15] The belief-sensitivity of conditionals is emphasized in Stalnaker [1975]; see also Harper [1976].

[16] In Lindström's argument, the notion of acceptance is spelled out in the framework of AGM theory (cf. Gärdenfors [1988]). See in the same vein Lindström and Rabinowicz [1995, Sect. 5.4].

[17] See MacFarlane [2012] for a useful overview of recent proposals.

why, in the literature on conditionals, the result has received but scant attention. However, the empirical data relating to SH that have been gathered in the past ten years should have been reason to take van Fraassen's result more seriously, given that this result entails that the said data need not be explained away and can be taken to show what they seem to show. The experimental data reported in Douven and Verbrugge [2013] lend still further support to van Fraassen's idea that the interpretation of the conditional may be belief-sensitive, in view of the fact that these data reveal as empirically inadequate a thesis – GSH – that follows from the conjunction of (i) the negation of van Fraassen's idea, (ii) SH, a thesis for which considerable support has accrued over the years, and (iii) a fairly uncontentious assumption about the class of rational probability functions (closure under conditionalization). To be sure, these data do not thereby constitute conclusive evidence for the correctness of van Fraassen's idea. But they support it strongly enough, I submit, to warrant a thorough rethinking of what are generally regarded as some of the most solid results of twentieth-century analytic philosophy.

As an aside, I note that although, as mentioned previously, there is no known clear counterexample to the IE principle, Douven and Verbrugge's results reported above do constitute evidence against it. It was mentioned in note 11 that, because probability theory is supposed to respect logic, IE entails that, for all φ, ψ, and χ, $\Pr(\text{If } \varphi, \text{ then if } \psi, \text{ then } \chi)$ must equal $\Pr(\text{If } \varphi \text{ and } \psi, \text{ then } \chi)$. If SH holds indeed, as a wealth of data seem to indicate, and as we *can* conclude from those data without running into triviality, then, as was stated in the same footnote, it should also hold that $\Pr(\text{If } \psi, \text{ then } \chi \mid \varphi)$ equals $\Pr(\chi \mid \varphi \wedge \psi)$. But that equality is GSH, which was precisely the focus of Douven and Verbrugge's study, and which their data refuted.

3.4 The return of triviality?

It is time to return to the proviso I made when I summarized van Fraassen's tenability result, that, in view of that result, all triviality arguments, present and future, must assume that the interpretation of the conditional-forming operator is independent of belief states, *unless* they impose certain restrictions on the probability functions representing those belief states. That van Fraassen's result can be circumvented in this way follows from a number of arguments which are all conveniently surveyed in Hájek and Hall [1994]. Here, I consider only the argument originally put forward in Hájek [1989], but the general point to be made in response to this applies to the other arguments as well.

Hájek's [1989] paper presents a triviality argument that does *not* assume the fixedness of the interpretation of the conditional, though it does assume that at least some people's belief states can be represented – at least some of the time – by means of a probability function that is definable on a finite set of possible worlds. Instead of going through the various steps of this argument, I give a simple illustration of it.[18] Let a person's degrees-of-belief function be representable by means of three equiprobable possible worlds, w_1, w_2, and w_3. Then all unconditional probabilities must be multiples of $1/3$. By contrast, some conditional probabilities have the value .5. For instance, where $\varphi := \{w_1, w_2\}$ and $\psi := \{w_1\}$, $\Pr(\psi \mid \varphi) = .5$. As a result, there can be no proposition expressed by "If φ, then ψ" such that its unconditional probability matches the corresponding conditional probability. Hájek's argument is a generalization of this simple idea, leading to the conclusion that if a person's degrees-of-belief function can be represented by means of a probability assignment to $n \geqslant 3$ possible worlds, then there will be conditional probabilities that cannot be matched with any unconditional probabilities.

How problematic is it that, if we want to keep SH in light of the empirical support it has received, we must assume rational people's belief states to be representable only by infinite algebras? It is certainly not a priori that people's belief states are ever representable by means of probability functions defined on only finitely many possible worlds. Naturally, for certain practical purposes, it may be convenient to consider only part of a person's belief state, and it may be possible to model that part by reference to only finitely many possible worlds. But, for all anyone has shown, a full representation of a person's belief state requires an assignment of probabilities to all models of the person's language, which will realistically mean: to infinitely many models.

That this is true for all anyone has shown is no guarantee that it is true. However, if we accept the methodological tenets of traditional Bayesianism, then we do have independent grounds for holding that our degrees-of-belief functions are to be modeled by infinite means. For according to traditional Bayesian thinking, we will, when prompted, be able to come up with a fair betting rate for (say) the proposition that tomorrow the sun will set between six o'clock and one minute past six in Amsterdam, even if we have never actively considered this proposition. Still according

---

[18] I owe the following illustration to Alan Hájek.

to traditional Bayesian thinking, this fact evidences a pre-existing disposition to bet on, and thus a degree of belief in, the designated proposition. Given that the same will hold for each proposition that differs from the aforementioned one only in referring to a different time interval, it follows that we have degrees of belief in infinitely many propositions concerning at what time the sun will set in Amsterdam tomorrow, whether or not these propositions have ever consciously crossed our minds.

Those who disagree with the broadly behaviorist assumptions of the foregoing argument may still be persuaded to accept its conclusion by the observation that, if for no other reason, the fact itself that – as the data show – people's degrees of belief accord with SH but not with GSH seems, in view of Hájek's argument, to constitute a legitimate reason for holding that those degrees of belief are to be represented by infinite means. Indeed, it is worth putting this point in more general terms, so as to make it apply equally to the other arguments that have sought to maintain triviality in the face of van Fraassen's result. In these more general terms, the point is that if the simplest account of a wide range of data – some of which pertain to SH, some to GSH – represents people's degrees-of-belief functions as belonging to a certain class of functions, where we have neither empirical nor theoretical reasons for believing that they do not belong to that class, then that fact itself provides indirect empirical support for holding that people's degrees-of-belief functions do belong to the given class.

Some readers may have as little sympathy for the abductive reasoning underlying this second argument as they have for the behaviorist bent of the first. Perhaps the following "transcendental" argument, which appeals to a version of the principle of charity, can sway even these readers. Van Fraassen's result and the responses it elicited show that if people's (nontrivial) degrees of belief conform to SH, then these degrees of belief are probabilities only if they require infinite means for their representation. Rationality requires people's degrees of belief to be probabilities. So, given that people's degrees of belief do conform to SH, either people are irrational or their degrees of belief are representable by infinite means only. And hence, finally, given that charity dictates that we assume people to be rational if at all possible, we must assume that people's degrees-of-belief functions are representable by infinite means only.[19]

---

[19] Note that there is no tension between this argument and Hájek's [2001:380] remark that it is hard to see why rationality should require people to have degrees-of-belief functions that can only be modeled by infinite means. What is involved in the argument is not the claim that rationality requires people's degrees-of-belief functions to be of the said sort but rather the weaker claim that *if* people's (nontrivial) degrees-of-belief functions conform to SH, *then* rationality requires these

There are a number of more detailed points worth making with respect to the responses to van Fraassen's result. Here, I confine myself to one comment on the argument from Hájek [1989]. The comment is to the effect that even if it had to be granted that at least some belief states can be modeled by finite means, Hájek's argument would still not give reason to think that the empirical results concerning the probabilities of conditionals exhibit flawed probabilistic reasoning, and so should be grouped with the experiments, mentioned earlier, which showed that people sometimes give more credibility to a conjunction than to its conjuncts. To see why not, first note that, given n equiprobable worlds, the divergence between the probability of a conditional and the corresponding conditional probability need never exceed $1/2n$. So, for instance, if $n = 99$, then even though there is no proposition that has a probability of exactly .5, there are propositions that have a probability that is within .005 of .5. That divergence is certainly smaller than any experiments of the kind that have been hitherto conducted, and perhaps simply *any* experiments, could detect.[20]

Of course, it is no assumption of Hájek's argument that all worlds are equiprobable. But if they are not, then that does not necessarily mean that the divergence between probabilities of conditionals and conditional probabilities must be, or at least must sometimes be, *greater* than $1/2n$. In fact, quite the opposite may hold! Thus, unless the assumption is not so much that some belief states are representable by finitely many possible worlds but rather that some belief states are representable by just a handful of possible worlds, we should not expect that experiments conducted to compare the probabilities of conditionals and the corresponding conditional probabilities will show a significant difference between these variables. So, even given the assumption that at least some belief states can be modeled by finite means – an assumption which, for all Hájek has told us, we are under no obligation to make – Hájek's argument leaves unscathed at least the approximate version of SH. And that, as said earlier, is all that the empirical results support anyway.[21]

functions to be of that sort. The latter claim follows directly from van Fraassen's results and Hájek's and others' responses to it in conjunction with the at least in the context of the current debate uncontested claim that rational degrees of belief are probabilities; like Hájek, I am not aware of any argument supporting the former claim.

[20] In this connection, it should be noted that many of the experiments about the probabilities of conditionals used Likert scales (labeled, typically, from "highly probable" to "highly improbable," as in the example from Douven and Verbrugge [2013] on p. 66 above) to measure participants' probabilities. Those experiments that did not use Likert scales asked participants to indicate their probabilities in terms of percentages, which will have invited these participants to indicate their probabilities up to a hundredth only.

[21] It is also worth mentioning Hájek's [1994] so-called perturbation argument, another attempt to challenge van Fraassen's result. The perturbation argument does require uniformity of the meaning

3.5 Bradley's preservation argument

Bradley's [2000] argument is the last on Bennett's list of reasons for abandoning the view that conditionals express propositions. The argument presents what is claimed to be an adequacy constraint on any account of conditionals and then aims to show that no truth-conditional semantics of conditionals can ensure the satisfaction of this constraint. Bradley calls the putative adequacy constraint "the preservation condition for conditionals." Given a language and a probability function Pr defined on it, the condition is that for all sentences φ and ψ of the language the following holds:

> PRESERVATION CONDITION (PC) $\Pr(\text{If } \varphi, \text{ then } \psi) = 0$ if $\Pr(\varphi) > 0$ and $\Pr(\psi) = 0$.

Note that this is a consequence of SH, but not vice versa. PC is not only weaker than SH; according to Bradley it is "immediately and rationally compelling in a way that [SH] is not" (p. 219).[22] Nevertheless, Bradley claims, no truth-conditional semantics can guarantee that PC holds: any such semantics is compatible with the falsity of PC. He admits that PC might still hold in virtue of something other than, or additional to, the semantics of conditionals. But Bradley does not see anything forthcoming that could plausibly fill this role.

It is good to be clear about a crucial difference between Bradley's argument and the triviality arguments discussed earlier. Above we saw that it is reasonable to take the Pr operator in SH to range over *rational* degrees-of-belief functions only. Now suppose, just for the sake of the argument, that we impose SH itself as a further rationality constraint on degrees-of-belief functions. Then it follows from the triviality arguments in conjunction

of "if" across belief states, but Hájek takes this argument to show that there is no way to ensure that SH holds if the meaning of "if" is allowed to vary other than simply to impose SH as a requirement on probability functions. For our present concerns, however, this is unproblematic. It is not as though we have to delineate on a priori grounds the class of degrees-of-belief functions for which SH holds. Rather, the task we face is to make sense of the fact that, for whatever precise reason, people's degrees-of-belief functions do seem to satisfy SH, or at least an approximate version thereof, and to do so in a way that does not imply that – supposing these degrees-of-belief functions to be probability functions – they must have features that they are known *not* to have as a matter of empirical fact (for example, that unconditional probabilities equal conditional probabilities).

[22] Kaufmann [2004] has recently argued that SH not only fails to be immediately compelling, but under certain specifiable conditions even departs quite starkly from intuition, whereas a different rule for determining the probabilities of conditionals, which Kaufmann proposes, does do justice to our intuitions. In Douven [2008b], I argued that, first, Kaufmann's alternative rule is inconsistent, and second, the intuitions that underlie his proposal are to be explained away rather than explained. In retrospect, and in the light of some of Kaufmann's other publications (e.g., his [2005]), I may have dismissed too quickly the contextualist reading of his proposal that I discussed only in passing in the paper.

with van Fraassen's tenability argument that that cannot be done *unless* one is prepared to relinquish the thought that the conditional-forming operator has a fixed interpretation from one belief state to another; otherwise the degrees-of-belief functions are bound to have properties that still rule them out as candidates for representing rational people's belief states. Nothing of the like follows from Bradley's argument. For all it shows, one *can* adopt PC as a rationality constraint without this leading to other problems with our degrees-of-belief functions, even supposing the fixedness of the interpretation of the conditional. Instead, what Bradley's argument purports to show is that there is nothing in a Boolean semantics that, possibly in combination with the probability axioms, could *guarantee* the holding of PC. Bradley views this as a problem, given that the principle appears so compelling to him.

Even granting that PC ought to hold for all rational degrees-of-belief functions, why should this follow from semantic or probabilistic facts? Moorean sentences of the form "φ, but I do not believe φ" are consistent (supposing φ to be consistent), and so probability theory does not prevent us from believing them to the maximal degree. As argued in Douven [2009], however, doing so would be irrational – for reasons that can be only partly spelled out in semantic and probabilistic terms.

That does not answer the question in virtue of what PC holds, supposing it does hold. If we assume a semantics of conditionals in the manner of van Fraassen's proposal and take the empirical results concerning SH at face value, then one response could be that PC holds in virtue of the fact that SH holds, given that SH entails PC. That might seem to answer Bradley's challenge in a way that is consistent with conditionals having truth conditions. But Bradley would doubtless complain that this is just to push the problem back. For what guarantees the holding of SH? As said previously, there is no known normative argument for SH, other than that it sounds right, which is not much of an argument at all. And for all the experimental work on SH, so far none of it has addressed the question of *why* people obey SH (even though I cannot think of a reason why this question could not be subjected to empirical investigation). In short, we do not know why SH holds or why it should hold.

Bradley goes beyond this conclusion in declaring that he fails to see any extra-semantic facts in virtue of which PC might hold. A fortiori, he cannot see any extra-semantic facts in virtue of which SH might hold. But why is it not a perfectly good answer to say that PC strikes us as (in Bradley's words) immediately and rationally compelling, and so we *set* our degrees of belief in accordance with it? Compare: there are no semantic *cum* probabilistic facts that prevent me from believing Moorean sentences to a perfect degree; but I *see* that it would be irrational to do so and hence I *set* my degrees of belief in such sentences to values lower than 1. That will not make sense to anyone who holds that doxastic rationality must be reducible to semantic *cum* probabilistic facts, but the analysis of Moorean sentences given in Douven [2009] casts aspersions on precisely that position.

In fact, going on in this way, it might be possible to arrive at an answer to the question that, we just said, is still wide open, to wit, the question of why people obey SH. There might be constraints other than PC that strike us as compelling and that equally follow from SH. If there are, then an efficient way to ensure that one's degrees of belief satisfy these constraints is to adopt SH as a normative principle.

This is one reason why PC may be of interest even if nothing about this principle entails that conditionals cannot have a truth-conditional semantics. A possibly more important reason is that PC might yield a further piece of evidence against the material conditional account. After all, it is not merely *possible* that $\Pr(\overline{\varphi} \vee \psi) > 0$ while $\Pr(\psi) = 0$; given any sentence φ such that $\Pr(\varphi) \neq 1$, it simply *must* hold that $\Pr(\overline{\varphi} \vee \psi) > 0$, whatever the probability of ψ. So on the mere assumption that there exist sentences φ and ψ such that $\Pr(\varphi) \neq 1$ and $\Pr(\psi) = 0$, the material conditional account is not just compatible with, but entails, the falsity of PC.

Naturally, all this is so only on the condition that PC is compelling indeed. Is it really?[23]

---

[23] Niels Skovgaard Olsen suggested to me that, given my inferentialist leanings (see Section 2.2), I should be inclined to answer this question in the positive. This is because – he believes – given inferentialism, one must assign a conditional zero probability of being true whenever one assigns its consequent zero probability of being true, "because then the probability of there being an inferential procedure from the antecedent to the consequent is equally zero" (personal communication). As he points out, this would at once provide the semantic foundation of PC that Bradley claims to be missing (even if the semantics cannot be a standard possible worlds semantics). Now, according to the version of inferentialism that I favor, there must be a valid argument from antecedent to consequent for a conditional to be true, where the intended notion of validity is broader than deductive validity. I could well imagine holding to some degree that if the village is flooded, the dam has broken, given that the breaking of the dam is the best explanation for the village being flooded (if it is flooded). Given that, in this case, the inferential connection between antecedent and consequent is abductive rather than deductive, I see no inconsistency in assigning some positive probability to the conditional "If the village is flooded, the dam has broken" while assigning a vanishingly small but positive probability to its antecedent and zero probability to its consequent (obviously this would be inconsistent if the inferential connection were deductive). Again, absent a worked-out account of abductive inference, it is hard to say anything very definite on this matter. Be this as it may, given that inferentialism currently enjoys little popularity, and sticking to the

Bradley appears to find PC *so* compelling that in his view it requires no more than a single example by way of support. The example he gives is this: "You cannot . . . hold that we might go to the beach, but that we certainly won't go swimming and at the same time consider it possible that if we go to the beach we will go swimming" (Bradley [2000:220]). For, he claims, "[t]o do so would reveal a misunderstanding of the indicative conditional (or just plain inconsistency)" (*ibid.*). I agree, but still do not think the example commits us to PC. My point is not that the example seems to involve modal-epistemic, rather than probabilistic, claims. Supposing, plausibly, and as Bradley must be (tacitly) doing as well, that a sentence is epistemically possible for an agent iff it has positive probability for the agent, and epistemically certain for the agent iff it has probability 1 for him or her, of course it cannot be reasonable to assign probabilities violating PC if the modal claims cannot be jointly held. Instead my claim is that there is no inconsistency in the example, and that, insofar as the example points to a misunderstanding of the conditional, this concerns the pragmatics, and not (necessarily) the semantics, of conditionals.

To make the point about consistency, assume, without loss of generality, the material conditional account, for whose proponents Bradley's argument should be of particular concern, as we saw. Furthermore, let *B* mean that we go to the beach, and *S* that we go swimming, and let the operators $\Box$ and $\Diamond$ express epistemic certainty and possibility, respectively. Then Bradley's contention, a bit more formally expressed, is that one cannot jointly hold the following:

(3.4) a. $\Diamond$(If *B*, then *S*);
       b. $\Diamond B$;
       c. $\Box \bar{S}$.

Note, however, that on the assumed semantics of conditionals, (3.4a) is equivalent to $\Diamond(\bar{B} \lor S)$. Note further that, given the connection between modalities and probabilities we are assuming, and given that it holds by the probability calculus for any probability function Pr that, first, if φ is a theorem of propositional logic, then $\Pr(\varphi) = 1$, and second, if $\Pr(\varphi) = 1$ and $\Pr(\varphi \supset \psi) = 1$, then $\Pr(\psi) = 1$ (where $\supset$ still denotes the material conditional), the logic of epistemic possibility and certainty must be an

plan not to assume inferentialism in these chapters on epistemology (p. 43), I address Bradley's challenge in the following from a more neutral perspective.

extension of **K**.[24] By consequence, the logic is a normal modal logic. Finally note that in any normal modal logic the following holds:

$$(3.5) \quad \Box \overline{S} \vdash \Diamond(\overline{B} \vee S) \leftrightarrow \Diamond \overline{B}.$$

As a result, the conjunction of (3.4a)–(3.4c) is, given any normal modal logic, and therefore also given the logic that governs our modal-epistemic operators, equivalent to

$$(3.6) \quad \Diamond B \wedge \Diamond \overline{B} \wedge \Box \overline{S},$$

that is, that we may or may not go to the beach, and whichever we do, we certainly will not swim. Surely that can be an eminently reasonable thing to believe. It would thus seem that any modal-epistemic logic on which (3.6) comes out as being inconsistent must be unacceptable. So we can safely assume that, whatever precisely the details of the logic of epistemic possibility and certainty, it will declare (3.6) to be consistent.[25]

But if anything, this makes it more pressing to explain the felt oddness of the example. To a first approximation, then, the explanation is that while there is nothing wrong with holding, in the sense of believing, (3.4a)–(3.4c), we are lured into thinking that these sentences cannot be jointly held true by the fact that one cannot reasonably assert them – which we may take to include stating or writing down – in conjunction. The latter has to do with pragmatic reasons, however, and therefore does not show that any probability assignment that fails to honor PC is somehow defective. The details of the explanation may (slightly) differ, depending on one's exact view of the pragmatics of conditionals.

[24] In fact, given some widely accepted assumptions about agents' introspective capacities (see, e.g., Sobel [1987] and Milne [1991]; but see also Douven [2007]), it is reasonable to think that the logic of epistemic possibility and certainty is **KD45**. One easily verifies that the properties of **KD45** displayed by Propositions 2.6.1 and 2.6.2 in Meyer and van der Hoek [1995:73 f] are all desirable ones, given our interpretation of the diamond (which corresponds to Meyer and van der Hoek's operator M). It is particularly noteworthy that the properties of logical omniscience enumerated by the second proposition, which are generally regarded as being problematic from the perspective of epistemic logic, are exactly as they should be for our purposes, given that probabilistically coherent agents are supposed to be logically omniscient. Incidentally, if we make the additional assumption that rational degrees of belief are strictly coherent in the sense that a rational person is certain of a proposition iff that proposition is a logical truth (cf. Kemeny [1955]), we can add the T schema to the logic, thereby obtaining **S5** (cf. also Gärdenfors [1975]). But for the sake of Bradley's argument, we must already reject strict coherence; for some principled reasons against strict coherence, see, e.g., Howson [2000:134 f].

[25] If we assume **KD45** as our logic, then (3.6) is clearly consistent; for instance, it is even valid in the **KD45**-model $\langle W, R, v \rangle$ with $W = \{w_1, w_2\}$, $R = \{\langle w_1, w_1 \rangle, \langle w_1, w_2 \rangle, \langle w_2, w_1 \rangle, \langle w_2, w_2 \rangle\}$, $v(B, w_1) = 1$, and $v(B, w_2) = v(S, w_1) = v(S, w_2) = 0$.

A straight Gricean explanation would have it that from (3.5), in tandem with some incontrovertible principles of good conversational practice, it follows that if one is certain that we will not swim, then by asserting that it is possible that if we go to the beach we will swim, one is being uncooperative. After all, by so doing one will implicate that one is not in a position to assert the stronger claim that it is possible that we will not go to the beach. And that implicature will appear misleading to any even minimally attentive listener, given that apparently one *is* in the position to assert that we certainly will not swim. For, quite patently, a speaker in that position who asserts that it is possible that if we go to the beach we will swim, is also in the position to assert instead what by her own lights must be more informative, namely, that we may not go to the beach. Of course, it is not generally true that one ought to make one's contribution to a conversation maximally informative; unnecessary information may confuse the hearer (Grice [1989b:26 f]). But in the present case one is, by asserting (3.4a), being less informative than one could be, to no discernible advantage. Rather there is a clear disadvantage: asserting that we may or may not go to the beach but certainly will not swim is both clearer and more succinct than asserting the conjunction of (3.4a)–(3.4c). In short, by asserting the latter, one will be flouting Grice's first maxim of Quantity in the most overt way conceivable (cf. Grice [1989b:26], and, specifically in relation to conditionals, [1989a:61 f]).

According to Jackson [1979], the first maxim of Quantity, when applied to conditionals, does not always give the right results. On his own, arguably more sophisticated, proposal, the explanation we are after would run as follows: By asserting a conditional, a speaker conventionally implicates that the probability of the consequent given the antecedent is high. Still assuming the above connection between epistemic modalities and probabilities, a hearer may be expected to infer from an assertion of (3.4c) that $\Pr(S) = 0$ (where Pr is the probability function representing the speaker's degrees of belief). It then follows from probability theory that $\Pr(S \mid \varphi) = 0$ for all sentences φ, so in particular $\Pr(S \mid B) = 0$ (the latter assumes that $\Pr(S \mid B)$ is defined, and thus that $\Pr(B) > 0$, but this must be the case for anyone in the position to assert (3.4b)). The clash we feel when (3.4a) and (3.4c) are asserted in the same breath, or when one is read close enough after the other, is then explained as follows: First, an assertion of "If we go to the beach, we will go swimming" implicates that $\Pr(S \mid B)$ is high. Second, while there may be few *general* principles concerning the embedding of implicatures in modal and other contexts that can be defended (cf. Récanati [2003]), the following *specific* principle seems utterly plausible:

(3.7) Let i be a conventional implicature of an utterance of φ. Then by asserting "It may be that φ" the speaker implicates (among other things perhaps) that it may be that i.

For instance, to assert "It may be that Jane will come to the party but that nevertheless John will stay home" when one does not at least believe that there may be a contrast between Jane's (possible) coming to the party and John's (possible) staying home, would be misleading; so would be to assert "It may be that Sarah hasn't arrived yet" when one does not at least believe that she may still arrive. Thus, by asserting (3.4a), a speaker implicates that it may be that his or her degree of belief in swimming conditional on going to the beach, $\Pr(S \mid B)$, is high.[26,27] On the other hand, by asserting (3.4c), the speaker implies that that same degree of belief equals 0. There is obviously something very odd, even if not inconsistent, about implicating that a given conditional degree of belief may be high and, in one and the same breath, implying that that conditional degree of belief equals 0.

It is worth mentioning an apparent advantage of the latter explanation over the Gricean one. That someone asserting (3.4a) is not in the position to make the stronger assertion that we will not go to the beach is what Grice calls a "conversational implicature" of that assertion. Among the distinctive features of conversational implicatures is that they are cancelable. One way to cancel such an implicature is to assert something that is inconsistent with it, or has itself an implicature that is inconsistent with the first. And one might wonder whether this is not simply what according to Grice should be going on in asserting, one after the other, (3.4a)–(3.4c). If it is, then the explanation of what is odd about Bradley's example would not seem to work, since normally we do not experience a cancellation of an

---

[26] Since we can unproblematically assign probabilities to probability statements, this can be rendered as: the speaker implicates that on his or her degrees-of-belief function Pr, $\Pr(\Pr(S \mid B) \text{ is high}) > 0$.

[27] It is worth noting that instead of appealing to (3.7), we could have appealed to Green's [1998:77] Embedded Implicature Hypothesis, which states that "[i]f assertion of a sentence S conveys the implicatum that p with nearly universal regularity, then when S is embedded the content that is usually understood to be embedded for semantic purposes is the proposition $(S \& p)$" (though strictly speaking the hypothesis is meant to apply to conversational implicatures that are conveyed nearly universally, there is nothing in Green's discussion to suggest that it could not similarly apply to conventional implicatures, which are conveyed not just *nearly* universally, of course). Given this principle, that one's degree of belief in swimming conditional on going to the beach is high is even part of the proposition embedded in "It may be that if we go to the beach, we will swim." However, because of its greater generality Green's principle already seems harder to defend than (3.7).

implicature as something odd happening. Here the Gricean might try to appeal to the order in which the sentences are asserted, arguing as follows:

> Perhaps the assertion of (3.4c) could be taken to cancel the implicature generated by the assertion of (3.4a) in
>
>> (3.8) We may go to the beach, and it may be that if we do, we will swim. In fact, I'm sure we won't swim.
>
> in which the assertion of (3.4a) precedes that of (3.4c). However, here already the more natural interpretation might be the one according to which the speaker, in between the two sentences in (3.8), changes his or her mind about the possibility of swimming. But this seems to be the only plausible interpretation if (3.4c) is asserted (or, as in the example, read) before (3.4a); at any rate, no cancellation seems to take place in that event. It is well known that order matters to whether or not an implicature is successfully canceled. Compare "John may have four children. In fact, he has three" with "John has three children, or possibly four." The latter is fine, and in it the implicature that John has exactly three children is successfully canceled. Of the former we can only make sense by assuming that in between the two sentences, the speaker suddenly remembers, or at least thinks he or she remembers, the exact number of John's children.

Be this as it may, for the other explanation offered above, the objection does not even arise, simply because on Jackson's proposal it is due to the conventional meaning of the word "if" that by asserting a conditional a speaker implicates that the conditional's consequent is highly probable given its antecedent. And conventional implicatures are not cancellable (see, e.g., Levinson [1983:128]).

As a further comment, I should like to address a possible objection to the pragmatic explanation of our intuitive response to Bradley's example.[28] Let Pr be my current degrees-of-belief function, and suppose that $\Pr(B)$ is low but positive and $\Pr(S) = 0$. Then, provided I obey the axioms of probability theory, $\Pr(\overline{B} \vee S)$ is high and thus, given the material conditional account that we are supposing for the sake of the argument, so must be $\Pr(\text{If } B, \text{ then } S)$. Given, for instance, Jackson's account of conditionals, the conditional is still unassertable for me, for $\Pr(S \mid B) = 0$. However, we may assume that $\Pr(\overline{B} \vee S)$ is high enough for $\overline{B} \vee S$ to qualify as acceptable.[29] So suppose I believe that disjunction. Then even though I should

---

[28] Thanks to Richard Bradley for pressing me on this.

[29] The connection between high probability and acceptability that is assumed here is not without problems. I come back to this in the next chapter. But here it may be granted for the sake of the objection.

not assert that if we go to the beach, we will go for a swim, I *should* be willing to assert that

(3.9)   I believe that if we go to the beach we will go for a swim.

But given that I am sure that we will not swim, I am *not* willing to assert (3.9). The objection then is that the only plausible explanation for this is that (3.9) would misrepresent what I believe, contrary to what is implied by the semantics of conditionals we are supposing here.

The response to this objection starts by pointing to the following principle, which should appear plausible:

(3.10)   By asserting "I believe that φ," a speaker reports her belief in φ and in addition implicates that she believes the implicatures that an assertion of φ generates or would generate in the given context of utterance.

For example, it seems evident that when I say that I believe that John has three children, I am implicating that I believe John has exactly three children; were I to believe that John has exactly four children, then the assertion, though not strictly speaking false, would be misleading. Similarly, when I say that I believe that, although Sue does not like Brahms' music, she will go to the concert, I am implicating that I believe there to be a contrast between Sue's not liking Brahms' music and her going to the concert; indeed, one would reasonably infer from my assertion that the concert program features one or more pieces by Brahms. Applied to the example of the objection, and assuming Jackson's account of conditionals, (3.10) says that by asserting (3.9) I shall implicate that I believe that our going for a swim is highly probable, conditional on our going to the beach. But given that, as the objection assumes, $\Pr(S) = 0$, I must regard that implicature as utterly misleading. Thus, we can readily extend the pragmatic explanation given above to one that explains our reluctance to assert (3.9), too.[30]

---

[30] There are ways to extend the explanation and reach the same conclusion about sentence (3.9) other than via principle (3.10). For example, on Green's Embedded Implicature Hypothesis cited in note 27, "I believe that our going for a swim is highly probable conditional on our going to the beach" even comes out as being a conjunct of the proposition embedded in (3.9). Incidentally, while not required for our present purposes, generalizing (3.10) to belief ascriptions to persons other than oneself is certainly possible. Thus generalized, the principle would for instance account for the phenomenon that when someone reports "Paul believes that the King has died and that a Republic has been declared," that person "suggests that, according to Paul, [the two events] took

In summary, there is little hope that we can appeal to PC in trying to explain why people's degrees-of-belief functions tend to be in agreement with SH, or that the principle provides extra ammunition against the material conditional account. At least, Bradley's argument gives us no reason for believing that we are committed to PC. The principle appears plausible, to be sure, but broadly Gricean grounds suffice to explain that appearance.

place in that order" (Récanati [2003:312]). But Soames [2003:203 n] seems right to note that it may depend on context whether when a speaker has uttered a sentence of the form "Person P believes that φ" it is more plausible to attribute an implicature of an utterance of φ to P or rather to the speaker. It is patent that such an ambiguity cannot attach to utterances of the form "I believe that φ."

CHAPTER 4

Acceptability

As I understand the term "acceptability," it designates justified or rational believability. To say that a given proposition is acceptable for a person is to say that it is epistemically all right for the person to adopt that proposition as a belief. In Section 3.2, it was already mentioned that the term "acceptability" is used both in a categorical and in a graded sense. Both the categorical and the graded notion of acceptability play a vital role in our epistemic life; we go routinely back and forth between thinking and speaking about *what* we deem acceptable and about the *degrees* to which we deem various things acceptable. Neither mode is to be dismissed off-hand as being loose talking and thinking, nor is it even clear on what grounds one mode could be said to be inferior or subservient to the other. Accordingly, many philosophers hold that we need both an epistemology of belief and an epistemology of degrees of belief.

It would seem that we can have both the attitude of deeming categorically acceptable and the attitude of deeming acceptable to a certain degree vis-à-vis conditionals as well. That, at any rate, is what a number of authors have been supposing in their work on either the categorical acceptability conditions of conditionals or their graded acceptability conditions (or both). It was noted in Section 1.1 that the issue of the acceptability of conditionals is one of the rare topics on which philosophers tend to agree. In the previous chapter, we saw that most philosophers agree – wrongly, as was argued – on what the probabilities of conditionals cannot be, whereas the question of what these probabilities *are* is a matter of ongoing debate. With respect to the issue of acceptability, the agreement is more substantial. Many philosophers agree on what the graded acceptability conditions of conditionals are, and there is also a good deal of agreement on the categorical acceptability conditions.

Thus one might think that if a whole chapter of this book is to be devoted at all to issues – graded and categorical acceptability of conditionals – on which virtually everyone agrees, the chapter will be a short one. Instead, this chapter is the longest in the book. The reason for this is that I believe the near-consensus on both issues to be misguided, and arguing against the mainstream requires proper backing. Thus, I will provide, next to theoretical considerations, rather unambiguous empirical data *against* the popular accounts of the graded and categorical acceptability conditions of conditionals and *for* specific amendments to these accounts.

The term "amendments" suggests, and is meant to suggest, that I am still in broad agreement with the mainstream on the acceptability of conditionals. In particular, like the mainstream, I hold that the acceptability of a conditional depends on there being an epistemically significant relationship between the conditional's antecedent and its consequent. This relationship is typically one to the effect that a change in a person's epistemic position vis-à-vis a conditional's antecedent places, or would place, that person in a certain epistemic position vis-à-vis that conditional's consequent, all else remaining equal.[1,2]

A famous source of inspiration for thinking in this way about the acceptability of conditionals is a footnote in Ramsey [1929/1990]. There he describes the assessment of the acceptability of a conditional as relying on a process of hypothetical updating:

> If two people are arguing "If p will q?" and are both in doubt as to p, they are adding p hypothetically to their stock of knowledge and arguing on that basis about q; so that in a sense "If p, q" and "If p, $\neg q$" are contradictories. We can say they are fixing their degrees of belief in q given p. (Ramsey [1929/1990:155 n])

Specifically, Ramsey has been interpreted as suggesting in this passage that whether we accept a conditional depends on how we assess the consequent when we temporarily push ourselves into the fiction of having come to know (or, as some prefer, having come to believe) the antecedent. Thus interpreted, the footnote is commonly regarded to contain the first formulation of the Ramsey test.

It is important to note, however, that neither the notion of hypothetical updating on the antecedent nor that of assessing the consequent in the hypothetically updated knowledge (or belief) state – "arguing on that basis about q" – is specified in any detail by Ramsey. As a result, the above

---

[1] The ceteris paribus clause is meant to take care of such conditionals as "If Reagan worked for the KGB, no one will ever find out." Here, an epistemic change vis-à-vis the antecedent might lead one to give up the conditional rather than to change one's epistemic attitude vis-à-vis the consequent; see Section 4.4.

[2] See, for instance, Gärdenfors [1988:147]: "[C]onditional sentences in various forms are about changes of states of belief."

passage leaves room for a number of different explications. In principle, a theory according to which "If φ, then ψ" is acceptable to a person iff the person's coming to know φ would place that person in the position to know ψ (if he or she is not already in that position) could qualify as conforming to the idea behind the Ramsey test; the same could be said of a theory according to which the conditional is acceptable iff, or to the extent that, what would justify the person in believing φ would also justify him or her in believing ψ. But Ramsey's reference to the fixing of conditional probabilities ("degrees of belief in q given p") has led most to believe that for Ramsey the acceptability of conditionals was to be spelled out in probabilistic terms, specifically by reference to the notion of conditional probability.

I am again with the mainstream in believing that probabilities must play at least a key role in the statement of both the graded and the categorical acceptability conditions of conditionals. Where I depart from mainstream thinking is on the exact statements of these conditions. Section 4.1 deals with graded acceptability, and Sections 4.2–4.7 deal with categorical acceptability.

4.1 Graded acceptability

Before Stalnaker proposed SH as an adequacy condition for semantics of conditionals, Adams [1965] had already proposed a thesis that looks almost identical, and which now goes by his name:

> ADAMS' THESIS (AT) $\Pr(\text{If } \varphi, \text{ then } \psi) = \Pr(\psi \mid \varphi)$, for all simple conditionals "If φ, then ψ" such that $\Pr(\varphi) \neq 0$; if $\Pr(\varphi) = 0$, then $\Pr(\text{If } \varphi, \text{ then } \psi) = 1$.

One difference between AT and SH is immediately obvious: the former is restricted to simple conditionals, while the latter is not. This restriction was motivated by Adams' skepticism with regard to the idea that conditionals express propositions. Were AT to hold unrestrictedly, then, where φ or ψ is a conditional, and given the ratio definition of conditional probability, the probability of "If φ, then ψ" would equal $\Pr(\varphi \wedge \psi)/\Pr(\varphi)$, according to AT. That is, the probability of the conditional would equal a ratio whose numerator contains a conjunction, at least one of whose conjuncts is a conditional. But, as pointed out earlier, to admit that conditionals can figure as conjuncts in conjunctions commits one to the view that conditionals express propositions.

Adams' non-propositional view of conditionals has a further consequence, one that is not apparent from AT as usually stated. It is hard to
make sense of the idea that conditionals could have a probability of truth
if they cannot be true to begin with. Therefore, as Adams realized, given
non-propositionalism, the probability operator cannot apply literally to
conditionals. He thus proposed that we think of $Pr(If \varphi, then \psi)$ as indicating the *degree of assertability* of "If φ, then ψ"; this, he thought, was
measured by the corresponding conditional probability $Pr(\psi \mid \varphi)$.[3] Later,
Adams came to think of $Pr(If \varphi, then \psi)$ as indicating rather the *degree of
acceptability* of the conditional. Thus, it might be clearer to state Adams'
Thesis as $As(If \varphi, then \psi) = Pr(\psi \mid \varphi)$, as Jackson [1987:11] does, or better still, as in Douven and Verbrugge [2010:305], as $Ac(If \varphi, then \psi) =
Pr(\psi \mid \varphi)$, where, of course, the provisos of AT are still supposed to hold.

The non-propositional view of conditionals protects AT against all
extant triviality arguments, even if conditionals have a fixed interpretation across belief states. Nearly all of these arguments are blocked by the
fact that conditionals cannot occur in Boolean combinations if they do
not express propositions. For instance, in that case the law of total probability – or an analog of it for Adams' assertability/acceptability operator –
cannot be applied to conditionals, which immediately blocks Lewis' first
triviality result rehearsed in the introduction to Chapter 3. And although
Hájek's [1989] argument does not require any embedding of conditionals
in Boolean combinations, it too is blocked because if conditionals do not
express propositions, they cannot be equated with sets of possible worlds
whose degree of assertability might otherwise somehow equal the sum of
the degrees of assertability assigned to their members. A fortiori, Hájek
cannot argue that, assuming that a person's belief state can be represented
by means of a finite algebra of propositions, the number of distinct values
of the person's conditional probabilities must exceed the number of degrees
of assertability that this person attaches to the various propositions.

What is the status of AT? Is it meant as a normative thesis, or is it
supposed to be descriptively correct, or both? Just as there is no known
argument for the claim that SH is normatively compelling, there is no
known argument for the claim that AT is normatively compelling. According to almost all commentators, however, the thesis is at least descriptively
correct. Jackson [1987:12] is very explicit in this respect:[4]

---

[3] We are supposed to abstract here from Gricean and other broadly social considerations. The thesis
could in effect be said to concern what Jackson [1987:10] calls "assertibility."

[4] In the meantime, Jackson has distanced himself from AT. Jackson [2006] argues that $Pr(\psi \mid \varphi)$
gives the "intuitive probability" of "If φ, then ψ." In his view, this intuitive probability is really an

There is a great deal of evidence for [AT]. There is head-counting evidence. Very many philosophers of otherwise differing opinions have found [AT] highly intuitive. There is case-by-case evidence. Take a conditional which is highly assertible ...; it will invariably be one whose consequent is highly probable given its antecedent.

Similarly, McGee [1989:485] says that "[AT] describes what English speakers assert and accept with unfailing accuracy," and that "[t]he numerical values [Adams assigns to conditionals] accurately measure the assertability and acceptability of conditionals." Indeed, Edgington [1995:280], who shares Adams' view on conditionals, appears to be the only commentator who is more cautious on the descriptive adequacy of AT, saying that "[i]t is an empirical question how well [AT] fits our practice of assessing conditionals."[5,6]

Despite what the citations from Jackson and McGee might suggest, they are not based on any systematic investigation of AT's empirical adequacy. Until very recently, experimentalists have paid no attention to AT. Perhaps they thought that it would make no difference whether one asked people to judge the degrees of assertability or acceptability of conditionals instead of the probabilities.[7] Adams' own work may even have suggested as much, given that he sticks to the use of the probability operator before conditionals, which is then to be interpreted as an acceptability or assertability operator. Still, the assertion that asking for a conditional's probability and asking for its degree of acceptability or assertability will yield the same result is itself an empirical claim, which it would seem well worth checking. It is in a way curious, therefore, that the first experimental findings that explicitly pertain to AT were reported only a few years ago, in Douven and Verbrugge [2010].

The conditionals that figure in the stimuli of the experiments that Douven and Verbrugge conducted are all what some linguists call "inferential conditionals," that is, conditionals that express a reasoning process, having

---

illusion: the folk are collectively mistaken in thinking that conditionals have probabilities satisfying SH. Intuitive probability cannot be real probability, Jackson believes, in the light of Lewis' and others' triviality arguments. That is itself a mistake, as we saw in the previous chapter.

[5] She had made basically the same remark in her [1992:195], though there she adds that AT is "not *far* off the mark: there would not be *much* difference, if any, between uses of 'if' according to [AT] and actual uses."

[6] Many authors who take AT to be descriptively correct at the same time agree with McGee [1989:485] that the thesis is disappointingly weak, given that it says nothing about compounds of conditionals. McGee's paper is actually an attempt to extend AT to right-nested conditionals, though, according to Lance [1991] and Dietz and Douven [2010], not a successful one.

[7] Though note that the citations are from publications predating the empirical work on the probabilities of conditionals discussed in the previous chapter.

the conditional's antecedent as a premise and its consequent as a conclusion. In the linguistics literature, it is customary to distinguish inferential conditionals from so-called content conditionals, though the latter do not seem to form a particularly well-delineated class. Its members are sometimes loosely defined as describing relations between states of affairs or events as they obtain, or respectively happen, in reality. However, examples adduced in the literature suggest a rather mixed bag, including such diverse conditionals as conditional threats and promises as well as conditionals stating law-like regularities.[8] Fortunately, for the purposes of Douven and Verbrugge's study, it is not really important whether the distinction between inferential and content conditionals is well founded. All that matters is that many conditionals satisfy the definition of inferential conditionals.[9]

For linguists, the distinction between inferential and content conditionals typically only serves as a starting point. They have proposed various finer-grained typologies, especially of inferential conditionals, mostly based on grammatical features of the sentences. Douven and Verbrugge introduce a different typology of inferential conditionals, one based on the type of inference a conditional reflects, where the relevant types are deductive, inductive, and abductive inference, and where the type may depend on the background assumptions that are being made in the context in which a conditional is asserted or evaluated. More exactly, they distinguish between: deductive inferential (DI) conditionals, in which the consequent follows deductively from the antecedent, possibly in conjunction with background premises; inductive inferential (II) conditionals, in which the consequent follows inductively from the antecedent and, possibly, background premises, where the notion of following inductively is understood in terms of high statistical probability; and abductive inferential (AI) conditionals, in which the consequent follows abductively from the antecedent and, possibly, background premises, where this is understood to imply that either the consequent best explains the antecedent in light of the background premises (if there are any) or the consequent best explains something in the background in light of the antecedent.[10]

---

[8] See, e.g., Dancygier [1998], Declerck and Reed [2001], and Haegeman [2003]. Inferential conditionals have also been discussed in the psychology of reasoning literature; see, e.g., Politzer and Bonnefon [2006] and Verbrugge et al. [2007].

[9] If conditionals require for their truth the presence of an inferential relation between their antecedent and consequent, as has been suggested (see Section 2.2), then it would seem that any conditional that is to stand a chance of being true must qualify as an inferential one.

[10] Douven and Verbrugge begin their typology by first distinguishing between certain and uncertain inferential conditionals; they then divide the latter further into inductive and abductive inferential

For example, of these conditionals:

(4.1)   a. If $a + 1 = 7$, then $a = 6$.
   b. If John lives in Chelsea, he is rich.
   c. If Tim and Hank are jogging together, they must have patched up their recent quarrel.

(4.1a) is clearly a DI conditional. On the other hand, (4.1b) is plausibly thought of as reflecting an inductive inference, leading to the conclusion that John is rich on the basis of the premise that he lives in Chelsea, given the background assumption that most people living in Chelsea are rich; so (4.1b) belongs to the class of II conditionals. Finally, supposing a context in which it is believed that old friends Tim and Hank recently had a serious quarrel which, it seemed, ended their friendship for good, (4.1c) is grouped most naturally with the AI conditionals, given that, in the said kind of context, their having patched up their quarrel best explains the (presumed) fact that Tim and Hank are jogging together.

Douven and Verbrugge use conditionals of all three types not only in testing AT but also in testing a number of weaker theses, which might be closer than AT to what some authors have in mind when they discuss Adams' work on conditionals. Note that, as it stands, AT is very strict in that it requires the degree of acceptability of a conditional to *equal* the corresponding conditional probability. But clearly, one can acknowledge that acceptability is or can be a matter of degree, and also subscribe to the thought that, at least in general, the degree of acceptability of a conditional "goes by" its conditional probability (as Lewis [1976:133] puts it), without having to subscribe to a strict equality between Ac(If φ, then ψ) and Pr($\psi \mid \varphi$), as AT postulates, or even to the following slightly weaker version of the thesis:

WEAK ADAMS' THESIS 1 (WAT1)   Ac(If φ, then ψ) $\approx$ Pr($\psi \mid \varphi$).[11]

What are apparently meant as paraphrases of AT in the literature suggest that various authors also conceive of the relevant connection in a looser

conditionals. If the truncated argument view of conditionals is right, not all uncertain conditionals should be expected to be either of the inductive or of the abductive type, given that non-deductively valid arguments may contain both inductive and abductive steps. So, on this view, it would make sense to add a mixed inductive/abductive category of inferential conditionals. Be this as it may, the uncertain inferential conditionals that Douven and Verbrugge used in their stimuli all fall into one of the two pure categories of II and AI conditionals.

[11]   It is taken as read that in WAT1, and also in the further variants of AT to be stated below in the text, "If φ, then ψ" stands for a simple conditional. The proviso that Pr(φ) $\neq$ 0 also applies here and below.

way. Purportedly stating Adams' view – with which he proclaims to agree –
Bennett [2003:46] writes: "[T]he assertability or acceptability of 'If φ, then
ψ' for a person at a time *is governed by* the probability the person then
assigns to ψ on the supposition of φ" (notation altered for uniformity
of reading; my italics). This can be interpreted in a number of ways. For
instance, Bennett might have in mind something like

> WEAK ADAMS' THESIS 2 (WAT2)   Ac(If φ, ψ) is high/middling/low iff
> $\Pr(\psi \mid \varphi)$ is high/middling/low.

This, in any event, is the version of Adams' Thesis that McGee [1989:487 f]
aims to defend; he thinks that, thus interpreted, Adams' Thesis "dis-
plays uncanny accuracy" (p. 488).[12] Alternatively, Bennett's assertion that
Ac(If φ, then ψ) is governed by $\Pr(\psi \mid \varphi)$ could be taken to mean

> WEAK ADAMS' THESIS 3 (WAT3)   Ac(If φ, then ψ) highly correlates
> with $\Pr(\psi \mid \varphi)$.

Or perhaps it even just means

> WEAK ADAMS' THESIS 4 (WAT4)   Ac(If φ, then ψ) is at least moder-
> ately correlated with $\Pr(\psi \mid \varphi)$.

(Presumably on no plausible reading of "being governed by" could
Ac(If φ, then ψ) be said to be governed by $\Pr(\psi \mid \varphi)$ if there is but a weak
correlation between them.)

  Naturally, if AT holds, then so do WAT1–WAT4. But any of these latter
theses might hold without AT holding. A priori, it is also possible that
different theses hold for different restricted domains; that, for instance,
one thesis holds for DI conditionals, a second for II conditionals, and a
third for AI conditionals.

  Douven and Verbrugge's main experiment is again a between-
participants experiment: The participants in one group were given thirty
items, consisting of context–conditional pairs $\langle C_i, \text{"If } \varphi_i, \text{ then } \psi_i\text{"} \rangle$ (1 $\leqslant$
$i \leqslant$ 30), with 10 DI, 10 II, and 10 AI conditionals; participants were asked
to rate the acceptability of each conditional "If φ_i, then ψ_i" in light of context C_i. The thirty context–conditional pairs were used to construct thirty
context–sentence pairs of the schematic form $\langle C_i + \text{"Suppose } \varphi_i\text{"}, \psi_i \rangle$.
These were presented to a second group of participants, who were asked

---

[12] Hájek and Hall [1994:101] think that, while WAT2 may be plausible, it is not very interesting, given
    that "it seems unlikely that it could play a very useful role in the development of probability logic,
    or in other philosophical projects." Naturally, insofar as one's interest is in the descriptive adequacy
    of AT or any of its variants, such considerations are beside the point.

to rate the probability of each ψ_i in light of context C_i + "Suppose φ_i," thereby yielding conditional probability ratings of ψ_i given φ_i in C_i, for all i.

The following is one of their items asking for the acceptability of conditionals, in this case an II conditional:

Context: According to a recent report written on the authority of the Dutch government, many primary school students in the province of Friesland (where many people still mainly speak Frisian) have difficulty with spelling. Jitske is a student of a primary school somewhere in the Netherlands.

Conditional: If Jitske goes to a Frisian primary school, then she has difficulty with spelling.

Indicate how acceptable you find this conditional in the given context:

　　Highly unacceptable　1　2　3　4　5　6　7　Highly acceptable[13]

The other group received the corresponding question asking for the conditional probability:

Context: According to a recent report written on the authority of the Dutch government, many primary school students in the province of Friesland (where many people still mainly speak Frisian) have difficulty with spelling. Jitske is a student of a primary school somewhere in the Netherlands. Suppose, in fact, that Jitske goes to a Frisian primary school.

Sentence: Jitske has difficulty with spelling.

Indicate how probable you find this sentence in the given context:

　　Highly improbable　1　2　3　4　5　6　7　Highly probable

The results documented in Douven and Verbrugge's paper are mixed, but mostly negative. When taken over all inferential conditionals, the results show that the acceptability of a conditional does not equal the corresponding conditional probability, and that the two are not even approximately equal (on any plausible reading of "approximately"). Hence, the results manifestly refute Adams' Thesis, both in its strict form AT and in its approximate form WAT1. In fact, the data even refute the still weaker thesis WAT2, according to which the acceptability of a conditional

---

[13] The numbers 2–6 were again labeled in the obvious way (2 = Unacceptable, 3 = Somewhat unacceptable, etc.).

and the corresponding conditional probability are at least in the same range (high, middling, or low). On the other hand, the data do support WAT3: Douven and Verbrugge found a high correlation ($r = .83, p < .05$) between acceptability judgments and judgments of corresponding conditional probabilities.

As stated, these are the results taken over all their materials. When the types of inferential conditionals are considered separately, the results are partly better, partly worse. For DI conditionals, AT does hold (or at any rate the approximate version of that thesis). For AI conditionals, the most that can be said is, again, that acceptability of conditionals highly correlates with conditional probability ($r = .81, p < .05$). However, for II conditionals not even that much is true: for these conditionals, there was at best a moderate correlation ($r = .65, p < .05$) between acceptability and conditional probability judgments. So, for II conditionals, only the exceedingly weak WAT4 holds. Note that if inferential conditionals do not exhaust the class of conditionals – for instance, because the class of content conditionals is non-empty (see above) – then the picture may come to look still more fragmented when further types of conditionals are taken into account.

Ironically, while SH had never been tested specifically in relation to inferential conditionals, Douven and Verbrugge, in one of their control experiments, used the same stimuli for testing SH that they had used for testing AT, with the result of finding more support for SH. That is to say, when they asked a third group of participants to rate the probability (instead of the acceptability) of each "If φ_i, then ψ_i" in light of C_i, they found a close to perfect match between those ratings and the corresponding conditional probability ratings of their second group of participants.

The results reported in Douven and Verbrugge [2010] in effect create an even more fundamental problem for Adams and those who, like him, wish to maintain that we can make sense of a probability operator as pertaining to a conditional even if conditionals do not express propositions – namely, by interpreting it as indicating the degree of acceptability of the conditional. For Douven and Verbrugge also found a significant difference between the *probability* and the *acceptability* ratings of conditionals. So, apparently, people do *not* interpret the probability operator when it occurs in front of a conditional as indicating degree of acceptability.[14]

It thus appears that a popular strand of philosophical theorizing about the use conditions of conditionals needs substantial rethinking. We saw

---

[14] Here in particular it is worth mentioning that Douven and Verbrugge also conducted a control experiment to verify that their participants had understood the notion of acceptability in the intended (epistemic) sense, and not as, for example, social acceptability or political correctness.

that many philosophers assume explicitly – though presumably merely on the basis of casual introspection – that AT, or at least some attenuated version thereof, is descriptively correct. But this assumption is not warranted by Douven and Verbrugge's empirical findings. These suggest a messier picture of the relation between a conditional's degree of acceptability and the corresponding conditional probability and, to repeat, the picture may get messier still if other conditionals beyond inferential conditionals are to be taken into account. *If* we want to put something in place of AT that is of the same generality, it should be the thesis that there is a high correlation between the degrees to which conditionals are deemed acceptable and the corresponding conditional probabilities. But if we do so, we should often enough remind ourselves that the thesis is rather crude, and does not apply to the same extent across all types of conditionals.

Of course, future research may give us a clearer picture of the graded acceptability conditions of conditionals. It does not follow from Douven and Verbrugge's study that these cannot be stated entirely in terms of probabilities; perhaps they can, but just not as straightforwardly as AT makes it seem. Still, further studies should certainly be open to the possibility that non-probabilistic factors may be involved as well.

To end this section on a more positive note, it should be mentioned that Douven and Verbrugge found a significant effect of type of conditional on acceptability ratings, the mean acceptability rating for the DI items being the highest, that for the II items being the lowest. This effect is plausibly explained by, and thereby gives some support to, the broadly shared view about the epistemic nature of the acceptability conditions of conditionals. For it is natural to suppose that these differences among the three types of conditionals are due to the fact that the types of inference that underlie the DI/II/AI typology differ from an epistemological viewpoint in that they may put us in different epistemic positions vis-à-vis the conclusions we reach by them on the basis of known or accepted premises. For instance, coming to know φ will normally put us in an epistemic position vis-à-vis ψ that is weaker if ψ follows inductively from φ than if ψ follows deductively from φ. Of course, this is rather speculative, given that not much is known at this point about how different types of inferences may give rise to different doxastic attitudes, or different degrees to which we have a given doxastic attitude, even though these questions seem amenable to empirical research. At the same time, everyone would be surprised if deductive inference would not in general result in a stronger epistemic position than either inductive or abductive inference, assuming the same epistemic position vis-à-vis the premises on which the inference is based.

4.2 Qualitative Adams' Thesis

AT is a quantitative thesis, relating the *degree* of acceptability of a conditional to the corresponding conditional probability. As mentioned, however, although we do talk and think in terms of degrees of acceptability, we also use "acceptability" and "acceptable" (and kindred terms) in a categorical sense: statements can be said to be acceptable, respectively unacceptable, *tout court*. Accordingly, we can ask under what circumstances a conditional is acceptable, categorically speaking. For those who were (or still are) attracted to AT, the most natural answer may be provided by the following qualitative version of that thesis:

QUALITATIVE ADAMS' THESIS (QAT)   A simple conditional "If φ, then ψ" is acceptable iff $\Pr(\psi \mid \varphi) > \theta$,[15]

where θ is a threshold value meant to explicate the notion of high probability. This is a vague notion, so only by way of idealization can we pin an exact value on θ. However, unless we would want to grant that there can be propositions φ and ψ such that "If φ, then ψ" and "If φ, then not ψ" are both acceptable, or that "If φ, then ψ" can be acceptable even though, given φ, it is more likely that $\overline{\psi}$ than that ψ, we will have to set $\theta \geqslant .5$. And just as a proposition can be acceptable in the absence of full certainty – as almost all agree[16] – so it would seem that a conditional can be acceptable even if its consequent is not fully certain conditional on its antecedent. Thus, we will want to set $\theta < 1$.

Lewis [1976] and Jackson [1979], [1987:31] advocate a principle that reads just like QAT except that it has "assertable" where QAT has "acceptable"; there is nothing to suggest that they would find the acceptability reading objectionable. Gibbard [1981:229] endorses the principle that one *accepts* a conditional iff one assigns its consequent a high probability conditional on its antecedent. Also, Chalmers and Hájek [2007] state QAT (without the restriction to simple conditionals) as a possible explication of Ramsey's footnote cited earlier in this chapter (p. 92).[17]

---

[15] Here, as well as in all similar theses to be stated below, "acceptable" is taken to mean acceptable to a given person, and the Pr operator to refer to this person's subjective probability function.

[16] See, among others, Foley [1992], Edgington [1995:287 n50], DeRose [1996], and Douven [2006]; Williamson [2000] seems to be the only dissenter here, holding that one should accept something only if one knows it (p. 255 f), and that knowledge requires a degree of belief of 1 (Chs. 9, 10).

[17] In their paper, Chalmers and Hájek criticize another interpretation of that footnote, according to which a conditional is acceptable to a person iff, were the person to accept the antecedent and consider the consequent, he or she would accept the consequent. Chalmers and Hájek argue that this version of the Ramsey test commits one to the acceptability of all instances of "If φ, then I believe that φ" as well as of all instances of "If I believe that φ, then φ," which would seem to imply

In view of our results concerning SH in the previous chapter, the implicit support for QAT may be broader still. In the introduction to this chapter, it was remarked that many philosophers hold that we need an epistemology of belief as well as an epistemology of degrees of belief. Given that there are obvious and close pretheoretical ties between a person's beliefs and her degrees of belief – for instance, someone telling us that she believes (categorically) a proposition, of which she also tells us that she believes it to a degree of zero, would seem hopelessly confused if not downright irrational – epistemologists have been concerned with stating exactly how the two modes of thinking and talking about our doxastic states constrain one another. As part of this endeavor, some have proposed the following thesis:[18]

LOCKEAN THESIS (LT)   A proposition φ is acceptable iff $\Pr(\varphi) > \theta$.[19]

If it is unclear what the probabilities of conditionals are, then LT is uninformative about when a conditional is acceptable. If, by contrast, SH holds, contrary to what is generally believed, but in line with what was argued in the previous chapter, or if SH holds at least for simple conditionals, then QAT straightforwardly follows from LT.

However natural and plausible QAT may appear, and in spite of all the (explicit or implicit) support it may enjoy, there is an a priori reason to

that one is both omniscient and infallible. The reason they offer for their claim is that rejecting any of the designated instances is tantamount to accepting the Moore-paradoxical "φ and I do not believe that φ," respectively the equally Moore-paradoxical "Not-φ and I believe φ." Be this as it may, in a footnote they admit that the interpretation of Ramsey's footnote that basically amounts to QAT avoids the omniscience problem. They could have added that QAT avoids the infallibility problem as well. For given QAT, to deny that every instance of "If I believe φ, then φ" must be acceptable to me is just to say that, for some φ, my degree of belief in φ conditional on my believing φ may not be high. Surely saying this does not commit me to the Moore-paradoxical "Not-φ and I believe φ," for any φ. Just consider some φ such that I do not believe φ and I am fully aware of my not believing φ. Then my rational degree of belief in my believing φ will be 0 and, consequently, my degree of belief in φ conditional on my believing φ will be undefined. A fortiori, my degree of belief in φ conditional on my believing φ is not high and so, by QAT, "If I believe φ, then φ" is not acceptable to me. However, given that rationality requires my degree of belief in "Not-φ and I believe φ" to be 0 as well, it is hard to see how I could be committed to this statement. Lest it be thought that the point hinges on the relevant conditional degree of belief being undefined (which might be deemed a special type of situation), consider the following: I may not be able to fully rule out that I believe that my best friend is disloyal to me; there is a chance that I am suppressing that belief. Yet my degree of belief that my best friend is disloyal to me, conditional on my believing that he is, is low. If I do believe, deep down, that he is disloyal to me, then this may, instead, be evidence of a paranoid trait in my character.

18   To the best of my knowledge, the name "Lockean Thesis" was coined by Foley [1992].
19   By again using θ as a threshold parameter, I am not suggesting that QAT and LT *must* postulate the same threshold value, but given that the threshold in both these theses serves to formalize the same notion of high probability, it is reasonable to assume that QAT and LT, as well as the theses EST and CAST to be introduced shortly, do in fact postulate the same threshold.

doubt its material adequacy. As we saw earlier, all of the more popular accounts of the acceptability conditions of conditionals are motivated by the fundamental idea that, for a conditional to be acceptable, there must be some sort of epistemic connection between its antecedent and consequent. And while QAT's requirement of high conditional probability may seem to secure the presence of just such a connection, it does not really do that. Any proposition that is highly probable unconditionally is also highly probable conditional on any other proposition that is probabilistically independent of it, and often the absence of probabilistic relevance signals the absence of relevance in a broader sense.

In Douven [2008c:21], I illustrate this point by dint of the following example about a fair coin that is to be tossed at least 1,000,000 times:

(4.2) There will be at least one heads in the first 1,000,000 tosses of this fair coin

$$
\text{if} \left\{ \begin{array}{ll} \text{there is a heads in the first 10 tosses.} & (\alpha) \\ \text{Chelsea wins the Champions League.} & (\beta) \end{array} \right.
$$

Making no special assumptions about the context in which these sentences are evaluated, $(4.2\text{-}\alpha)$, though not a deep truth perhaps, appears perfectly acceptable while $(4.2\text{-}\beta)$ does not. Plausibly, this is because the truth of (β) is entirely irrelevant to the truth of the consequent of (4.2), whereas the truth of (α) is obviously relevant to the truth of the consequent.[20]

These data pose an obvious difficulty for QAT. That there will be at least one heads in the first 1,000,000 tosses has a very high a priori probability, namely, $1 - 1/2^{1,000,000} \approx 1$. (That the coin is fair is taken to imply that the tosses are probabilistically independent.) Conditional on (α), the truth of the consequent of (4.2) is of course certain. But Chelsea's winning the Champions League is, we may assume, probabilistically independent

---

[20] Precisely because the truth of (β) appears irrelevant to the truth of the consequent of (4.2), one might be tempted to read $(4.2\text{-}\beta)$ as a non-interference conditional. Indeed, some contexts might strongly invite this reading. (See p. 14 for the point that whether a conditional qualifies as standard or as, for instance, a non-interference conditional is sensitive to context.) Suppose, for instance, that we had been discussing the question what would be an acceptable price for a certain bet that pays big if there is at least one heads in the first 1,000,000 tosses of the coin, and that someone had suddenly changed the topic of the conversation by starting to talk about Chelsea's chances of winning the Champions League. We might then quite appropriately assert $(4.2\text{-}\beta)$ to bring the conversation back to our previous discussion. However, that is not the intended reading here. To resist the temptation to interpret $(4.2\text{-}\beta)$ as a non-interference conditional, it should help to rephrase the sentence as "If Chelsea wins the Champions League, then there will be at least one heads in the first 1,000,000 tosses of this fair coin." (See p. 13 on non-interference conditionals not taking the pronoun "then.")

of there being at least one heads in the first 1,000,000 tosses. So, conditional on either (α) or (β) the probability of the consequent of (4.2) being true is at most marginally different from 1. Furthermore, we can bring the probability of (variants of) the consequent of (4.2) conditional on (β) as close as we like to that of the consequent of (4.2) conditional on (α) by supplanting the number 1,000,000 in (4.2) by a larger one. Consequently, given QAT, we can make (4.2–β) or a variant of this sentence come out as having the same status as regards acceptability as (4.2–α) has, whatever one's preferred value of θ (still supposing that it is unequal to 1). This is so even though, pretheoretically, the two sentences do *not* have the same status in this respect.

Note that the above example also constitutes a problem for AT (though it may no longer be so surprising, after what was seen earlier in this chapter, to find that this thesis faces problems). After all, given that thesis, (4.2–α) and (4.2–β) ought to be highly acceptable for any rational person, for we may assume that for any such person Pr(there will be a heads in the first 1,000,000 tosses of this fair coin | Chelsea wins the Champions League) $\approx$ Pr(there will be a heads in the first 1,000,000 tosses of this fair coin | there is a heads in the first 10 tosses) = 1. Of course, on Adams' account (4.2–α) is *perfectly* acceptable while (4.2–β) is not. But the account predicts that the difference in acceptability is only minute, and that is manifestly wrong. It further predicts – for reasons mentioned in the previous paragraph – that by making some suitable substitution the acceptability of (variants of) (4.2–β) can be brought arbitrarily close to the perfect acceptability of (4.2–α), which appears wrong too, for it seems that the intuitive unacceptability of (4.2–β) is fairly independent of the exact number of times the coin is presumed to be tossed.

Advocates of QAT (or AT) might object to the conclusions I draw from the above example, claiming that I am mistaking an intuition about the asymmetry in the *assertability* conditions of (4.2–α) and (4.2–β) for one about the asymmetry in the *acceptability* conditions of these sentences, and that the former asymmetry has an explanation purely in Gricean terms. But for this objection to get off the ground, it should at a minimum be pointed out how the putative Gricean explanation goes.

At first blush, a Gricean explanation of the asymmetry might seem straightforward. For (4.2–β) might seem to be unassertable on the grounds that it suggests a connection between Chelsea winning the Champions League and there being a heads in the first 1,000,000 tosses, a connection that, we may reasonably assume, does not exist, so that the suggestion is misleading. And it is one of the core insights of Gricean pragmatics that even a true sentence may be unassertable because by asserting it a speaker would mislead her audience by suggesting something false. No such problem seems to attach to (4.2-α). Still, assuming the Gricean machinery, how exactly is the suggestion of there existing a connection between the truth of the consequent of (4.2) and that of (β) supposed to come about?

It may be tempting to invoke Grice's first maxim of Quantity here, according to which we should make our contribution to a conversation as informative as is required for the purposes of the conversation, or, in Jackson's [1979:112] more specific formulation, we should "[a]ssert the [logically] stronger instead of the weaker (when probabilities are close)." First note, though, that whether the consequent of (4.2) on its own really *is* logically stronger than (4.2-β) will depend on what the truth conditions of these sentences are, if the latter has any at all. If we grant Grice, Jackson, Lewis, and a few others that, as they think, the conditional "If φ, then ψ" has the truth conditions of $\varphi \supset \psi$, then the consequent of (4.2) is indeed logically stronger than (4.2-β), and the probabilities of that consequent and of (4.2-β) are very close to each other. But even so, the strategy seems hopeless, for given the present assumption, the consequent of (4.2) is also logically stronger than (4.2-α), and the probability of the consequent is very close to that of (4.2-α) as well. Accordingly, the proposed Gricean explanation would seem to explain both too much and too little: it would "explain" why (4.2-α) is unassertable – while (4.2-α) actually appears assertable – and it would thereby fail to explain the asymmetry in the assertability of (4.2-α) and (4.2-β).

Another maxim to consider in this connection is the second maxim of Quality, according to which we should have adequate evidence for what we say (Grice [1989b:27]). Supposing that (4.2-β) has the truth conditions of the corresponding material conditional, and thus those of "Either Chelsea does not win the Champions League or there will be at least one heads in the first 1,000,000 tosses of this coin (or both)," there seems to be an immediate problem with this suggestion. For I do have excellent evidence for the disjunction, and thus, given the current supposition, for (4.2-β), namely, all the evidence I have for the second disjunct, that is, the consequent of (4.2). But Grice [1989a:61 f] is clearly aware of this problem and demands that the evidence for the conditional must be of a non-truth-functional kind, meaning that it must not be just evidence for either the consequent or the negation of the antecedent. Why is that? Well, otherwise I am clearly violating the first maxim of Quantity, for if I have excellent evidence for, say, the consequent, then I should assert *that*, and not the logically weaker conditional. As we just saw, however, this cannot be right. For if it were, $(4.2–\alpha)$ should be unassertable, which patently it is not.

Some might intuit that an appeal to the maxim of Relevance (or Relation) might be helpful here.[21] This maxim, about which Grice [1989a], [1989b] is exceedingly brief, simply states that we should make our contribution to a conversation a relevant one. And while it may be that asserting $(4.2–\beta)$ could only be of relevance if its antecedent and consequent were related in some intuitive way, and would hence create the – given the minimal suppositions we made about the context of utterance – misleading implicature that they are in fact thus related, *that* one will usually make an irrelevant contribution to a conversation by asserting a conditional whose antecedent and consequent fail to be related (in the requisite sense) is not something that follows from the maxim of Relevance, nor, it seems, from any other of Grice's maxims. In fact, it rather seems to be the sort of thing to be explained by a theory of the use conditions of conditionals. At a minimum, a theory of that kind that can explain *why* it is an irrelevant contribution to a conversation to assert a conditional whose antecedent is irrelevant to its consequent is, all else being equal, to be preferred to one that must accept the foregoing as a primitive fact.

4.3 The role of evidential support

Motivated by this kind of consideration, I proposed in my [2008c] an account of the categorical acceptability conditions of conditionals that analyzes the unacceptability of $(4.2–\beta)$ in terms of a lack of relevance of the antecedent to the consequent indeed, but then explains this lack of relevance in more basic terms, specifically, in terms of evidential support, where this is understood along standard Bayesian lines.

The proposal is not simply that a conditional is acceptable iff its antecedent is evidence – in the Bayesian sense – for its consequent. That would not work. My colleague Henry's quitting his job is evidence that I shall teach next year's introductory course in social philosophy, because conditional on the former the latter is a bit more probable than it is unconditionally. But even the conditional probability is still exceedingly low, given that I simply lack the requisite background for teaching such a course. It is in effect much more likely that Tom, my other colleague, who

---

[21] Though Grice apparently did not. His own paper on conditionals [1989a] does not contain a single reference to the maxim of Relevance.

has a specialization in social philosophy, will teach the course if Henry quits his job. Thus,

(4.3) If Henry quits his job, I shall teach next year's introductory course in social philosophy.

is not acceptable to me, notwithstanding that its antecedent is evidence for its consequent.

Nor is the proposal that the antecedent must make the consequent certain.[22] For example,

(4.4) If Henry quits his job, then Tom will teach next year's introductory course in social philosophy.

is perfectly acceptable to me. But although the antecedent is evidence, and indeed very strong evidence, for the consequent, it is not true that conditional on the antecedent the consequent has perfect probability. Even if Henry quits his job, a welter of things could happen to Tom, or to the department (or both), that would prevent him from teaching the course. As already mentioned, it seems too strong a requirement that a conditional's antecedent make its consequent certain for the conditional to be acceptable, just as it is too strong a requirement that a proposition have probability 1 for it to be acceptable.

Rather, according to the proposal, QAT is right in making high, but not perfect, conditional probability a requirement for the acceptability of a conditional. Where it goes wrong is in lumping together all cases in which the probability of the consequent, given the antecedent, is high regardless of whether that probability is *higher* than the unconditional probability of the consequent, that is, regardless of whether the antecedent is evidence for the consequent. This diagnosis suggests an obvious fix, which results in the following thesis:[23]

EVIDENTIAL SUPPORT THESIS (EST) A simple conditional "If φ, then ψ" is acceptable iff (i) $\Pr(\psi \mid \varphi) > \theta$ and (ii) $\Pr(\psi \mid \varphi) > \Pr(\psi)$.

In other words, the consequent ought not only be *highly* probable conditional on the antecedent, it also ought to be *more* probable conditional

---

[22] See Dudman [1992] for a proposal to this effect.
[23] Rott [1986], [1986] and Spohn [2013] contain similar proposals. Rott's proposal is in the context of AGM theory; Spohn's relies on the framework of ranking theory (see also Olsen [2014]).

on the antecedent than it is unconditionally. The additional requirement of evidential support is thought to secure the intuitively requisite kind of epistemic connection between antecedent and consequent. (The proposal of Douven [2008c] is actually a bit more complicated in that there is an extra condition that is supposed to prevent so-called lottery conditionals from qualifying as acceptable; we come to this complication in Section 4.7.)

EST manifestly makes the right prediction both regarding (4.2–α) and regarding (4.2–β): Without loss of generality, we may assume the consequent of (4.2) conditional on antecedent (β) to be above the threshold value θ. However, (β) is not *evidence* for that consequent. By contrast, not only is the probability of the consequent of (4.2) conditional on (α) above θ, that probability is also greater than the marginal probability of the consequent of (4.2), meaning that (α) *is* evidence for that consequent. As a result, (4.2–α) comes out as being acceptable on EST, (4.2–β) as being unacceptable, as required.

4.4 Anticipated objections

Jackson [1987:44] comes close to considering something like EST for assertability by considering the view that for "If φ, then ψ" to be highly assertable $\Pr(\psi \mid \varphi)$ must not only be high but also significantly higher than $\Pr(\psi)$. He is very brief about this idea, however, because he thinks it can be dismissed out of hand, on the basis of one alleged counterexample, to wit, the conditional

(4.5) If Reagan is bald, no one in the press knows it.

He seems right to note that (4.5) is highly assertable even though "the absolute probability of 'No one in the press knows Reagan is bald' is higher than its conditional probability given he is bald" (*ibid.*). It would compromise the present proposal if an unacceptable conditional can be highly assertable, especially if one endorses – as I do – the view that warranted assertion requires acceptability (see p. 7).

Note, though, that (4.5) is a clear instance of a conditional whose intuitive assertability would, if anything, go up were we to replace "if" in it by "even if," or by "whether or not," or by "regardless of whether." Moreover, making the consequent begin with the pronoun "then" would clearly affect the meaning of the sentence. That is to say, the example passes the litmus tests for non-interference conditionals with flying colors. I therefore take the conditional to be an abnormal one and hence to be outside the intended scope of our theory.

But there seem to be similar examples that need not be interpreted as non-interference conditionals. Note, for instance, that it might be wrong to dismiss (4.6) as a non-interference conditional:

(4.6) If Reagan worked for the KGB, there will be no evidence to be found for that.

Although we can certainly imagine contexts in which it would be most naturally interpreted as one, there are others in which it could not be thus interpreted. Imagine, for instance, that it has just been asserted that if Reagan worked for the CIA, then, sooner or later, we will come to have evidence for that. "On the other hand," it might then be added, "if he worked for the KGB, we will never find any evidence for that." In that context, it would sound quite wrong if "if" in (4.6) were replaced by "even if" or by "whether or not."

We can well understand how (4.6) could be perfectly acceptable to someone, but on my proposal its acceptability might at first seem something of a mystery, for the proposal may seem to imply both that there could be evidence for a proposition and that if there really is evidence for that proposition, then it must be concluded that there is no evidence for the proposition.

That is not really implied, however, for it is perfectly compatible to suppose *both* that the consequent of (4.6) has a probability above θ given the antecedent and also that the antecedent is evidence for the consequent *and* that if someone came to know – and thus to have excellent evidence – that Reagan worked for the KGB, she would not "detach" the consequent of (4.6). As several authors have noted, conditionalization (as Bayesians say) is not the only possible rational response to the receipt of new information; another is to revise one's conditional degree(s) of belief given the new information.[24] Sentence (4.6) illustrates this point: if we were to find out that Reagan worked for the KGB, and thus were to get evidence for that, we would revise – in fact lower to 0 – our degree of belief in the proposition that there is no evidence that Reagan worked for the KGB conditional on the proposition that he did work for the KGB. Accordingly, the conditional in that case would no longer be acceptable. There is no inconsistency with our *now* finding it acceptable or even accepting it.

---

[24] See, for instance, Jackson [1979:123 f] and Howson [2000:139]; see also Chapter 6.

There are still other possible objections to EST to be considered. A first possible objection comes from a claim Mellor [1993:235 f, 247 f] makes about future-referring conditionals, such as

(4.7)   If Oswald doesn't kill Kennedy, someone else will.

According to Mellor, Oswald, prior to his decision to make the antecedent true, may have had *no* degree of belief in the antecedent and hence – Mellor's suggestion is – he can have had no conditional degree of belief in the consequent given the antecedent. Nevertheless, it is at least imaginable that (4.7) was acceptable to Oswald prior to his decision to kill Kennedy. If Mellor's suggestion is correct, then according to my proposal (4.7) could not possibly have been acceptable to Oswald.

In response, let me first note that it is not quite so evident that Oswald may have had no degree of belief whatsoever in the antecedent. Even if he was still to decide what to do, we may suppose that he had *some* inkling of the outcome of his deliberations, however vague perhaps. So he may well have been able to assign at least a vague (interval-valued) probability to the antecedent.[25]

More importantly, what matters for my proposal to work in this case is that, *pace* Mellor, Oswald can plausibly be supposed to have had a degree of belief (if perhaps only a vague one) in the consequent as well as a conditional degree of belief (which may also have been vague) in the consequent given the antecedent. As to the former, the question whether the consequent of (4.7) is true will have been highly relevant to Oswald while he was still pondering whether to kill Kennedy. We may thus assume that Oswald had a (possibly vague) unconditional degree of belief in the consequent of (4.7). As to the latter, Mellor's supposition that if Oswald had no degree of belief in the antecedent, he can have had no conditional degree of belief in the consequent given the antecedent, is of course true if we assume that that conditional degree of belief is the ratio of Oswald's degree of belief in the conjunction of the antecedent and the consequent and his degree of belief in the antecedent. But note that I may be completely unable to say something definite about my degree of belief in φ as well as about my degree of belief in $\varphi \wedge \psi$, and yet I may be very clear about their ratio and thus about my conditional degree of belief in ψ given φ. Suppose, for instance, you are told that from a large but unspecified number n of lottery tickets, numbered 1 through n, all of which have

[25] Cf. Levi [1974].

the same chance of being drawn, precisely one is to be drawn. Since you have not been informed about the exact number of tickets in the lottery, there is no way to determine a credence in "Ticket no. 1 will be drawn"; all you will be able to say is that it must be small. Still, you will have no difficulty determining your conditional degree of belief in "Ticket no. 1 will be drawn given that one of tickets nos. 1 and 2 will be drawn." Even more to the point, suppose Oswald indeed had no degree of belief in the antecedent of (4.7), as per Mellor's suggestion. Would he have had difficulty determining his degree of belief in the proposition that Oswald does not kill Kennedy conditional on the proposition that Oswald does not kill Kennedy? Surely Oswald must have thought that it is 1. I suspect that, even if Mellor is right about Oswald's possibly not having had a degree of belief in the antecedent of (4.7), Oswald would still have been able to answer the question whether he thinks it is more likely that someone will kill Kennedy, given the supposition that *he* does *not* kill Kennedy, than that someone will kill Kennedy, period, and also the question whether he thinks it is very likely or not quite so likely that someone will kill Kennedy given that he (Oswald) will not do it.

So, even if it is true that we may sometimes be entirely in the dark about our degree of belief in a proposition, it still does not follow that there may be conditionals for which we fail to have a corresponding degree of belief in the consequent conditional upon the antecedent, nor that, if we do have such a conditional degree of belief, we may be unable to say that it is greater than our unconditional degree of belief in the consequent or that it is greater than a given threshold value.[26]

A second objection, or rather a number of related objections, might come from the fact that, on a probabilistic understanding of evidence, φ can only be evidence for ψ if both φ and ψ have non-extreme probabilities. This means that, supposing EST, conditionals whose antecedent or consequent has either probability 0 or probability 1 for a given person are not acceptable to that person. Does this accord with intuition? Let us consider the possible cases.

There is general agreement that conditionals are what Bennett [2003:54–57] calls *zero-intolerant*, meaning that "nobody has any use for 'If φ, then ψ' when for him $\Pr(\varphi) = 0$" (p. 55; italics omitted and notation adapted

---

[26] According to Mellor [1993:235 f], (4.7) refutes what he calls "the belief-in-Adams theory," that is, the theory that states that to accept a conditional is to believe that one has a high conditional credence in the consequent given the antecedent. It might seem that those wanting to defend the theory can save it from Mellor's objection by appealing to my defense, too. That still does not save the belief-in-Adams theory, however, for as a moment's reflection suffices to make plain, (4.2) is a counterexample to the former as well.

for uniformity of reading).[27] So what the theory says about conditionals with probability 0 antecedents is clearly right.

But how about conditionals with probability 0 consequents? Being confident that John did not pass the exam, I may reasonably hold that if John passed the exam, then I am Peter Pan. (This is a Dutchman conditional, but being Dutch, I cannot use "then I am Dutch" in the consequent, at least not with the same effect.) I am very sure that I am not Peter Pan, so the antecedent cannot possibly be evidence for the consequent. How, then, do I explain the apparent acceptability of the conditional? Given that it is so obvious to anyone that I am not Peter Pan, and thus also that there can be no evidence for my being Peter Pan, the designated conditional will be understood as implicating that, *per impossibile*, John's passing the exam would be evidence for my being Peter Pan, and hence as really conveying that I am confident that John did not pass the exam. Given that I *am* confident that John did not pass the exam, the conditional is acceptable.

I find it difficult to think of acceptable conditionals whose antecedents or consequents have probability 1. It does not help if there is a clear connection between antecedent and consequent, as for example in

(4.8) If Obama is president of the United States, his residence is the White House.

This sentence still strikes me as odd, despite the apparent connection. In general, where the antecedent has probability 1, we feel that "if" should have been replaced by "given that," "since," or "as," to avoid the misleading suggestion that the truth of the antecedent is a matter of uncertainty for the speaker. Equally, someone who asserts a conditional of whose consequent she is certain will generally be convicted of misleading us by making it seem as if the truth of the consequent depended on something the truth of which is still to be settled.

It might be thought that this just cannot be right, at least not from the perspective of anyone who holds that warranted assertability requires (at least) acceptability. After all, it might be said, conditionals with

---

[27] This is generally, but not universally, agreed upon. Some think that one may believe that Oswald killed Kennedy and at the same time reasonably believe that if Oswald did not kill Kennedy then someone else did (see, e.g., Gillies [2004:585 f]). That seems right to me only if we are using "believe" in a rather loose way. It seems perfectly alright, for instance, to say that I believe that Oswald killed Kennedy if that is to mean that I am relatively confident (but not necessarily near to sure) that he did, and that I believe also that if he did not do it, someone else did. By way of test, one may compare "Oswald killed Kennedy, at least I'm relatively confident of that; but if he didn't, then someone else did" with "Oswald killed Kennedy, but if he didn't, then someone else did." The former sounds more or less okay to my ears; the latter sounds positively odd.

probability 1 antecedents or consequents *can* be assertable. Suppose, for instance, that I try to explain to someone that Chelsea cannot fail to win the championship, now that it has a seven-point lead on Arsenal, which is in second position, and there are only two more matches to go, but the person thinks I am wrong, although she knows that Chelsea has a seven-point lead and that there are only two matches to be played. Then I may well say: "But if Chelsea is seven points ahead of Arsenal, and in each match there are at most three points to be gained, then the championship cannot escape Chelsea. Can it?" Here both the antecedent and the consequent have probability 1 for me. So how can the conditional be assertable for me, as it surely is? The right answer is that, in such cases, one does not assert anything conditional but rather gives a kind of demonstration to the addressee of how he or she ought to reason to arrive at a conclusion we are fully convinced of but that for him or her is still a matter of doubt.[28]

The final possible objection to be considered has to do with the fact – as it appears to be – that we may be unsure about the acceptability of a conditional. The problem is to explain how this can be, on my account, for it seems that in order to find out whether a conditional is acceptable to me I just have to check (so to speak) my degrees-of-belief function at the relevant "locations." So, how could I be unsure whether or not my degree of belief in the consequent given the antecedent of a particular conditional is both above my unconditional degree of belief in the consequent and above θ?

This problem is only compelling as long as we assume the standard Bayesian picture of what it is to have degrees of belief. On that picture, we

---

[28] See, in this vein, also Edgington [1997b:112]. The same may apply with respect to conditionals such as "If $7 + 5 = 12$, then $7 + 6 = 13$," which seem perfectly assertable (see Atlas [2005:89]). In fact, the same may also apply with respect to conditionals such as "If $23^5 = 121^3$, then $0 = 1$," which might occur as part of a reductio argument, and which might otherwise seem to give the lie to Bennett's claim, cited in the text above, that we do not have any use for conditionals with probability 0 antecedents. (Thanks to Niels Skovgaard Olsen here.)

Note, though, that this need not be our general response to conditionals whose antecedents and consequents are mathematical truths/falsehoods. While according to standard probability theory, all logical and mathematical truths are to receive probability 1 and all logical and mathematical falsehoods probability 0, there is a pretheoretically clear sense of probability in which it can be reasonable to assign, for instance, a probability other than 1 to a mathematical truth. Prior to the enunciation of Wiles' proof of Fermat's Last Theorem, it was certainly reasonable (in the pretheoretical sense) to assign that theorem some probability lower than 1. Given this notion of probability, there is of course no difficulty accommodating conditionals of the designated type within our general approach. Alternatively, we might treat the notion of mathematical evidence as being *sui generis*, and requiring an account of its own (see Martin [1998] for some first steps toward such an account). That might allow us to say that, for instance, "If ZFC is consistent, then so is ZFC + $V = L$" is assertable/acceptable because the antecedent is *very strong mathematical evidence* for the consequent.

have at any moment of our (mature) conscious lives determinate degrees of belief in all propositions that are expressible in our language, and hence, at least given the ratio definition of conditional probability, we also have determinate conditional degrees of belief in all propositions given any other proposition (to be exact: given any other proposition with non-zero probability). However, it is widely recognized (and we already implicitly granted it in our discussion of future-referring conditionals) that this picture is starkly idealized. In reality, we often have only vague – sometimes only very vague – degrees of belief in many propositions. And if I have only a vague degree of belief in some proposition ψ, or a vague degree of belief in that proposition conditional on a second proposition φ, then I may well be unable to determine whether φ is evidence for ψ, or whether ψ has a probability above θ conditional on φ.

Even leaving vagueness aside, there is the problem that the Bayesian picture assumes our degrees of belief to be directly accessible to us at any moment. As is explained in Douven and Uffink [2003], this may have been a reasonable assumption in the operationalist/behaviorist climate in which (modern) Bayesianism emerged,[29] and in which degrees of belief were equated with dispositions to engage in acts of certain kinds, but it ceases to be reasonable once we grant, as many nowadays think we should, that a person's degrees of belief correspond to certain states of her mind. Given such a realist attitude toward degrees of belief, it is no less plausible to hold that some of our degrees of belief may at least sometimes be inaccessible to us, or at least not fully accessible to us, than that, for instance, our desires are not always fully accessible to us – which has the status of a near-truism in contemporary psychology.

4.5 Aside: the acceptability of counterfactuals

Not only do I think that EST withstands the above objections, it also seems to me that it can easily be extended to an account of the acceptability conditions of (simple normal) *counterfactual* conditionals, that is, subjunctives whose antecedent we believe, or know, to be false. (As far as I can see, EST applies to the remaining subjunctive conditionals as it stands.) The crucial additional concept needed for that extension is the concept of counterfactual probabilities, as it has surfaced in discussions of the so-called problem of old evidence in Bayesian confirmation theory. As

---

[29] Though even this may be contestable; see Douven [2007].

intimated earlier, nothing that has probability 1 can be evidence for anything. That is a problem for Bayesian confirmation theory, for it seems that
sometimes theories are supported by data that were already known when
the theory was conceived.[30] To accommodate this fact within Bayesian
confirmation theory, various authors have proposed that in such cases we
should consider not the scientist's actual degrees-of-belief function, but the
degrees-of-belief function he or she would have had at the time he or she
conceived the theory had he or she been unaware of the data. For instance,
let E be the relevant data, T the theory, and Pr the scientist's degrees-of-
belief function given his or her actual background knowledge. Then we
may denote by Pr_E^- the degrees-of-belief function the scientist would have
had, had he or she not known E; in other words, Pr_E^- is the scientist's
counterfactual degrees-of-belief function which "brackets" the truth of E.
We may take this to imply that $\mathrm{Pr}_E^-(E) \neq 1$, so that E can be said to be
evidence for T for the scientist in the sense that $\mathrm{Pr}_E^-(T \mid E) > \mathrm{Pr}_E^-(T)$.[31]

It may already be obvious how this idea can be fruitfully exploited in an
analysis of counterfactuals. In the kind of cases that give rise to the problem
of old evidence, we are asked to imagine what probability we would assign
to something conditional on something else we know to be true if we had
not known the latter to be true. That is not fundamentally different from
imagining what probability we would assign to something conditional on
something we know to be false had we not known the latter to be false.
And, while on the standard Bayesian account, something known to be
false cannot be evidence for anything anymore than something known to
be true can be evidence for anything, we will often enough be able to
answer the question of whether something would have been evidence for a
given theory, say, had we not known the former to be false. Consequently,
there seems to be no impediment to stating the acceptability conditions of
counterfactuals in perfect analogy to EST, as follows:

> COUNTERFACTUAL EVIDENTIAL SUPPORT THESIS (CEST) A simple
> counterfactual conditional "If φ were/had been the case, then ψ
> would be/have been the case" is acceptable iff (i) $\mathrm{Pr}_{\overline{\varphi}}^-(\psi \mid \varphi) > \theta$
> and (ii) $\mathrm{Pr}_{\overline{\varphi}}^-(\psi \mid \varphi) > \mathrm{Pr}_{\overline{\varphi}}^-(\psi)$.

---

[30] The example standardly adduced in this connection is that of Mercury's perihelion, which Einstein
took to be evidence for his General Theory of Relativity – and rightly so, intuition has us say – even
though he knew what the perihelion was when he set out to work on the theory. See Earman [1992,
Ch. 5] for a thorough discussion of the problem of old evidence.

[31] See Horwich [1982], Howson [1984], [1985], and Howson and Urbach [1993:403 ff] for a solution
to the problem of old evidence along the lines sketched in the text.

The notion of counterfactual degrees of belief has been challenged. Most importantly, it has been questioned whether we in general have such determinate degrees of belief.[32] My rather cautious remark that we "often enough" are able to determine whether one thing would have been evidence for a second thing, had the former not known to be false, may already flag some doubt on my part that the answer to the question of the previous sentence is a resounding "yes." Note, however, that even if the answer is negative, this seems more of a problem for Bayesian confirmation theory than for CEST. For although we may generally be able to answer determinately the question whether certain data known at the time a theory was propounded support that theory, questions whether a given counterfactual conditional is acceptable seem relatively frequently *not* to have a determinate answer.[33] So, far from undermining it, the critique that sometimes we do not have determinate counterfactual degrees of belief would in effect seem to buttress CEST, for it would explain the indeterminacy we at times experience in our judgments regarding particular counterfactuals.

This book being about indicative conditionals, I have only presented CEST here as a possible avenue for future research and will let it rest for now.

4.6 Testing the role of evidential support

It is a clear point in favor of EST that it makes the right predictions about the acceptability of both $(4.2-\alpha)$ and $(4.2-\beta)$, whereas the known accounts get $(4.2-\beta)$ wrong. On the other hand, it is to be acknowledged that $(4.2-\beta)$ could be an exception, a linguistic curiosity, and therefore of little theoretical significance, given that theses about natural language (such as EST is surely meant to be) should not be expected to hold unexceptionably. To convince oneself that ordinary usage provides more evidence for EST, one may consider any number of further examples of conditionals and register one's responses to them. But a general lesson to be learned from the empirical work on AT discussed above is that philosophers' intuitions regarding the acceptability or unacceptability of conditionals are anything but failsafe. The way to gain more definite insight into the status of theses such as QAT and EST is to subject them to the same kind of testing to which SH and AT have been subjected.

---

[32] See, for instance, van Fraassen [1988].
[33] Cf. Lewis [1979:34]: "Counterfactuals are infected with vagueness, as everyone agrees."

Some indirect empirical evidence for EST is already to be found in Over et al. [2007]. These authors investigated the probabilities of both indicative and subjunctive real world conditionals (see above, on p. 67) and found strong support for SH. However, their experiments also showed a modest effect of evidential connection between antecedent and consequent. (Over et al. do not speak in terms of evidence but in terms of the so-called Δp-rule, which measures the difference between the conditional probability of the consequent given the antecedent and the conditional probability of the consequent given the negation of the antecedent. This has been defended as a measure of evidential support in Joyce [1999:205 ff].) A plausible thought is that, at least insofar as their results concern indicative conditionals, this effect is due to the fact that the evidential connection between antecedent and consequent is crucially involved in the use conditions of such conditionals. For it is natural to suppose, as Over et al. [2007:92] also remark, that there may be some intrusion of pragmatic factors in the assignment of probabilities. To use a well-worn example, according to standard semantic theorizing,

(4.9) They married and she got pregnant.

and

(4.10) She got pregnant and they married.

have the same semantic content (they express the same proposition). That we sense a difference in meaning nonetheless is said to be due to pragmatic factors; according to standard pragmatic theorizing, it is due to Grice's [1989b:27] maxim to be orderly, in particular to recount events in the order in which they occurred. Probabilistically, such pragmatic factors are supposed not to matter: probability theory respects logic and disallows the assignment of different probabilities to logically equivalent propositions. But surely that is an idealization. To the best of my knowledge, no work has been done so far on the connection between people's probability judgments and pragmatic factors of the kind just alluded to. However, it seems reasonable to expect that, placing (4.9) and (4.10) in a context in which "they" refers to children of conservative Catholic parents, say, many people will not assign these sentences the same probability.

As indicated earlier, Over et al.'s studies offer some *indirect* evidence for EST. More recently, Douven and Verbrugge [2012] have empirically investigated the issue of the acceptability of conditionals head-on. In fact, in their paper, Douven and Verbrugge not only consider the predictive accuracy of QAT and EST but also the possibility that the notion of evidential support is the key to distinguishing between the acceptability of an *indicative* conditional and the acceptability of the corresponding *concessive* conditional, that is, the conditional with "if" replaced by "even if" (or with "still" inserted in the consequent). In particular, they offer the following thesis as a complement to EST:

> CONCESSIVE ABSENCE OF SUPPORT THESIS (CAST) A simple normal indicative concessive conditional "If φ, then still ψ," or "Even if φ, ψ," is acceptable iff (i) $\Pr(\psi \mid \varphi) > \theta$ and (ii) $\Pr(\psi \mid \varphi) \leqslant \Pr(\psi)$.

So, together EST and CAST imply that for a conditional and the corresponding concessive to be acceptable, their shared consequent must be highly probable given their shared antecedent. However, where the acceptability of the conditional requires the antecedent to be evidence for the consequent, the acceptability of the concessive requires the antecedent *not* to be evidence for the consequent.[34]

Douven and Verbrugge conducted a within-participants experiment designed to test all three of QAT, EST, and CAST. In this experiment, the participants were presented a number of items, each centering on a different conditional. The items consisted of three parts. The first part asked for the unconditional probability of the consequent of the item's corresponding conditional. The second part asked for the conditional probability of the consequent given the antecedent of the same conditional. And the third part showed the indicative conditional together with the corresponding concessive conditional and asked whether the participant accepted only the former, only the latter, both, or neither; for instance, the following is the third part of one of the items used in the study:

Consider the following statements:

1. If some second-rate actor plays the role of James Bond in the next Bond movie, that movie will become a box office hit.
2. Even if some second-rate actor plays the role of James Bond in the next Bond movie, that movie will become a box office hit.

---

[34] It is worth noting that, just as combining EST with the notion of counterfactual degrees of belief yields CEST, an analysis of the acceptability conditions of counterfactual "if"-conditionals, combining something like CAST with the notion of counterfactual degrees of belief may yield acceptability conditions for "even if"-counterfactuals.

Of these statements:

☐ I accept only 1.
☐ I accept only 2.
☐ I accept both.
☐ I accept neither.

The results Douven and Verbrugge obtained are evidence *against* QAT and *for* EST and CAST. While participants did find some conditionals with a high corresponding conditional probability acceptable, they found many others with an equally high or even higher corresponding conditional probability unacceptable, thereby casting doubt on QAT. The data were also consistent with the hypothesis that the vast majority of participants regarded high conditional probability as a necessary or at least close-to-necessary condition for the acceptability of the corresponding indicative or concessive conditional, as predicted by EST and, respectively, CAST. Finally, the data confirmed the prediction, following from the conjunction of EST and CAST, that if people judge $\Pr(\psi \mid \varphi)$ to be high, their preference for either "If φ, then ψ" or "Even if φ, ψ" depends on whether or not they judge φ to be evidence for ψ.

4.7 Refining the proposal?

In closing this chapter, I want to come back to an earlier parenthetical remark that the version of EST proposed in Douven [2008c] is actually a bit more complicated than the version given in Section 4.2.

The complication has to do with conditionals like this:

(4.11)   If there is only one winner in the lottery, then your ticket is a loser.

Assume this to be said of a lottery that is known to consist of 100 tickets, each having the same chance of winning. Also assume that it is unknown how many winners there will be. What is known is that *either* there will be a unique winner *or* half of the tickets will end up being winners, and that the chances of either of these possibilities obtaining are equal. On this scenario, it can be easily calculated that the probability that your ticket will lose equals $149/200 = .745$. Suppose, just for purposes of illustration, that $\theta = .9$. Then the consequent of (4.11) has a probability conditional on its antecedent that is greater than its marginal probability and also greater than θ: $\Pr(\text{Your ticket is a loser} \mid \text{There is only one winner}) = .99 > \theta >$

.745 = Pr(Your ticket is a loser). As a result, the conditional comes out as being acceptable on my proposal.

This is a problem, at least from the viewpoint of all those who hold that, for instance,

(4.12)   Your ticket is a loser.

is unacceptable previous to the drawing of the lottery and on the supposition that there is exactly one winner.[35] After all, were we to accept (4.11) and then come to learn, still previous to the drawing, that the lottery has a unique winner, it would be reasonable and also normal to detach the consequent of (4.11) (i.e., to apply Modus Ponens), whereby we would accept (4.12) previous to the drawing.

Intuitions diverge on the issue of whether (4.12) can be acceptable before the drawing takes place. According to many philosophers, the answer is "yes."[36] Many others hold the opposite position on (4.12) and kindred propositions.[37] So, similarly one might expect two opposed camps on the issue of whether conditionals like (4.11) are acceptable.

In my [2008c], I sided with the naysayers and kept (4.11) and similar conditionals from qualifying as acceptable by adding a defeater to EST. However, the defeater was described only functionally, in terms of what it had to accomplish, and as such was a placeholder for something that I did not, and do not, know what it should look like. Philosophers attracted to LT, but wanting to do justice to their intuition that (4.12) and other "lottery propositions" are unacceptable, have given detailed descriptions of defeaters that are meant to disqualify as selectively as possible such lottery propositions. One could consider adding some such defeater to EST, possibly in a modified form, given that it is to apply to conditionals. Unfortunately, Douven and Williamson [2006] have shown that all proposals to add a defeater to LT boil down either to the claim that only propositions of

---

[35] See DeRose [1999:416 n7]. But see also the discussion of the urn example in Appiah [1985:171 f], which involves a lottery by another name.

[36] See, e.g., Kyburg [1961], Foley [1979], [1992], Klein [1985], Moser and Tlumac [1985], Hunter [1996], Achinstein [2001], Swinburne [2001], and Weintraub [2001]. Jackson is probably also in this group, unless in his view warranted assertion does not require at least acceptability, for he says: " 'At least one of the five tosses will be a head' [said of a fair coin to be tossed five times] is probable enough . . . to warrant assertion" (Jackson [1979:118]). Of course, the probability that there will be at least one heads in five tosses with a fair coin is higher (to wit, .96875) than .745, the probability that (4.12) has in our scenario. But the numbers here are inessential; we can easily change the scenario, and the point about (4.12) would remain.

[37] See, e.g., Lehrer [1975], [1990], Kaplan [1981a], [1981b], [1996], Stalnaker [1984], Pollock [1990], Ryan [1996], Evnine [1999], Nelkin [2000], Adler [2002], and Douven [2002a].

which one is certain are acceptable to one, or to the claim that the inconsistent proposition is acceptable. At least, that is so if the defeater is to come from the class of defeaters that are definable in broadly logical and mathematical terms – which is the class that all defeaters that have been seriously considered so far fall into, and that indeed one would expect any serious candidate to fall into.[38] There is no reason to expect that the same problem would not crop up for defeaters that might be considered as additions to EST.

There are other ways to respond to conditionals like (4.11). One is to side with the yea-sayers on the issue of the possible acceptability of such conditionals and to explain any intuition to the contrary that one might have by arguing that lottery conditionals are, just like lottery propositions, unassertable for Gricean reasons, and that in feeling pulled toward the negative answer we are conflating unassertability with unacceptability. Philosophers have argued for the unassertability of lottery propositions on the grounds that, by asserting them, one misleadingly implicates the possession of insider knowledge. For instance, by asserting (4.12) one would seem to be suggesting that one has information going beyond the publicly available information that the addressee may be expected to be aware of. Arguably, by asserting (4.11) one would seem to be making exactly the same suggestion.[39]

A second possible response goes along with the first in arguing that lottery conditionals are unassertable on Gricean grounds, but then goes on to claim that those same grounds make them unacceptable, too. This response relies on the idea that Gricean considerations pertain to what is acceptable no less than to what is assertable, an idea that, under the name of "pragmatics of belief," is defended in Douven [2010], [2012], and [2013b]. It is to be admitted, though, that the idea of a pragmatics of belief is at this point still entirely speculative, lacking any empirical backing.

---

[38] See Smith [2010] for a strengthening of Douven and Williamson's result. See Chandler [2010] for a critical discussion.

[39] See Weiner [2005], Lackey [2007], and Douven [2012] for arguments to the effect that lottery propositions are unassertable for Gricean reasons. This claim has been criticized by Williamson [1996], but see Weiner [2005] and Douven [2012] for responses.

CHAPTER 5

Closure

It was said earlier that the Lockean Thesis (LT) is meant as an answer to the question of how the epistemology of belief and the epistemology of degrees of belief are connected. As such an answer, the thesis is generally judged to be plausible, even though, as was seen in the last section of the previous chapter, some hold that it gives intuitively wrong verdicts about the acceptability of lottery propositions. Kyburg, one of the main advocates of LT, discovered that this thesis actually gives rise to more than a little friction with pretheoretical judgment, at least when it is combined with a prima facie equally plausible principle, to wit,

> CLOSURE PRINCIPLE (CP)   If it is rational for a person to accept each $\varphi \in \Phi$, and ψ follows logically from Φ, then it is rational for the person to accept ψ.

Specifically, Kyburg [1961:197] showed that the conjunction of LT and CP gives rise to (what is now known as) the Lottery Paradox. In a nutshell, the paradox is that, given a large enough fair lottery with only one winner, LT makes it rational to accept of each single ticket that it will lose, and then CP makes it rational to accept that all tickets will lose, even if it is known – and a fortiori rationally acceptable – that one ticket is going to win. Not long after the discovery of the Lottery Paradox, Makinson [1965] discovered a similar paradox, the so-called Preface Paradox: By LT, an author can rationally accept each of a number of claims that he or she has carefully researched and which, accordingly, he or she believes to a degree exceeding θ. Then CP makes it rational to accept the conjunction of all these claims. This is so even if, as may easily be the case, the author's degree of belief in that conjunction does *not* exceed θ and thus, according to LT again, is not rationally acceptable.[1]

---

[1] This is not quite how Makinson presents the paradox, but for our purposes the version given here is the more relevant one; see Douven and Uffink [2003] for a comparison of the two versions.

There is no unanimity in the philosophical community concerning how best to deal with these paradoxes: some authors advocate abandoning LT, at least in its present, unadorned form, while others hold that CP must go. Those in the former group have typically tried to find a defeater that, when added to LT, will keep the Lottery and Preface Paradoxes at bay. A few pages back it was said, however, that this approach does not look very promising in view of recent impossibility results. On the other hand, to abandon CP is to abandon a principle we appear to rely on in many of our everyday deliberations.

I will not try here to adjudicate between these options. Instead, I want to point out a problem besetting CP that is unrelated to the Lottery and Preface Paradoxes, to wit, that this principle is substantially incomplete if it is to apply to a language that contains a conditional operator whose semantics is not given by the truth table for the material conditional, and so, as most theorists nowadays agree, if CP is to apply to our own language. For CP is standardly taken to refer to the consequence relation of classical logic. As a result, CP fails to answer such obviously legitimate and real questions as to whether it is rational to accept that ψ whenever it is rational to accept that φ and also rational to accept that if φ then ψ, or whether it is rational to accept that χ if $\varphi \wedge \psi$ whenever it is rational to accept that $\psi \wedge \chi$ if φ.

The answer to such questions will depend, of course, on the account of acceptability of conditionals that is assumed. Not surprisingly, I will assume the one presented in the previous chapter, which was seen to enjoy considerable backing, both theoretical and empirical. The question of which closure conditions go with EST is of interest in itself. But it becomes a pressing one if we allow lottery conditionals, like (4.11), to qualify as acceptable, which, as suggested at the end of the previous chapter, we may well have reason to do. For then, depending on the exact conditions under which acceptability is closed, conditional versions of the Lottery and Preface Paradoxes loom.

5.1 The Lottery and Preface Paradoxes, conditional versions

Consider a fair n-ticket lottery $\mathcal{L}$ of which it is still to be determined whether it will have three winners, two winners, only one winner, or no winner at all, with these possibilities being equally likely, and with n such that $(n-1)/n > \theta$. By EST, and supposing n to be large enough,

(5.1) If $\mathcal{L}$ will have exactly one winner, then ticket number i will lose.

is acceptable for each $i \in \{1, \ldots, n\}$, at least for anyone who is informed about the setup of $\mathcal{L}$ and who aligns his or her degrees of belief with information about chances. After all, n is such that

$$\text{Pr(Ticket number } i \text{ will lose} \mid \mathcal{L} \text{ will have exactly one winner)} = 1 - \frac{1}{n} > \theta.$$

Furthermore,[2]

$$\text{Pr(Ticket number } i \text{ will lose)} = 1 - \left(\frac{1}{4n} + \frac{2}{4n} + \frac{3}{4n} \right) = 1 - \frac{3}{2n} < 1 - \frac{1}{n}.$$

Thus, the conditions of EST are satisfied.

Now assume that acceptability is closed under the principle that in the literature mostly goes under the label "CC." This principle licenses the inference of "If φ, then ψ and χ" from "If φ, then ψ" and "If φ, then χ." CC has been said to be highly plausible and is also validated by all of the better-known conditional logics.[3]

However, when conjoined with EST, the assumption that acceptability is closed under CC spells trouble. For, by repeated application of this principle, we derive (5.2) from the whole of the instances of (5.1):

(5.2) If $\mathcal{L}$ will have exactly one winner, then ticket number 1 will lose, ticket number 2 will lose, . . . , and ticket number n will lose.

So, given our closure assumption, (5.2) is acceptable. But the corresponding conditional probability is zero. Because EST makes high conditional probability necessary for acceptability, it rules (5.2) unacceptable. Hence, it follows from EST that (5.1) both is and is not acceptable. (Note, incidentally, that all steps go through if we assume QAT instead of EST.)

In a similar manner, one derives from EST a conditional version of the Preface Paradox. Suppose an author has excellent evidence for each of the n claims she makes in her new book – good enough, in any case, to make each of those claims highly probable in the sense of EST. Then EST implies that

---

[2] If the following is not clear, note that if there will be m winners, with $m \in \{0, \ldots, 3\}$, the chance for any given ticket to lose is $1 - m/n$. The lottery is equally likely to have no, one, two, or three winners. So the chance for a ticket to win equals $(1/4)(1 - 0/n) + (1/4)(1 - 1/n) + (1/4)(1 - 2/n) + (1/4)(1 - 3n)$, which, with some algebra, can be seen to equal $1 - 1/4n - 2/4n - 3/4n = 1 - 3/2n$.

[3] Segerberg [1989] even goes so far as to claim that every "reasonable" system of conditional logic includes CC.

(5.3) If my evidence is non-misleading, then the i-th claim I make in the book is correct.

is acceptable to her for each $i \in \{1, \ldots, n\}$. Given the closure assumption, it follows that

(5.4) If my evidence is non-misleading, then the first claim is correct, the second claim is correct, ..., and the last claim is correct.

is acceptable to the author as well. This is so even if the conjunction of the n claims – the consequent of (5.4) – is highly *im*probable conditional on her evidence (and thus conditional on her evidence being non-misleading). And this it may well be, even though individually the claims are highly probable conditional on the evidence.[4] Without loss of generality, suppose this to be the case for our author. Then (5.4) is *not* acceptable to her, according to EST. Consequently, it follows from EST that (5.4) both is and is not acceptable. (Note again that all steps go through on the assumption of QAT in place of EST.)

Does this mean that EST is to be abandoned, or that it needs to be modified, at least? It is presumably fair to say that the sufficiency direction of LT enjoys greater popularity in the literature than the necessity direction.[5] So perhaps some might, in view of the above, be willing to sacrifice the necessity direction of EST and content themselves with the claim that high conditional probability of ψ given φ, together with φ being evidence for ψ, is enough for "If φ, then ψ" to be acceptable. However, all we need to derive a paradox from this sufficiency thesis is the assumption that acceptability is closed not only under CC but also under the principle RCEC, which licenses substitutions of logically equivalent propositions in consequents of conditionals,[6] and under the principle CNC, which, it will be recalled from Section 2.5 (p. 54), is the principle that "If φ, then ψ" and "If φ, then not ψ" together license inferring the inconsistent proposition (on condition that φ is consistent). Like CC, the principles RCEC and CNC hold in the main conditional logics.

---

[4] For example, let each of the n claims have high but non-unit probability conditional on the evidence, and let the claims be mutually probabilistically independent conditional on the evidence. Then the probability of the consequent of (5.4) conditional on the evidence equals the product of the conditional probabilities of the individual claims given the evidence, and that product can be made arbitrarily small by taking n large enough.

[5] See Douven [2013c] for an overview of the relevant literature.

[6] RCEC could in effect be weakened by having it permit substitutions only of propositions that are *patently* logically equivalent.

Given the assumption that acceptability is closed under RCEC, it follows from (5.2) that

(5.5)   If $\mathcal{L}$ will have exactly one winner, then none of its tickets will win.

is acceptable.[7] Further note that a priori the probability that some of $\mathcal{L}$'s tickets will win is 3/4. Supposing that $\mathcal{L}$ will have exactly one winner, it is of course certain that some of its tickets will win. Hence, by the sufficiency direction of EST,

(5.6)   If $\mathcal{L}$ will have exactly one winner, then some of its tickets will win.

is acceptable as well. By CNC, it follows from (5.5) and (5.6) that the inconsistent proposition is acceptable, which cannot be right.

Should we abandon EST altogether then? It is to be noted that, however plausible CC appears, EST appears plausible too, and we saw that it is backed by empirical results. To be sure, abandoning CC would appear an uncomfortable move as well, in view of the principle's seeming naturalness. However, in Section 5.4.2 I will try to explain how CC can be invalid as a closure principle and yet appear intuitive. Thus, for the moment at least, I propose to stick to EST unadorned and turn to an investigation of the question of which closure principles it does validate.

5.2 Closure principles: analytical results

This section's aim is to investigate closure principles analytically. It will be proven which principles are acceptability-preserving and which are not. The next section will propose a generalization of the notion of acceptability preservation which turns it into a graded notion. Computer simulations and survey studies are then used to determine the degrees to which the various principles that our analytical results show to be not *strictly* acceptability-preserving do preserve acceptability.

A fair amount of work on the closure conditions for QAT can already be found in the literature; see, for instance, Adams [1986], Schurz [1998], Hawthorne and Makinson [2007], Schurz and Thorn [2012], and Thorn

---

7   To bring out more clearly the logical equivalence of the consequents of (5.2) and (5.5), and thus the applicability of RCEC in this case, one might want to spell out "ticket number 1 will lose" as "ticket number 1 of *n*-ticket lottery $\mathcal{L}$ will lose," and so on.

and Schurz [2015].[8] But a systematic investigation of the closure conditions for EST is still to be undertaken. To fill this lacuna, I have gone through a list of *all* candidate closure principles that I have been able to find in the literature – basically any inferential principle that has been discussed in the context of conditional reasoning – and have proved which of those are acceptability-preserving and which are not, on the assumption of EST.

Specifically, I have considered the thirty-six principles listed in Table 5.1.[9] I am using $\to$ to symbolize the indicative-conditional-forming operator and (as previously) $\supset$ to symbolize the material-conditional-forming operator. Furthermore, $\vdash \varphi$ indicates that φ is a (classical) logical truth, $\bot$ designates an arbitrary contradiction, and $(\varphi \equiv \psi)$ is defined to be equivalent to $(\varphi \supset \psi) \wedge (\psi \supset \varphi)$. One final point: I present the principles as premise–conclusion rules of the form "Whenever Γ, then Δ," with $\Gamma = \emptyset$ for zero-premise rules. Many of these principles are to be found in the survey articles on conditional logics by Nute and Cross [2001] and Arló-Costa [2007].[10] The list contains the axioms of all the standard and even some not-so-standard conditional logics, including Stalnaker's [1968] system C2, Adams' [1975] and Kraus, Lehmann, and Magidor's [1990] system P, Lewis' [1973a] systems V, VC, and VW, Burgess' [1981] system B, Pollock's [1981] system SS, and Hawthorne and Makinson's [2007] system O.

From here on, assume that acceptability for conditionals goes by EST and acceptability for non-conditional propositions (or for propositions in general, if conditionals fail to express propositions) goes by LT. Note that although none of the principles involves iterated conditionals, a fair number of them refer to embedded conditionals, on which EST is silent as well. That is no reason to set these principles aside for present purposes,

---

[8] Hannes Leitgeb (personal communication) has observed that, supposing evidential support to play the role in the acceptability of conditionals and concessives that was hypothesized and confirmed in Douven and Verbrugge [2012], the papers cited in the text actually concern closure principles for disjunctions of the form "If φ, then ψ, *or even if* φ, ψ."

[9] Recall that we are concerned with simple conditionals only. Therefore, the list is limited to possible closure principles for such conditionals. So, for instance, the Import–Export principle encountered in Chapter 3 does not occur on the list, as it involves iterated conditionals.

[10] I have used common labels for the various principles, though it is to be noted that the labeling in the literature is not entirely uniform. For instance, ANT (Antecedence) also goes by the name "Absorption," CS is sometimes called "Centering" (see Section 2.2), and some authors use "Supraclassicality" as a name for RCE. Most confusingly, sometimes the label "CC," which here stands for "Conjunction in the Consequent," is used as an abbreviation for "Cautious Cut," which is another name for the principle here labeled "CT" (Cumulative Transitivity). See Unterhuber [2013, Ch. 5] for more on the names in use for principles of conditional reasoning and also for an explanation of what most of the labels in Table 5.1 abbreviate. The labels "BR1" and "BR2" are mine and refer to the fact that these principles are stated (for the first time, to my knowledge) in Bradley [2002].

Table 5.1. *Candidate closure principles*

Label	Principle
ANT	Whenever $\varphi \to \psi$, then $\varphi \to (\varphi \wedge \psi)$.
BR1	Whenever $\top \to \varphi$, then φ.
BR2	Whenever φ, then $\top \to \varphi$.
CC	Whenever $\varphi \to \psi$ and $\varphi \to \chi$, then $\varphi \to (\psi \wedge \chi)$.
CEM	Whenever $\emptyset$, then $\varphi \to \psi$ or $\varphi \to \overline{\psi}$ (or both).
CM	Whenever $\varphi \to (\psi \wedge \chi)$, then $\varphi \to \psi$ and $\varphi \to \chi$.
CMon	Whenever $\varphi \to \psi$ and $\varphi \to \chi$, then $(\varphi \wedge \psi) \to \chi$.
CN	Whenever $\emptyset$, then $\varphi \to \top$.
CNC	Whenever $\varphi \nvdash \bot$, $\varphi \to \psi$, and $\varphi \to \overline{\psi}$, then $\bot$.
Contraposition	Whenever $\varphi \to \overline{\psi}$, then $\psi \to \overline{\varphi}$.
CS	Whenever $\varphi \wedge \psi$, then $\varphi \to \psi$.
CSO	Whenever $\varphi \to \psi$ and $\psi \to \varphi$, then $(\varphi \to \chi) \equiv (\psi \to \chi)$.
CT	Whenever $\varphi \to \psi$ and $(\varphi \wedge \psi) \to \chi$, then $\varphi \to \chi$.
CV	Whenever $\varphi \to \psi$ and $\overline{\varphi \to \overline{\chi}}$, then $(\varphi \wedge \chi) \to \psi$.
DEDUC	Whenever $(\varphi \wedge \psi) \to \chi$, then $\varphi \to (\overline{\psi} \vee \chi)$.
MOD	Whenever $\overline{\varphi} \to \varphi$, then $\psi \to \varphi$.
Modus Ponens	Whenever φ and $\varphi \to \psi$, then ψ.
Modus Tollens	Whenever $\varphi \to \psi$ and $\overline{\psi}$, then $\overline{\varphi}$.
MP	Whenever $\varphi \to \psi$, then $\varphi \supset \psi$.
NR	Whenever $\varphi \to \psi$, then $(\varphi \wedge \chi) \to \psi$ or $(\varphi \wedge \overline{\chi}) \to \overline{\psi}$ (or both).
OR	Whenever $\varphi \to \psi$ and $\chi \to \psi$, then $(\varphi \vee \chi) \to \psi$.
Or-to-if	Whenever $\varphi \vee \psi$, then $\overline{\varphi} \to \psi$.
RCE	Whenever $\vdash \varphi \supset \psi$, then $\varphi \to \psi$.
RCEA	Whenever $\vdash \varphi \equiv \psi$, then $(\varphi \to \chi) \equiv (\psi \to \chi)$.
RCEC	Whenever $\vdash \varphi \equiv \psi$, then $(\chi \to \varphi) \equiv (\chi \to \psi)$.
RCK	Whenever $\vdash (\varphi_1 \wedge \cdots \wedge \varphi_n) \supset \psi$, $\chi \to \varphi_1$, $\chi \to \varphi_2, \ldots,$ and $\chi \to \varphi_n$, then $\chi \to \psi$.
RCM	Whenever $\vdash \psi \supset \chi$ and $\varphi \to \psi$, then $\varphi \to \chi$.
REF	Whenever $\emptyset$, then $\varphi \to \varphi$.
ROR	Whenever $\varphi \to (\psi \vee \chi)$, then $\varphi \to \psi$ or $\varphi \to \chi$ (or both).
SA	Whenever $\varphi \to \psi$, then $(\varphi \wedge \chi) \to \psi$.
SDA	Whenever $(\varphi \vee \psi) \to \chi$, then $\varphi \to \chi$ and $\psi \to \chi$.
Trans	Whenever $\varphi \to \psi$ and $\psi \to \chi$, then $\varphi \to \chi$.
VCM	Whenever $\varphi \to (\psi \wedge \chi)$, then $(\varphi \wedge \psi) \to \chi$.
WAND	Whenever $\varphi \to \psi$ and $(\varphi \wedge \overline{\chi}) \to \bot$, then $\varphi \to (\psi \wedge \chi)$.
XOR	Whenever $\vdash \overline{\varphi \wedge \psi}$, $\varphi \to \chi$, and $\psi \to \chi$, then $(\varphi \vee \psi) \to \chi$.
Xor-to-if	Whenever $\varphi \vee \psi$ and $\overline{\varphi \wedge \psi}$, then $\overline{\varphi} \to \psi$.

because it is straightforward to make sense of them as candidate closure principles even in the context of EST, to wit, by interpreting the claim that two conditionals are materially equivalent as requiring that one of them is acceptable iff the other is acceptable; interpreting $\overline{\varphi \to \overline{\chi}}$, which occurs as a premise in CV, as requiring that $\varphi \to \overline{\chi}$ not be acceptable; and interpreting the conjunctions and disjunctions in the conclusions of CEM, CM, NR, ROR, and SDA as requiring that both conjuncts, respectively at least one disjunct, be acceptable. That, at any rate, is how these principles are to be interpreted in the following.

Say that a principle is *valid for t* iff it is acceptability-preserving for $\theta = t$, that is to say, on the assumption that $\theta = t$, its conclusion is acceptable whenever its premise or premises are acceptable; otherwise it is *invalid for t*. Say that a principle is *valid* (*invalid*) simpliciter iff it is valid (invalid) for all $t \in [.5, 1)$. Then the analytical investigations can be summarized by the following theorem, the proof of which is given in Appendix A:

Theorem 5.2.1 *The following principles in Table 5.1 are valid: ANT, BR1, (the principal part of) CNC, MP, MOD, (the principal part of) RCE, RCEA, RCEC, (the principal part of) REF, WAND, and XOR; all other principles in the table are invalid.*

Saying that the principal part of a given principle is valid means that that principle is valid if we exclude certain trivial cases. Specifically, CNC is valid for all conditionals barring those with probability 0 antecedents, and RCE and REF are valid for all conditionals barring those with probability 1 consequents. In view of what was said in Section 4.4 about conditionals whose antecedent or consequent have an extreme probability, I could as well have considered each principle only insofar as it pertains to conditionals whose antecedent and consequent have non-extreme probabilities. But it will not hurt to have a proof of the slightly more general Theorem 5.2.1.

A number of comments on this theorem follow below. First, it merits remark that the proof of the theorem does not assume CP. Otherwise, MP could not be valid. After all, given CP, the acceptability of ψ would follow from the joint acceptability of φ and $\varphi \supset \psi$, and thus, given MP, from the joint acceptability of φ and "If φ, then ψ." But, as the proof shows, Modus Ponens is not a valid principle on our proposal. It was said earlier that some theorists have taken the Lottery and Preface Paradoxes as reasons to abandon CP. Actually, those paradoxes require for their derivation only (what is sometimes called) the Conjunction Principle, according to which a conjunction is acceptable if its conjuncts are. However, it would be wrong to conclude from this that the Conjunction Principle is the only problematic part of CP. Indeed, it is easy to see that the principle that from φ and $\varphi \supset \psi$ one may infer ψ – Modus Ponens for the material conditional, that is – is not acceptability-preserving either. To illustrate, suppose that $\theta = .9$ and that $\Pr(\varphi) = \Pr(\varphi \supset \psi) = .91$. Thus, both φ

and $\varphi \supset \psi$ are acceptable, according to LT. However, if we now suppose that $\varphi \wedge \psi \vdash \bot$ – as it may well be – then it follows from the foregoing assumptions that $\Pr(\psi) = .82 \not> \theta$. And thus ψ is not acceptable, according to LT.[11]

Second, many believe that if conditionals have truth conditions at all, these must be somewhere in between the truth conditions of the material conditional and those of the so-called strict conditional, that is, the material conditional in the scope of a necessity operator.[12] While I want to keep my promise to remain noncommittal on the question of the truth conditions of conditionals, I would still like to note that, in view of the fact that both MP and RCE are valid, the *acceptability* conditions for a strict conditional are at least as strong as the acceptability conditions for the corresponding conditional, which are in turn at least as strong as the acceptability conditions for the corresponding material conditional. In fact, because Contraposition, for instance, is invalid on our proposal, the acceptability conditions of a conditional are strictly weaker than those of the corresponding strict conditional, and because Or-to-if is invalid as well, the acceptability conditions of a conditional are strictly stronger than those of the corresponding material conditional.

Third, it is to be noted that none of the standard conditional logics has all of its axioms validated by our proposal of EST. The systems C2, SS, V, VC, and VW all count the invalid principles CSO and RCK among their axioms; in addition, C2, V, and VC have CV as an axiom, SS and VC have CS as an axiom, and C2 has CEM as an axiom, all of which are invalid by Theorem 5.2.1. System P has two valid axioms – RCEA and REF – and four invalid ones, to wit, CC, CMon, OR, and RCM. System B has half of its axioms – ANT, RCEA, REF – validated; the other half – consisting of DEDUC, RCM, and VCM – is invalid. Of the better-known systems, O does best, with two of its axioms – RCM and VCM – coming out invalid, the other axioms – RCEA, REF, WAND, and XOR – being valid. Moreover, all standard conditional logics are conservative over classical logic, meaning that any theorem of classical logic is also a theorem

---

[11] To solve the Lottery Paradox, Kyburg [1970] abandons CP in favor of what he calls "the Weak Deduction Principle," according to which every logical consequence of an acceptable proposition is itself acceptable. While he is right to point out that this principle together with the Conjunction Principle yields CP again, it is not true that abandoning the Conjunction Principle must leave one with the Weak Deduction Principle. For example, one goes beyond this principle by adding to it the principle that acceptability is closed under Modus Ponens for the material conditional, but this will still not allow one to recover the Conjunction Principle.

[12] As we saw in Section 2.2 (p. 42), not *all* believe this. In particular, not all believe that a conditional must be false whenever the corresponding material conditional is false.

of any of the standard conditional logics. But we already know from the Lottery and Preface Paradoxes that, if LT is assumed, not all classically valid inferences preserve acceptability. Naturally, nothing of this should be considered as a criticism of these logics, nor as a reason to prefer one conditional logic over the other, given that none of them was proposed as an axiomatization of the conditions under which *acceptability* is closed.[13] It is still useful to know that none of the standard logics of conditionals *could* serve as such an axiomatization.

Fourth, while Theorem 5.2.1 can be considered as establishing a soundness result, one would like to have a corresponding completeness result. Specifically, one would like to know the answer to the following question: if φ is acceptable in all probability models in which all $\psi \in \Psi$ are acceptable – supposing LT and EST – can φ be derived from Ψ using only the inferential principles that are valid according to Theorem 5.2.1? I must leave this question unanswered here. Indeed, it is an open question whether a result establishing either completeness or incompleteness in the previous sense can be obtained at all.

And fifth, Theorem 5.2.1 states which principles in Table 5.1 are acceptability-preserving when the arrow occurring in these principles is interpreted as standing for the indicative-conditional-forming operator. As was mentioned in Section 4.6, the acceptability conditions of concessives do not entirely coincide with those of conditionals. A concessive and the corresponding conditional both require for their acceptability a high conditional probability of the consequent given the antecedent, but whereas the conditional is acceptable only if that conditional probability is *higher* than the unconditional probability of the consequent, the concessive is acceptable only if that is *not* the case. Inspection of the proof of Theorem 5.2.1 shows that some results will continue to hold if we assume the acceptability conditions of concessives instead of those of conditionals. But not all results carry over. Thus, the question of which of the principles on our list are acceptability-preserving if the arrow is interpreted as standing for the concessive-forming operator is not answered by Theorem 5.2.1, and similarly for the question of which other principles might qualify as closure principles for that operator. As for the latter question, note that at least one principle *not* on the list is presumably valid for concessives but certainly invalid for conditionals, to wit, the principle that ψ whenever "Even if φ,

---

[13] At least, none of them was meant as an axiomatization of the conditions under which acceptability is closed, supposing acceptability is defined for conditionals by EST. Though he does not put it this way, Adams seems to have meant system P as an axiomatization of the conditions under which acceptability is closed, given that acceptability is defined for conditionals by QAT.

ψ" (with ψ being factive).[14] For the acceptability of the concessive requires the probability of the consequent given the antecedent to be above θ, yet not above the unconditional probability of the consequent. A fortiori, it requires the unconditional probability of the consequent to be above θ as well. Given LT, this is enough to make the consequent acceptable. Insofar as it accords with intuition that a concessive's consequent is acceptable whenever the concessive is acceptable, the foregoing is a point in favor of the conjunction of LT and the analysis of the acceptability conditions of concessives proposed in Douven and Verbrugge [2012]. However, these questions concerning concessives are mentioned here only to set them aside for present concerns. This chapter is focussed exclusively on closure principles for conditionals.

5.3 Going beyond strict validity: a conjecture

We already know, from Section 5.1, that CC is not valid on EST, even though – as we noticed – the principle does appear to be unproblematic, from a pretheoretical standpoint. Perhaps pretheoretical intuitions about the validity of principles such as CC are not really fueled by facts about validity in the strict sense.

As briefly mentioned, it is possible to generalize the notion of validity and turn it into one that permits of degrees. The proposal is but a straightforward generalization of Bamber's [2000] notion of entailment with near surety, which he develops for (what he calls) the language of high conditional probability assertions, and which requires, not that *every* model (as with classical entailment), but only *nearly* every model, that satisfies the premises satisfy the conclusion. Differently put,

> all but a "negligible" proportion of the models of the premises should be models of the conclusion. Thus, a randomly selected model of the premises should have only a negligible probability of failing to be a model of the conclusion. (Bamber [2000:4])

---

[14] See Lycan's [2001:101 f] and references given there. The reader will have no difficulty refuting the claim that the parallel principle for conditionals is valid. One might think that the principle is invalid for concessives too, in view of examples like this one: "Even if John drinks just a little, he will be fired." After all, it would seem that this sentence can be acceptable without its consequent being acceptable; for instance, John might manage to turn himself into a teetotaler. Note, however, that the given sentence is a conditional rather than a concessive. What it expresses is that if John drinks, *no matter how little*, he will be fired. In other words, in this sentence "even" takes scope only over "just a little," and not over the whole antecedent. See, for arguments in this vein, Bennett [1982] and Lycan [2001:102]. (These authors consider a subjunctive version of the example sentence, but that does not affect the main point.)

The notions of "negligible proportion" and "negligible probability" are made precise by standard measure-theoretic means; see Bamber [2000:16 ff]. For Bamber's purposes, only the notion of entailment with near surety is of interest, but he could easily have gone on and defined generally that a set of premises α-*entails* a conclusion iff the conclusion holds in a randomly selected model of the premises with (objective) probability α.

I will avail myself of this idea, applying it to our notion of validity. Say that a closure principle is *valid to a degree of* α iff α is the probability that its conclusion is acceptable in a randomly selected model in which its premises are acceptable. The terminology might suggest that a closure principle is better, in that it is closer to having the desirable status of being valid, the higher its degree of validity. But this suggestion is unintended. The degree of validity of a principle is simply hoped to provide a reliable indicator of the likelihood that one will be confronted in daily life with a counterexample to the principle, or – which may be directly related to the foregoing – that one will be able to conceive of a counterexample when pondering whether to apply the principle. Specifically, one would expect the two to be inversely related: the higher the degree of validity of a principle, the lower the likelihood that one will stumble upon a counterexample to it.

The point about CC hinted at earlier can now be stated more precisely, and also more generally, as the following conjecture: people are more likely to mistake an invalid principle for a valid one the higher the degree of validity of the principle is. For all that has been said so far, CC may be valid to a very high degree. If so, then that may explain why it appears so natural to us as a closure principle for acceptability, even though as such it is invalid. The same may hold for various other principles on our list that come out invalid in Theorem 5.2.1 but that intuitively "feel" valid. (If the conjecture is true, then it could be said that, in a sense, it is bad rather than good for us if an invalid principle has a high degree of validity, as it increases the chance that we misperceive the principle as a valid one.)

The idea underlying this conjecture is not altogether new. Famously, McGee [1985] presents a number of cases that, in his view, show Modus Ponens to be invalid in the classical sense of failing to preserve truth.[15] Various commentators have argued that the cases at most show that Modus Ponens does not preserve acceptability.[16] Besides, the conclusion of McGee's paper is meant to be limited to instances of Modus Ponens

---

[15] See Lycan [2001:58] for another alleged counterexample to Modus Ponens.
[16] See, e.g., Sinnott-Armstrong, Moor, and Fogelin [1986]. But see also Lycan [2001:66–69], who argues that McGee's cases are real counterexamples to Modus Ponens.

that have a right-nested conditional as their major premise. According to McGee [1985:468], "there is every reason to suppose that, restricted to [simple] conditionals, modus ponens is unexceptionable." McGee does not say what his reasons for this claim are. Whatever the reasons are, Theorem 5.2.1 shows that they cannot be cogent reasons to believe that Modus Ponens is unexceptionable when it comes to preserving acceptability, at least not if acceptability is spelled out in terms of EST and LT.[17] But the more relevant point in McGee's paper is his proposed explanation of why we have come to regard Modus Ponens as a core principle governing the use of conditionals, even though – in his opinion – the principle is invalid, to wit, that "[w]e encounter a great many conditionals in daily life, and we have noticed that, when we accept a conditional and we accept its antecedent, we are prone to accept the consequent as well" (*ibid.*). In McGee's diagnosis, we have been overhasty in generalizing from these observations. These remarks remain entirely speculative in McGee's paper, but the next section presents results that support them (to some extent).

In fact, there is already some indirect support for the conjecture to be found in the psychological literature. De Neys, Schaeken, and d'Ydewalle [2003] report experiments on the fallacies of Affirming the Consequent and Denying the Antecedent that were mentioned in Chapter 3 (p. 66). In their second experiment, they first pretested the participants by presenting them with a set of conditionals and asking them to write down as many "alternatives" to each conditional as they could think of, where an alternative to a conditional in their sense is a conditional with the same consequent but a different antecedent that plausibly leads to the truth of the consequent; to give one of their examples, an alternative to "If fertilizer is put on the plants, then they will grow quickly" would be "If the plants get a lot of sunlight, then they will grow quickly" (De Neys, Schaeken, and d'Ydewalle [2003:584]). Then, after approximately a month, they invited the same participants back and presented them with various instances of the aforementioned fallacies, each of which had as its major premise one of the conditionals that had been used in the pretest. The analysis of the results revealed that a participant was less likely to endorse an instance the more alternatives to the conditional figuring in the instance he or she had been able to generate in the pretest. De Neys et al. were not concerned with the notion of acceptability or that of degree of validity. But, given how we defined the latter notion, it is not unreasonable to suppose that

---

[17] It is also noteworthy that Lycan's counterexample to Modus Ponens does not involve any nested conditionals.

the number of alternatives the participants were able to think of was a function of the frequency with which they had come across counterexamples (in our sense) to Affirming the Consequent and Denying the Antecedent. Models in which many alternatives to a conditional are acceptable may easily be models in which both that conditional and its consequent are acceptable but its antecedent is not, or in which even the negation of the antecedent is acceptable. Such a model may represent the belief state of a person who takes the consequent to obtain because the antecedent of one of the alternative conditionals obtains. Whether this is the deeper explanation behind the results De Neys et al. report would itself be testable. However, as will be seen in Section 5.5, there may be more direct ways of testing the conjecture.

As a final comment on the conjecture, I note that, on the present definition of degree of validity, all counterexamples to an invalid principle are on a par. But some counterexamples could be argued to be more serious than others. For example, if a probability model validates the premises of a given principle but fails to validate the conclusion, because it assigns a conditional probability of exactly θ where a conditional probability greater than θ would be needed to validate the conclusion, then that would seem to constitute a less serious counterexample to the principle than a model that validates the premises but fails to validate the conclusion because it assigns a value of 0 to the relevant conditional probability. Although the idea that counterexamples can be more and less serious makes sense pretheoretically, it will be far from easy to devise a well-motivated measure of seriousness. However, supposing such a measure can be had, it might be worth considering a refinement of the conjecture in terms not just of the likelihood that we are confronted with a counterexample to a principle, but also the likelihood that we are confronted with a *serious* counterexample.[18]

5.4 Determining degrees of validity

For the above conjecture to have empirical content, it must be specified how the degrees of validity of the principles that are invalid according to our theorem are to be determined, or at least estimated. In outline, the procedure to be followed is straightforward enough: sample a number of randomly generated probability models in which the premise or premises of a given principle are acceptable and check in how many of those the

---

[18] I owe this suggestion to David Over.

conclusion is acceptable as well or, as we shall say henceforth, what proportion of randomly generated p(remise)-models are c(onclusion)-models. What is less straightforward is how to go about obtaining random probability models. One way to generate such models makes use of computer simulations. Another uses surveys to elicit people's degrees of belief in various randomly chosen propositions. There may be still further ways to obtain probability models that could be claimed to be randomly generated, but in the following I will limit myself to the aforementioned two methods.

Checking whether a random probability model is a p-model or a c-model of a principle requires that we settle on a value for θ. Philosophers who endorse LT or QAT or variant theses tend to be noncommittal on the exact value of the threshold to which these theses refer. If a value is mentioned at all – this is typically done only for purposes of illustration – it is most frequently .9, though .5 and .99 are also often mentioned.[19] On the other hand, Douven and Verbrugge's earlier-mentioned [2012] study suggests that $\theta = .5$ may be the more realistic assumption. In that study, the assumption of $\theta = .9$ would have led to the conclusion that almost none of the participants regarded a conditional probability above the threshold as a necessary condition for asserting the corresponding conditional (whether in its "if" or in its "even if" form). That would have been an implausible conclusion, whatever one's exact take on the relationship between acceptability and probability. Nevertheless, in the following, both .5 and .9 will be assumed in estimating degrees of validity.

Most of the principles in Table 5.1 involve three propositions; some involve two. So, for the most part we will want to generate random models that assign probabilities to at least three propositions as well as to their truth-functional combinations. Given propositions φ, ψ, and χ, call any instance of $\pm\varphi \wedge \pm\psi \wedge \pm\chi$ an *atom* of these propositions, where $\pm X$ indicates that the proposition X may occur either simpliciter or negated in the atom. For each triple of propositions, there are exactly eight different atoms. These are mutually exclusive (at most one of them can be true) and jointly exhaustive (one of them must be true). Given three propositions, call the set consisting of the eight different atoms the *atom matrix* of those propositions.

It is immediately obvious that the invalid principles BR2 and CN have a degree of validity of zero. After all, no proposition is supported by any

---

[19] Kaplan [1981:308], Moser and Tlumac [1985:128], and Kyburg [1990:64] mention .9; Foley [1992:113] mentions .99. Achinstein [2001:156] is the only author who strongly commits to a particular value of θ, to wit, .5.

tautology, and no tautology is supported by any proposition. So there are no probability models in which the conclusion of either BR2 or CN can hold (though there are models in which their premises can hold). Thus, there is no need to consider these principles further in the present section.

5.4.1 Computer simulations

In the computer simulations, which were carried out using *Mathematica* 8, random probability models were generated via the following procedure, which was applied to each of the invalid principles in Table 5.1, barring the aforementioned BR2 and CN. First, *Mathematica's* built-in random number generator was used to generate a random real number $r_i \in [0, 1]$ for each atom i in the atom matrix of propositions φ, ψ, and χ such that the eight numbers would sum to 1. This was done by picking seven random pairwise distinct points in the $[0, 1]$ interval and by assigning randomly the lengths of the eight segments into which these seven points divided the interval $[0, 1]$ as values to the eight atoms.[20] This process was repeated until 1,000 p-models had been obtained for whichever of the principles was being tested. Then it was checked how many of those 1,000 models were also c-models of the principle. This was repeated ten times, and finally the average number of c-models that were found among the p-models over the ten runs was determined. The process was in fact done twice over, once for $\theta = .5$ and once for $\theta = .9$. For RCK, which is the only principle that involves more than three propositions, the same procedure was carried out, except that models assigning probabilities to four propositions were generated.[21]

The results of the simulations are given in Table 5.2. These results show that there are clear differences between the various principles with respect to the average number of c-models that one finds among 1,000 of their p-models. The results also show that the choice of value for θ can make a big difference. In fact, there is only a moderate correlation ($r = .486$, $p = .02$) between the results for $\theta = .5$ and the results for $\theta = .9$.

As for the results for $\theta = .5$, if we interpret averages as estimates of the degrees of validity of the various principles (or rather, averages divided by

---

[20]　Thanks to Stephan Hartmann for pointing out to me that this is the proper way to generate the random probability models that I needed.

[21]　Recall that RCK is the principle that whenever $\vdash (\varphi_1 \wedge \cdots \wedge \varphi_n) \supset \psi$, $\chi \to \varphi_1$, $\chi \to \varphi_2$, $\ldots$, and $\chi \to \varphi_n$, then $\chi \to \psi$. Due to limitations of computing time, simulations were carried out only for the special case in which $n = 2$.

Table 5.2. Averages over 10 runs of 1,000 models; standard deviations appear in parentheses.

Principle	$\theta = .5$	$\theta = .9$
CC	606 (17)	512 (12)
CEM	755 (15)	184 (11)
CM	732 (12)	984 (3)
CMon	864 (6)	994 (1)
Contraposition	806 (13)	554 (9)
CS	835 (12)	975 (6)
CSO	763 (8)	967 (8)
CT	641 (7)	659 (18)
CV	798 (14)	721 (15)
DEDUC	764 (13)	932 (7)
Modus Ponens	842 (12)	691 (19)
Modus Tollens	751 (18)	989 (4)
NR	690 (21)	670 (18)
OR	887 (6)	832 (12)
Or-to-if	426 (15)	347 (14)
RCK	812 (13)	930 (28)
RCM	918 (9)	995 (2)
ROR	865 (9)	208 (15)
SA	703 (10)	679 (19)
SDA	449 (15)	461 (9)
Trans	651 (14)	681 (11)
VCM	949 (9)	998 (1)
Xor-to-if	686 (8)	673 (13)

100, given that we measure graded validity on a scale from 0 to 1), then it appears that a number of principles that are strictly invalid still have a high degree of validity; for instance, we see that VCM has an estimated degree of validity of .95. We also see that other principles have only a moderate or even low degree of validity. For $\theta = .9$, still more principles come out as having a near-to-perfect degree of validity. Indeed, for VCM the ten runs each generating 1,000 p-models yielded no more than a handful of models that were not c-models for this principle.

In the previous section it was remarked that none of the standard conditional logics contains only principles that are valid in the sense of acceptability-preserving. However, the simulation results show that if graded validity is understood in terms of computer-generated probability models, then some of those logics (above all, system O) consist of axioms, all of which are valid to a high degree, even to a very high degree if we assume $\theta = .9$.

5.4.2 Survey models

One might worry that many of the models obtained in these simulations
do not represent degrees-of-belief functions that any rational person could
plausibly be expected to have. And if there is a correlation to be found
at all between the extent to which people obey the various principles in
Table 5.1 and the degrees of validity of these principles, where degree of
validity is understood in terms of random probability models, then it is
more likely to be found when we consider random models that could realistically represent someone's degrees of belief than when we consider models
generated by means of computer simulations, many of which might not
look anything like a real degrees-of-belief function. To address the worry
that the models generated in the simulations might not be of the kind we
want, I conducted an experiment to obtain random probability models in
a different way as well.

In this experiment, participants were asked to rate the probabilities (in
percentages) of the elements of atom matrices of randomly selected propositions. They were explicitly instructed that the truth of any one of the
elements excluded the truth of all other elements and that one of the elements had to be true, and also that therefore the probabilities they assigned
to the elements had to sum to 100 percent.

More specifically, the experiment was carried out in two stages at two
different points in time. In the first stage, ten sentences were picked more
or less at random from the BBC, *The New York Times*, and *Los Angeles
Times* news sites in the last week of August 2012 (see Appendix B).[22]
Each of the $\binom{10}{3} = 120$ possible combinations of three different sentences from this set served as the basis of an atom matrix. In the first
week of September 2012, participants were recruited via CrowdFlower
(http://www.crowdflower.com), which directed them to the Qualtrics plat-
form (http://www.qualtrics.com), on which the survey was run. There
they received the instructions as explained and then were given at random
one of the 120 different atom matrices. They were paid a small amount
of money in return for their participation. Repeat participation was prevented. In this part of the experiment, there were 713 participants, all from
Australia, Canada, New Zealand, the United Kingdom, and the United
States. Thirty-two participants indicated that they were nonnative speakers
of English. Data from these participants were excluded from the analysis.

---

[22] The sentences were picked *more or less* at random, because they had to be relatively short, uncom-
pounded, and comprehensible outside the context of the article from which they were taken. Also,
for reasons of comprehensibility, here and there a word or two had to be changed.

The remaining 681 participants had a mean age of 32 (±14), with 47 percent female, and with 80 percent listing college or higher as their current education level, 19 percent listing high school, and 1 percent listing a lower education level.

The second stage of the experiment was simply a repetition of the first exactly one month later, and now with ten different sentences picked from the BBC, CNN, *The New York Times*, and *Los Angeles Times* news sites (see again Appendix B). In this second part of the experiment, there were 466 participants from Canada, New Zealand, the United Kingdom, and the United States, who also received some payment for their participation. Repeat participation was again prevented. As before, data from participants who indicated that they were nonnative speakers of English ($N = 17$) were excluded from the analysis. The remaining 449 participants had a mean age of 32 (±12), with 54 percent female, and with 80 percent listing college or higher as their current education level and 20 percent listing high school.

So, in total there were 1,179 participants,[23] and the analysis was based on data from the 1,130 participants who had identified themselves as native English speakers. The mean age of the latter group was 32 (±13); 49 percent of the participants in this group were female; 80 percent listed college or higher as their current education level, 19 percent listed high school, and 1 percent listed a lower education level. The 1,130 response sets that were obtained over the two stages of the experiment were analyzed in the same way in which we analyzed the models generated in the simulations. Thus, for each of the invalid principles, it was determined how many of the models that were p-models of the principle were also c-models of it. It is to be noted that in neither stage of the experiment was there among the sentences picked from the various news portals one that was classically entailed by some of the other sentences. For that reason, the degree of validity of the rule RCM could not be estimated in this experiment. The same was true for the rule RCK, given that people were asked to rate the probabilities of elements of atom matrices of three propositions only.

Before looking at the outcomes of the analysis, we mention two possible worries about the current method of obtaining random probability

---

[23] Actually, there were 1,179 response sets. At the time, CrowdFlower only offered the functionality to identify participants' public IP addresses, which do not uniquely identify participants and which may change over time (in the meantime, experimenters have been given access to participants' CrowdFlower identification numbers). It thus cannot be excluded that some people have participated in both stages of the experiment. Given that the stages were spaced one month apart from each other, it is hard to imagine how there could have been any carry-over effects. It therefore seemed safe to treat the response sets in the analysis as coming from unique participants.

models. The first worry is that the results may be too dependent on the particular selection of sentences and should thus not be considered to constitute genuinely random models (in spite of the fact that the sentences were selected randomly). The second worry is that the task presented to the participants in the experiment, which asks them to assess probabilities of conjunctions with three conjuncts, is cognitively quite demanding, and that therefore the responses may not accurately reflect the participants' real degrees of belief in the various conjunctions.

In response to the first worry, we may exploit the fact that the experiment was conducted in two stages, and especially that different materials were used at each stage. In particular, we can analyze the data from the two stages separately and then compare the outcomes. If these outcomes correlate well, that gives reason to hold that the results do not depend on the specific materials.

In response to the second worry, it could be said that the models we obtained in this experiment are still more likely to represent real degrees-of-belief functions (that is, real *partial* degrees-of-belief functions) than many of the models randomly generated by the procedure used in our computer simulations. But there is no need to be so concessive at this point, for given that some of the principles listed in Table 5.1 involve only two propositions, it is possible to compare some of the results from the above experiment with results obtained in a control experiment in which people were asked to assess the probabilities of the elements of atom matrices of only two propositions, which is cognitively not excessively demanding and which in any event is a rather standard procedure for eliciting people's probabilities. Specifically, we can for each of CEM, Contraposition, CS, Modus Ponens, Modus Tollens, Or-to-if, and Xor-to-if compare the percentage of models obtained in the main experiment that validate the given principle with the percentage of models obtained in the control experiment that validate that principle. If these percentages correlate well, then that gives reason to believe that the models obtained in the main experiment are not too far off from real degrees-of-belief functions.

In the control experiment, there were 275 participants, all from Canada, the United Kingdom, or the United States. They received some payment for their participation. Sixteen participants indicated that they were nonnative speakers of English. Data from these participants were excluded from the analysis. The remaining 259 participants had a mean age of 32 ($\pm$11), with 56 percent female, and with 76 percent listing college or higher as their current education level, 23 percent listing high school, and 1 percent listing a lower education level.

Each participant was asked to assess the probabilities of all instances of $\pm\varphi \wedge \pm\psi$ for exactly one randomly chosen element of the $\binom{10}{2} = 45$ different atom matrices of pairs of sentences chosen from the list of sentences that were used at the second stage of the main experiment. Otherwise, the procedure was the same as for the two stages of the main experiment.

Table 5.3 presents the results of the main experiment, also (separately) those of the different stages of that experiment, as well as the results of the control experiment. An analysis of these results shows there to be significant and very strong correlations between the outcomes of the two stages of the experiment: for $\theta = .5$, the results had $r = .915$, $p < .0001$; for $\theta = .9$, the results had $r = .917$, $p < .0001$; and all results taken together had $r = .916$, $p < .0001$. This should suffice to put to rest the first worry raised above. As for the second worry, there also exist significant and strong to very strong correlations between the outcomes of the main experiment and those of the control experiment: for $\theta = .5$, the results had $r = .937$, $p < .01$; for $\theta = .9$, the results had $r = .811$, $p = .05$; and the results taken together had $r = .864$, $p < .0001$. This supports the thought that the models obtained in the main experiment do reflect people's degrees of belief.

More generally, it is to be noted that the value of θ matters a great deal, as it did for the simulations, although here we do find a relatively strong correlation between the results for $\theta = .5$ and those for $\theta = .9$, namely, $r = .781$, $p < .0001$. What is more striking is that there is but a moderate correlation between the outcomes of the computer simulations for $\theta = .5$ and the outcomes of the above experiment for $\theta = .5$, to wit, $r = .446$, $p < .05$; for $\theta = .9$, there is no significant correlation between the results of the simulations and the results of the experiment. Furthermore, although we do not have data on RCK and RCM (for the reasons mentioned above), as far as the data we do have go, some of the standard conditional logics come out as having axioms that are either valid or valid to a high degree.

The most important finding is no doubt that among 1,130 random probability models, *there was not a single violation of CC*. To reiterate an earlier point, no degree of validity turns an invalid principle into a valid one, or even only helps to elevate it to the status of "being as good as valid" or "being valid for all practical purposes." But the finding may be the key to explaining why CC strikes us as compelling, despite the fact that, if EST is correct, the principle is invalid. If the experimentally determined random probability models give a good estimate of the degrees to which the various principles are valid, then the finding suggests that the conditional versions

Table 5.3. Results of survey experiment: ratios of p-models that are also c-models to all p-models; percentages appear in parentheses.

Principle	Total		Stage 1		Stage 2		Control	
	$\theta = .5$	$\theta = .9$	$\theta = .5$	$\theta = .9$	$\theta = .5$	$\theta = .9$	$\theta = .5$	$\theta = .9$
CC	134/134 (100)	24/24 (100)	86/86 (100)	18/18 (100)	48/48 (100)	6/6 (100)	–	–
CEM	454/1130 (40)	48/1130 (4)	288/681 (42)	35/681 (5)	166/449 (37)	13/449 (3)	91/259 (35)	20/259 (8)
CM	94/134 (70)	12/24 (50)	58/86 (67)	8/18 (44)	36/48 (75)	4/6 (67)	–	–
CMon	139/161 (86)	17/17 (100)	87/98 (89)	12/12 (100)	52/63 (83)	5/5 (100)	–	–
Contraposition	94/138 (70)	7/9 (78)	64/92 (70)	5/6 (83)	30/46 (65)	2/3 (67)	13/27 (48)	1/3 (33)
CS	107/268 (40)	4/102 (4)	62/146 (42)	3/56 (5)	45/122 (37)	1/46 (2)	31/76 (41)	1/20 (5)
CSO	188/252 (75)	19/19 (100)	114/159 (72)	13/13 (100)	74/93 (80)	6/6 (100)	–	–
CT	139/160 (87)	17/18 (94)	87/102 (85)	12/12 (100)	52/58 (90)	5/6 (83)	–	–
CV	215/259 (83)	38/39 (97)	139/164 (85)	28/29 (97)	76/95 (80)	10/10 (100)	–	–
DEDUC	242/317 (76)	54/66 (82)	154/197 (78)	33/38 (87)	88/120 (73)	21/28 (75)	–	–
Modus Ponens	187/206 (91)	7/9 (78)	115/127 (91)	5/6 (83)	72/79 (91)	2/3 (67)	47/49 (96)	1/1 (100)
Modus Tollens	21/35 (60)	0/0 (–)	16/22 (73)	0/0 (–)	5/10 (50)	0/0 (–)	0/0 (–)	0/0 (–)
NR	239/316 (76)	38/39 (97)	150/196 (77)	28/29 (97)	89/120 (74)	10/10 (100)	–	–
OR	126/151 (83)	10/17 (59)	71/91 (78)	7/12 (58)	55/60 (92)	3/5 (60)	–	–
Or-to-if	300/1060 (28)	39/412 (9)	180/636 (28)	21/229 (9)	120/424 (28)	18/183 (10)	55/249 (22)	12/109 (11)
ROR	290/355 (82)	35/158 (22)	172/212 (81)	22/97 (23)	118/143 (83)	13/61 (21)	–	–
SA	239/316 (76)	38/39 (97)	150/196 (77)	28/29 (97)	89/120 (74)	10/10 (100)	–	–
SDA	130/295 (44)	14/25 (56)	72/185 (39)	10/14 (71)	58/110 (53)	4/11 (36)	–	–
Trans	111/143 (78)	12/12 (100)	66/91 (73)	9/9 (100)	45/52 (87)	3/3 (100)	–	–
VCM	119/134 (89)	18/24 (75)	74/86 (86)	12/18 (67)	45/48 (94)	6/6 (100)	–	–
Xor-to-if	264/715 (37)	10/53 (19)	161/448 (36)	4/34 (12)	103/267 (39)	6/19 (32)	39/139 (28)	1/9 (11)

of the Lottery and Preface Paradoxes presented in Section 5.1 may well rest on the illusion that CC is valid – which we fall prey to because in everyday life we rarely (if ever) face counterexamples to the principle.

Finally, note that the survey results concerning Modus Ponens go some way toward underpinning McGee's speculation concerning why his examples strike us as so puzzling, to wit, that these examples may well be among the rare cases in which Modus Ponens does not in fact countenance the inference of an acceptable conclusion from acceptable premises; at least given $\theta = .5$, Modus Ponens has a very high degree of validity. Admittedly, these results concern simple conditionals only, and therefore do not strictly speaking pertain to the kind of cases that figure in McGee's paper. But we do not seem to have separate intuitions about Modus Ponens as an acceptability-preserving principle when applied to simple conditionals versus when applied to right-nested conditionals. So, given that applications of Modus Ponens involving right-nested conditionals probably are vastly outnumbered by applications of Modus Ponens involving only simple conditionals, we would be surprised by McGee's examples, even in the unlikely case that Modus Ponens has a low degree of validity when only right-nested conditionals are allowed to serve as its major premise.

5.5 Testing the conjecture: some pointers

It was conjectured that people more easily mistake an invalid principle for a valid one, the higher the degree of validity of the principle. The notion of degree of validity was operationalized – twice over, in fact – and people's mistaking (to a certain extent) an invalid principle for a valid one can plausibly be understood in terms of endorsement rates: the more highly an invalid principle is endorsed, the more easily it is mistaken for a valid one. Thus, the conjecture appears to be testable. However, actually testing it may be challenging in practical terms. For experimentalists who might want to take up the challenge, I would like to point at some potential methodological pitfalls, and I also want to be clearer than I have been so far about what I take the scope of the conjecture to be.

A major methodological difficulty is the lack of a well-established experimental paradigm for the investigation of conditional reasoning. At a general level, it seems clear enough how to proceed: present participants with premises and either ask what, if anything, follows from these premises (i.e., put to them so-called conclusion-production tasks), or also present a conclusion and ask the participants whether they agree, or how strongly they agree, that the conclusion follows from the premises (these are so-called conclusion-evaluation tasks). But different experimentalists hold different views on how to fill in the details, most notably, on whether one should present premises and conclusion using schematic letters or using made-up words, or whether one should use so-called content-rich materials.

The use of content-rich materials has a well-documented tendency of inviting the phenomenon known as "belief bias" – participants' ignoring the premises and simply judging by whether or not they accept the conclusion (see, e.g., Evans and Over [1996]) – as well as more subtle content effects (see, e.g., Cosmides [1989] and Politzer and Bourmaud [2002]). Fillenbaum [1975] conducted a study to investigate whether conditionals warrant the inference of their "obverse" (where "If not φ, then not ψ" is the obverse of "If φ, then ψ"), and also whether conditionals of the form "If not φ, then ψ" warrant the inference of "Unless φ, ψ." This study used content-rich materials and found that the content of the antecedent and consequent clauses made a significant difference in the likelihood with which the aforementioned types of inferences were judged to be acceptable.

In view of these and similar findings, the use of abstract materials seems recommended. In fact, given the hypothesis at issue, the use of such materials is *very strongly* recommended. After all, for a number of the principles in Table 5.1 it is easy to give instances which would, in all likelihood, skew the results in one or the other direction. To use Harper's example (p. 50), we should expect *much* higher endorsement rates for SA if we used as relevant materials "If you put sugar in your cup of tea, it'll taste fine; hence, if you put sugar and milk in your cup of tea, it'll taste fine" than if we used "If you put sugar in your cup of tea, it'll taste fine; hence, if you put sugar and diesel oil in your cup of tea, it'll taste fine." Analogous examples are known for other principles on the list (see, for instance, p. 7). One might try to circumvent this problem by choosing instances of the principles that are in some way neutral, but one would be hard pressed to clarify which instances count as neutral. Another way around the problem might be to present a great number of instances for the various rules, but that would probably make the experiment impractically large.

There is an even more fundamental reason for going with abstract materials. The idea behind the conjecture we are considering is that people are more prone to mistake an invalid principle for a valid one the higher the degree of validity of the principle, because the higher the degree of validity the fewer the counterexamples to the principles that one will be confronted with in daily practice. An abstract presentation of a principle is more likely to invite people to search for possible counterexamples than a concrete instance of the principle; when presented with the latter, people will be inclined to simply give their judgment on *that* instance, without trying to conceive of other instances that might shift their judgment.

On the other hand, it is known that experiments using abstract materials tend to be cognitively much more demanding than experiments using concrete materials (ceteris paribus, that is). For example, Wason and Shapiro [1971] found that whereas only 12 percent of their participants were able to solve the abstract version of the famous Wason selection task (which was in line with Wason's [1968] original findings), 62 percent of the participants were able to solve a concrete version of that same task.[24] Because the judgments of participants who are confused by the abstract setup, or who otherwise do not fully understand what they are being asked, may simply constitute noise, any experiment concerned with the conjecture should include tasks especially for the purpose of selecting the cognitively more able participants, and then base the analysis on those participants' responses. But if this leaves a percentage of participants in the range that Wason found to be able to solve the selection task, psychology journals might question the relevance of the results as lacking sufficient generality.

As far as the scope of the conjecture is concerned, I am not at all sure that it should pertain to all principles in Table 5.1. It may be no coincidence that, so far, experimental work on conditional reasoning has hardly strayed beyond the patterns of Modus Ponens and Modus Tollens, although some attention has also been given to Or-to-if and to Contraposition.[25] I have mostly mined the literature on conditional logics for principles of conditional reasoning. While that is a natural place to look for such principles, not all the principles one finds there may have psychological reality in the sense that actual people rely on them in their reasoning. Principles that a logician comes to find plausible, possibly guided by a formal semantic framework, need not strike the layperson as plausible. Indeed, some of the principles in Table 5.1 involve forms that we find rarely instantiated in ordinary parlance. This may also explain why there is no generally agreed-upon conditional logic, and why principles advocated by some logicians have been highly disputed by others (as is for instance the case with CEM).

---

[24] Later research showed that the percentage of participants who are able to solve the task can be made to vary by appropriately varying the content of the concrete materials (see, e.g., Cosmides [1989]).

[25] Miyamoto et al. [1989] experimentally studied CM, RCM, and VCM and found violations of all three principles. However, their study was only concerned with counterfactual conditionals.

Nevertheless, even if this may go some way toward explaining why experimentalists have mainly focussed on Modus Ponens and Modus Tollens, there are principles in Table 5.1 that are almost as simple and seemingly natural as Modus Ponens and Modus Tollens, and that should be no harder to test empirically than these are. To the extent that principles like CC, CMon, CS, OR, Trans, and VCM, which are not only of the aforementioned sort but also figure in some of the better-known conditional logics, have been neglected in the experimental literature, that is a serious omission.[26]

Spelling out further the content of the conjecture is complicated by the fact, noted toward the end of the previous section, that there is little congruity in our results on graded validity. What would it mean to say that people's judgments of the validity of principles of conditional reasoning reflect those principles' degrees of validity, if the different ways of determining such degrees point in different directions? On the other hand, the choice may be not so difficult to make: given that we are interested in *people's* judgments of the validity of principles, it would seem to make more sense to use the survey-based data, which derive from people's probability judgments, than the data from the computer simulations. Moreover, as noted earlier, in view of Douven and Verbrugge's [2012] results, it seems reasonable to set θ equal to .5 rather than to .9.

Note, though, that we can leave open the question of the value of θ, at least insofar as the choice is between .5 and .9, and still derive some interesting predictions from our conjecture. I did not mean the conjecture to be so specific as to imply that if one principle has a higher degree of validity than another principle, then the former will receive higher endorsement rates, *no matter how slight the difference in degree of validity* – as for some pairs of principles it is – even if the difference reaches statistical significance.[27] But irrespective of whether $\theta = .5$ or $\theta = .9$, there are relatively large differences – mostly of more than 50 percent, and all significant at $p < .0001$ – between, on the one hand, CC, CMon, Modus Ponens, and VCM, and, on the other hand, CEM, CS, Or-to-if, and Xor-to-if. There are further large and equally significant differences between, on the one hand, these two groups of principles and, on the other hand, BR2 and CN, which, as noted, have a degree of validity of 0. And I do mean the

---

[26] Milne [2012] voices a similar complaint.

[27] Table 5.3 gives actual frequency data, rather than just percentages, so that it can be readily calculated whether the difference between any two principles is significant. It is to be noted that, while many of the differences *are* significant, many of them are not. Thus, for instance, it means nothing that both on the assumption that $\theta = .5$ and on the assumption that $\theta = .9$, CMon has a higher degree of validity than CV, for on neither assumption is the difference between the principles significant.

conjecture to imply that, in view of the magnitude of these differences, the first group of principles will receive higher endorsement rates than the second group and than BR2 and CN, and the second group will receive higher endorsement rates than BR2 and CN.

It is worth noting that the extant data on Modus Ponens and Modus Tollens in conjunction with the data from the survey experiment conform with a rather stronger interpretation of our conjecture: in all known experiments on Modus Ponens and Modus Tollens, endorsement rates of Modus Tollens have been well below those of Modus Ponens, which are typically close to 100 percent.[28] So, even if the conjecture is not intended to imply that relatively small differences in the degree of validity of principles are reflected in endorsement rates, it might still be interesting to see how close the fit is between graded validity and endorsement rates.

It might be thought that, in view of the degree of validity of the Or-to-if principle, the conjecture in fact looks a priori very bad. For it predicts that endorsement rates for this principle, which philosophers have almost unanimously said to be eminently plausible, are low. However, there are some recent experimental data on this principle and they are not at all what one would expect. In particular, they show that people are much less willing to make the Or-to-if inference than one might expect if the principle were generally perceived as valid (see Over, Evans, and Elqayam [2010] and Gilio and Over [2012]).

---

[28] See Over, Douven, and Verbrugge [2013] and references given there.

CHAPTER 6

Updating

So far, we have focussed on "static" aspects of the epistemology of conditionals, on various epistemic attitudes that people may have vis-à-vis given conditionals at given points in time, and on the closure conditions for one of those attitudes. But there is an obvious dynamic aspect to that epistemology as well, in that some of the information we receive is of an essentially conditional sort, as when we learn, in our earlier example (on p. 8), that

(6.1) If Millie is not going to work harder, she will not pass her exam.

or that

(6.2) If it starts raining this afternoon, the match will be canceled.

Not only do we learn things like these and thereupon come to believe them; such things also tend to impact what else we believe. Learning (6.1) may make me believe that Millie is not as zealous a student as I had thought she was. Equally, learning (6.2) may raise my confidence that if it starts *snowing* this afternoon, the match will be canceled as well.

What is more, we sometimes have clear intuitions about how one *ought* to respond to the receipt of conditional information. For example, barring special circumstances, it would seem wrong to *lower* one's confidence that the match will be canceled if it starts snowing, upon learning (6.2). However, while we seem to routinely process incoming conditional information, the questions of *how* we process such information and to which normative constraints such processing is subject, have hardly been addressed by epistemologists.

Admittedly, the normative question has been addressed, to some extent, by logicians and computer scientists.[1] But first, they have considered the

---

[1] See, e.g., Boutilier and Goldszmidt [1995] and Kern-Isberner [1999].

question almost exclusively from the perspective of AGM theory, which tells at best only a very partial story about belief change.[2] And second, they have mostly sidestepped the issue of whether the resulting account of belief change, as far as it pertains to conditionals, is at least minimally materially adequate in that it does justice to the intuitions we have about how people should respond to the receipt of particular pieces of conditional information.

In this book, I have chosen a Bayesian perspective, for reasons explained in Section 1.3. This chapter confronts Bayesian epistemology with the above question about the receipt of conditional information. Thus, more specifically, the question is how updating on conditional information is to be accounted for within the Bayesian framework. The answer to be argued for is that, at a minimum, updating on conditionals is very different from standard Bayesian updating on non-conditional information, and that such updating may proceed on the basis of considerations that, according to orthodox Bayesians, have no home within their doctrine.

I begin by presenting data that one would like to be explained by an account of updating on conditionals (Section 6.1) and then argue that none of the main Bayesian candidates for such an account are satisfactory (Section 6.2). On the positive side, in Section 6.3 I propose a still broadly Bayesian model of updating on conditionals that identifies explanation as a potentially crucial factor in the revision of our degrees of belief on the basis of newly acquired conditional information; the model is shown to have clear empirical content and thus to be amenable to experimental testing.

6.1 The data

From a Bayesian perspective, and at least prima facie, there may seem to be clear a priori constraints on updates on conditionals, to wit, the familiar Bayesian constraints of probabilistic coherence. But apart from the fact that it is far from obvious how these constraints apply in the case of updating on conditionals, as will shortly be seen, it would be wrong to assume them from the start, given that the question before us is exactly whether or not such updating can be accounted for in strictly Bayesian terms. Indeed, also in line with our general naturalistic outlook, I prefer to conceive of

---

[2] See Kern-Isberner [2001, Ch. 5] for a notable exception. However, she models the updating of graded belief states on conditional information using the rule of relative entropy minimization, which is known to have counterintuitive consequences; see note 7 for more on this.

the current project not as one to be conducted purely on the basis of a priori considerations, but rather as one that is at least partly empirical in nature. For this reason, I will rely on something like the Baconian method. By considering and comparing hypothetical cases of updating on a conditional, I aim to uncover some of the chief factors governing this type of update and, on that basis, I aim to provide a model of updating on conditionals. This model may then be subjected to more extensive testing in future experimental work.

Consider the following examples, each of which describes a case in which a person receives conditional information:

Example 6.1.1 (Douven and Romeijn [2011]) Ann and her sister Marian have arranged to go for sundowners at the Westcliff hotel tomorrow. Ann feels there is some chance that it will rain, but thinks they can always enjoy the view from inside. To make sure, Marian consults the staff at the Westcliff hotel and finds out that in the event of rain, the inside area will be occupied by a wedding party. So she tells Ann:

(6.3)   If it rains tomorrow, we cannot have sundowners at the Westcliff.

Upon learning this conditional, Ann sets her probability for sundowners *and* rain to 0, but she does not adapt her probability for rain.   ♦

Example 6.1.2 (Douven and Dietz [2011]) Bill sees his friend Sue buying a skiing outfit. This surprises him a bit, because he did not know of any plans of hers to go on a skiing trip. He knows that she recently had an important exam and thinks it unlikely that she passed. Then he meets Tom, his best friend and also a friend of Sue's, who is just on his way to Sue to hear whether she passed the exam, and who tells him:

(6.4)   If Sue passed the exam, her father will take her on a skiing vacation.

Recalling his earlier observation, Bill now comes to find it more likely that Sue passed the exam.   ♦

Example 6.1.3 Cheryl knows that Kevin, the son of her neighbors, was to take his driving test yesterday. She has no idea whether or not Kevin is a good driver; she deems it about as likely as not that Kevin passed the test. Cheryl notices that her neighbors have started to spade their garden. Then her mother, who is friends with Kevin's parents, calls her and tells her the following:

(6.5) If Kevin passed the driving test, his parents will throw a garden party.

Cheryl figures that, given the spading that has just begun, it is doubtful (even if not wholly excluded) that a party can be held in the garden of Kevin's parents in the near future. As a result, Cheryl lowers her degree of belief for Kevin's having passed the driving test. ♦

It should be fairly uncontroversial that, assuming these stories to supply all relevant information, the responses of Ann, Bill, and Cheryl to learning, respectively, (6.3), (6.4), and (6.5) are eminently rational, insofar as these responses are described here. Put the other way around, on the assumption that Ann, Bill, and Cheryl are rational in some informal sense, we could have predicted whether or not they would adjust their degree of belief for the antecedent of the conditional that they learn, and if they do adjust it, whether they raise or lower it.

While our intuitions about Examples 6.1.1–6.1.3 are clear enough, it is less clear what underlies them. Which factor or factors implicit in these examples make us so utterly confident that Ann's updating on (6.3) should not prompt her to change the degree to which she believes the antecedent of that conditional; that Tom's assertion justifies Bill in raising his degree of belief for Sue's having passed the exam; and that, similarly, Cheryl is justified in lowering her degree of belief for Kevin's having passed the driving test, given her mother's assertion? I propose as a desideratum for any account of updating on conditionals that it be able to answer this question. More generally, one would expect such an account to inform us about when updating on a conditional should lead the updater to raise, lower, and leave unchanged his or her degree of belief for the antecedent of the conditional.

To see why the desideratum is a reasonable one to impose, consider an analogy. In the above stories, Ann, Bill, and Cheryl seem intuitively right to accept the conditional information they receive on the basis of their informants' say-so, if only because these informants belong to the types of people (friends, parents) that we tend to trust most. We can easily add details to these stories to bring the relevant intuitions further into relief. For example, we could add to the first story that Marian is a highly trustworthy person who would never lie to her sister, and that Ann knows as much. We would then be even more inclined to think that Ann is right to rely on Marian's testimony. By contrast, we could add to Example 6.1.2 that, although Tom is Bill's best friend, he has self-serving reasons for leading Bill to believe that Sue passed the exam, regardless of whether she did pass, and that Bill actually suspects that Tom has such reasons. In that case, we would become strongly *dis*inclined to think that Bill is right to rely on Tom's testimony. These intuitions are unarguably among the most basic and compelling ones we have about testimony, and we would be deeply dissatisfied with any account of testimony that is unable to explain them.[3] We should be no less dissatisfied with an account of updating on conditionals that failed to explain equally basic and compelling intuitions about such updating, such as, in our examples, that Ann's, Bill's, and Cheryl's responses to the conditional information they receive are – insofar they are specified – quite obviously right.

Even if hard-nosed Bayesians disagree, and do not see it as their business to explain data like those related to the above examples, it should appear uncontentious to any nonpartisan observer that if an account of updating on conditionals *can* explain those data, then that counts as a point in its favor. Indeed, this should also appear uncontentious to the psychologists of reasoning, whose work we encountered in previous chapters and who have recently been touting Bayesianism for being not just a normative theory of graded belief but also a predictively accurate theory of how people reason.

Needless to say, one will want much more from an account of updating on conditionals than that it explain our intuitions about how the updating on a conditional should affect the updater's degree of belief for the antecedent. But however narrow in itself, a focus on this aspect of the updating process will be seen to suffice for discrediting some prima facie plausible hypotheses about how we update on conditionals, and to be instrumental in developing a new model of such updates too.

6.2 Charting the field

This section discusses some candidate Bayesian accounts of updating on conditionals and argues that they all fail to satisfy the adequacy condition just presented.

---

[3] It is not surprising that all serious accounts of testimony are aimed at explaining precisely such intuitions. See Fricker [1987], [1995], [2006] and Burge [1993], [1997] for the two main competing views on testimony. In Fricker's internalist view, the said intuitions are explained in terms of the addressees' having reasons for believing their informants to be trustworthy, or believing them to be untrustworthy (as in the case in which Bill suspects Tom of having self-serving reasons for lying to him), respectively. In Burge's externalist view, the explanation is instead in terms of the addressees' having a defeasible a priori warrant to trust the informants, respectively, this warrant's being defeated.

6.2.1 *Conditionalizing on the material conditional*

Prima facie, it may seem reasonable to think that in the Bayesian literature there is so little to be found about updating on conditionals because there is nothing special about it: we update on conditionals just as we update on any other kind of information, namely, by conditionalization. Unfortunately, however, things are not that simple. For what Skyrms said back in 1980 still seems true today, to wit, that "we have no clear conception of what it might be to conditionalize on a conditional" (Skyrms [1980:169]).

One problem for the suggestion we are considering is that, as noted earlier, the jury is still out on what the correct semantics of conditionals is, and even on the question of whether or not conditionals express propositions at all. If conditionals do *not* express propositions, then there is an immediate problem, for then it is unclear from the start how conditionalization could apply to them. Conditionalization is defined in terms of conditional probability and, to reiterate an earlier point, conditional probability is standardly defined in terms of conjunction, which is a *propositional* operator.

We saw that not all agree that the ratio definition is the best definition of conditional probability, and that some believe that Ramsey's footnote cited in Chapter 4 (p. 92) contains a better definition. Even if so, however, this alternative definition does not really help with the present problem, for how are we to add hypothetically a conditional to our stock of knowledge or stock of beliefs if conditionals are not the sort of things that can be known or believed?[4] In short, if conditionals do not express propositions, then it is hard to make sense of expressions of the form $\Pr(\chi \mid \text{If } \varphi, \text{then } \psi)$. As a result, it is hard to see how one could conditionalize on a conditional.

Even granted that conditionals do express propositions, there is still the question of *which* proposition a given conditional expresses. In Chapter 2, we came across a number of weighty considerations against the once-popular material conditional account. We also saw, however, that the account has some attractive features. Given that none of the objections that were raised against it can be said to offer a knock-down argument, it is worth seeing how far we can get in answering the question at issue by

---

4 The problem does not vanish by adopting the less radical form of non-propositionalism, according to which conditionals have the truth value of their consequent if the antecedent is true and otherwise are neither true nor false. Combining this view with the Ramsey procedure for determining conditional probabilities would seem to imply that $\Pr(\chi \mid \text{If } \varphi, \text{then } \psi)$ equals $\Pr(\chi \mid \varphi \land \psi)$, which is certainly not what we want. For instance, my probability that Millie is a zealous student conditional on (6.1) is lower than it is unconditionally, but it is still higher than my conditional probability that Millie is a zealous student given that she is not going to work harder and will not pass her exam.

combining the material conditional account with the standard Bayesian position that updating proceeds via conditionalization. After all, that combination would seem to yield the possibly simplest answer to our target question, which in turn might be regarded as a point in favor of the material conditional account.

However attractive the said combination might otherwise be, it is, in view of the following observation, materially inadequate:

Fact 6.2.1 (Popper and Miller [1983]) For all φ and ψ such that $\Pr(\varphi) <$ 1 or $\Pr(\psi) > 0$ (or both), $\Pr(\varphi \mid \varphi \supset \psi) \leqslant \Pr(\varphi)$; for all φ and ψ such that $0 < \Pr(\varphi) < 1$ and $\Pr(\psi \mid \varphi) < 1$, $\Pr(\varphi \mid \varphi \supset \psi) < \Pr(\varphi)$.

It is an immediate consequence of this fact that if updating on a conditional proceeds by conditionalizing on the corresponding material conditional, then, under very general conditions, an update on a conditional always leads to a decrease in the probability of the conditional's antecedent. But consider Example 6.1.1 again. Without loss of generality, we may assume that Ann's initial degree of belief for rain tomorrow as well as her initial degree of belief for having sundowners at the Westcliff conditional on rain tomorrow have non-extreme values. It then follows from Fact 6.2.1 that if updating on conditionals goes by conditionalization on the corresponding material conditional, Ann should, after learning (6.3), lower her degree of belief for rain tomorrow – which is absurd. Hence, the view we are considering appears to have strongly counterintuitive consequences.

Naturally it would be wrong to take the foregoing as a conclusive refutation of either the material conditional account or the thesis that updating on conditionals goes by conditionalization. Even if (6.3) has the same truth conditions as the corresponding material conditional, Marian may, by asserting the sentence, convey more than just those truth conditions; that is a fundamental insight from Gricean pragmatics. And if she does, then Ann may conditionalize not on the proposition expressed by (6.3) but rather on some stronger proposition, which includes whatever an assertion of (6.3) may conversationally or conventionally implicate. That conditionalizing on the proposition expressed by (6.3) must lead Ann to lower her degree of belief for rain tomorrow (supposing, as we currently do, that that proposition is the corresponding material conditional) is compatible with her leaving the said degree of belief unaltered if the proposition she conditionalizes on is another, stronger one. Pragmatic considerations might equally help to explain why Bill's degree of belief for Sue's having passed the exam goes up after his update on (6.4).

Two points are to be noted, however. First, it is one thing to gesture at Gricean pragmatics; it is another to pinpoint the implicatures generated by Marian's assertion of (6.3) and explain in Gricean terms why Ann's degree of belief for rain tomorrow is not affected if she conditionalizes on the total content conveyed by that assertion. For instance, it may be that, as Lewis [1976] and Jackson [1979] claim, the assertion implicates that Marian's degree of belief for no sundowners at the Westcliff tomorrow is high conditional on rain tomorrow; or, perhaps in view of the results reported in Chapter 4, it might be suggested that the assertion implicates that Marian's degree of belief for no sundowners at the Westcliff tomorrow is not only high conditional on rain tomorrow, but also higher than it is unconditionally. But on neither suggestion is the extra information that is provided by the assertion of a sort to which conditionalization applies, at least not in any straightforward sense.

Second, what led us to reconsider the material conditional account, despite the known problems it faces, is that, in conjunction with the view that updating on conditionals goes by conditionalization, it promised to offer the possibly simplest answer to the question in play. However, if in addition this combined view needs an appeal to putative pragmatically generated content conveyed by asserting a conditional where it is still to be determined how this surplus content functions in the process of updating, then in the end little may be left of the view's initial alluring simplicity.

6.2.2 *Stalnaker conditionals*

It will be recalled that in Stalnaker's possible worlds semantics, a conditional is true (false) precisely if its consequent is true (false) in the closest possible world in which the conditional's antecedent is true, so that the proposition expressed by a conditional "If φ, then ψ" corresponds to the set of worlds whose closest φ-worlds are ψ-worlds. Given that the set of worlds in which $\varphi \supset \psi$ holds may be different from the set of worlds whose closest φ-worlds are ψ-worlds, conditionalizing on "If φ, then ψ," understood as a Stalnaker conditional, may yield a different new probability than conditionalizing on $\varphi \supset \psi$.

What is more, Lewis [1976:147] observed that the extra semantical structure in this model – the similarity relations between worlds – can be used to define an update operation akin to conditionalization, to wit, the imaging operation already briefly mentioned in note 45. As in the operation of conditionalizing on a proposition φ, in imaging on φ all and only $\overline{\varphi}$-worlds get "crossed out"; these worlds all come to have 0 as their new probability. However, where conditionalization determines the new probability for each φ-world by dividing its old probability by the old probability for φ (or, equivalently, by the sum of the old probabilities assigned to the φ-worlds), imaging transfers the old probability of every $\overline{\varphi}$-world to its closest φ-world; that is, each φ-world w receives as its new probability its old probability plus the old probabilities that were assigned to all $\overline{\varphi}$-worlds w', such that $f(w', \varphi) = w$ (where f is Stalnaker's selection function, as earlier defined on p. 32). It is customary to write $\mathrm{Pr}_\psi(\varphi)$ for the result of conditionalizing φ on ψ; I will use $\mathrm{Pr}(\varphi)[\psi]$ for the result of imaging φ on ψ.

Because it permits this extra update operation, the Stalnaker conditional already offers greater flexibility than the material conditional when it comes to modeling updates on conditionals. But regardless of whether one thinks conditionalization or imaging to be the update operation to go with the Stalnaker conditional, there is for this conditional no claim parallel to the one we derived from Fact 6.2.1 for the material conditional. To show this, it suffices to extend the possible worlds models depicted in Figure 2.1 earlier on and to register some basic facts about them. In Figure 2.1, the models only indicated the closest φ-world for each world. But of course "If φ, then ψ" is represented by a proposition in each of these models, and in each model the selection function will be defined for every pair of a world and the proposition representing the conditional. The models in Figure 6.1 also represent closeness relations for the conditional proposition. Supposing again that $\mathrm{Pr}(w_i) = p_i > 0$ for all $i \in \{1, \ldots, 4\}$ in models I–III, $\mathrm{Pr}(\varphi) = p_1 + p_2$ in these models. Table 6.1 then shows that imaging on "If φ, then ψ," interpreted as a Stalnaker conditional, leads to an increase in the probability for φ in model I, to a decrease in that probability in model II, and leaves the probability unaltered in model III. The table also shows that, in contrast to conditionalizing on the material conditional,

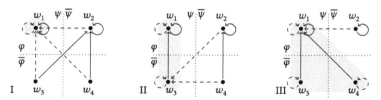

Figure 6.1 Solid arrows indicate closest A-worlds; dashed arrows indicate closest "If φ, then ψ"-worlds; gray areas indicate the Stalnakerian proposition expressed by "If φ, then ψ" in the respective models.

Table 6.1. *Probabilities assigned to φ in models I–III after imaging and conditionalizing, respectively, on the proposition expressed by "If φ, then ψ" in these models.*

	I	II	III
$\Pr(\varphi)[\text{If } \varphi, \text{ then } \psi]$	1	p_1	$p_1 + p_2$
$\Pr_{\text{If } \varphi, \text{ then } \psi}(\varphi)$	1	$\dfrac{p_1}{p_1 + p_3}$	$\dfrac{p_1}{p_1 + p_3 + p_4}$

conditionalizing on the designated proposition may lead to an increase in the probability for φ. (By making further assumptions about the values of $p_1, \ldots, p_4$, models II and III can be used to show that the probability for φ may also decrease or stay the same as a result of conditionalizing on "If φ, then ψ.")

While all this may seem to be good news, it really is not. We saw that the combination of the material conditional account with conditionalization makes the wrong predictions about Examples 6.1.1 and 6.1.2. The problem with the current account is that it makes no predictions at all about any of our examples. As far as it goes, anything may happen to Ann's, Bill's, and Cheryl's degrees of belief for the antecedent of the conditional they learn. That seems to exclude the possibility that Stalnaker's account offers an explanation of why the updates in those examples intuitively ought to have the effects they were said to have.

To see this, consider again Example 6.1.1, and in our models let φ stand for "rain tomorrow" and ψ for "no sundowners at the Westcliff." Can we rule out as not possibly representing Ann's (who, we may suppose, is pretheoretically rational) belief state all models *cum* probability assignments to the w_i's on which the probability for φ changes after imaging, respectively conditionalizing, on "If φ, then ψ"? It is not at all clear on which grounds that could be done.

Some might suggest that our intuitive verdict that the update should not affect Ann's degree of belief for the antecedent flows from the idea that Ann and Marian's not having sundowners at the Westcliff could not possibly cause, nor prohibit, rain tomorrow, and that this will be obvious to Ann. But while there are analyses of causality that build on exactly the same semantics as used by Stalnaker in his account of conditionals, they seem to offer no help with the present problem. The first and still best-known analysis of this kind is due to Lewis [1973b].[5] In this analysis, the presence

[5] Stalnaker [1984:155 f] appears sympathetic to this analysis. Since the publication of Lewis' paper, the proposal made therein has undergone several rounds of revision. See the papers in Collins, Hall,

(or absence) of any causal dependency of rain tomorrow on not having sundowners at the Westcliff hotel tomorrow is a matter of two things, to wit, first, whether rain tomorrow holds in the closest no-sundowners-at-the-Westcliff-worlds, and second, whether no rain tomorrow holds in the closest sundowners-at-the-Westcliff-worlds; both must be the case for rain tomorrow to depend causally on not having sundowners at the Westcliff. Now note that both closest ψ-world relations and closest $\overline{\psi}$-world relations can be specified in such a way in these models that, in all worlds, φ is causally independent of ψ: just let $f(w_1, \overline{\psi}) = w_2$ and $f(w_4, \psi) = w_3$. Then in no possible world is ψ causally dependent on φ: w_1 and w_2 have a closest $\overline{\psi}$-world in which φ occurs, and w_3 and w_4 have a closest ψ-world in which φ fails to occur. As a result, φ cannot possibly depend causally on ψ in these models. The final observation to be made is that the foregoing stipulation of closest ψ- and $\overline{\psi}$-worlds is consistent with the assumptions about closest φ-worlds and closest "If φ, then ψ"-worlds that were already made in models I–III. So, an appeal to causality is not going to help us in dismissing any of the above models as possible representations of Ann's belief system.

Nor is any help to be expected from the by-itself reasonable supposition that, for Ann, the antecedent and consequent of (6.3) are probabilistically independent of one another. For we can easily specify probabilities for the w_i's in models I–III such that φ and ψ do come out as being probabilistically independent; just let the worlds be equiprobable, for instance. Then models I and II give the wrong result for imaging, and models I and III give the wrong result for conditionalization.

In fact, to the best of my knowledge, nothing said by Stalnaker (or Lewis, or anyone else working on possible worlds semantics) implies either that, supposing that imaging is the update rule to go with Stalnaker's account, models I and II (in which the probability for φ changes after the update on the conditional) could not represent the belief state of a rational person in the context Ann is in; nor that, supposing conditionalization is the right update rule, models II and III could only represent such a person's belief state given assignments of probabilities to the worlds that ensure that $\Pr(\varphi) = \Pr_{\text{If } \varphi, \text{ then } \psi}(\varphi)$ (such assignments exist). In short, interpreting "If φ, then ψ" as the Stalnaker conditional and updating on it either by means of conditionalization or by means of imaging offers no guarantee that our intuitions are respected about what should happen –

---

and Paul [2004] for the current state of the art in analyses of causality along the lines of Lewis. As far as I can see, the proposed amendments are not essential to the point being made here.

or rather *not* happen – after the update on (6.3) to Ann's degree of belief for rain tomorrow. Naturally, it cannot be excluded that some of these models – and perhaps indeed all on which Ann's degree of belief in rain tomorrow changes as an effect of learning (6.3) – are to be ruled out on the basis of rationality constraints that I am presently overlooking, perhaps ones still to be uncovered, or at least still to be related to possible worlds semantics as a tool for modeling epistemic states.[6] It is left as a challenge to those attracted to the view considered here to point out such additional constraints.

6.2.3 *Adams conditioning and beyond*

Bradley [2005:351] presents the following rule – which he calls "Adams conditioning" – for updating one's degrees of belief in response to an induced change in a conditional degree of belief:

Definition 6.2.1 *Let φ and ψ be propositions such that, on one's initial degrees-of-belief function Pr, it holds that $0 < \Pr(\psi \mid \varphi) < 1$, and suppose that one is caused to change one's degree of belief in ψ conditional on φ from $\Pr(\psi \mid \varphi)$ to $\Pr^*(\psi \mid \varphi)$. Then one updates by Adams conditioning on this change iff, for all propositions χ,*

$$\Pr^*(\chi) \ = \ \Pr(\varphi \wedge \psi \wedge \chi) \frac{\Pr^*(\psi \mid \varphi)}{\Pr(\psi \mid \varphi)} + \Pr(\varphi \wedge \overline{\psi} \wedge \chi) \frac{\Pr^*(\overline{\psi} \mid \varphi)}{\Pr(\overline{\psi} \mid \varphi)} + \Pr(\overline{\varphi} \wedge \chi).$$

While Adams conditioning is not in itself a rule for updating on conditionals, but only for updating on shifts in one's conditional degrees of belief, in Douven and Romeijn [2011] it is argued that, with one minor addition, Adams conditioning does yield an update rule for conditionals. The addition is the assumption that, whenever we learn a conditional "If φ, then ψ," we set our degree of belief for ψ given φ equal to 1. Given this assumed connection between learning conditionals and shifts in conditional probabilities, an update by Adams conditioning on "If φ, then ψ" yields, for all χ,

(6.1) $\qquad \Pr^*(\chi) \ = \ \Pr(\chi \mid \overline{\varphi}) \Pr(\overline{\varphi}) + \Pr(\chi \mid \varphi \wedge \psi) \Pr(\varphi).$

---

[6] My own suggestion, to be elaborated in the next section, is that the intuitions about Example 6.1.1 (as well as those about the other examples) hinge on explanatory considerations. But the only theories of explanation I know of that analyze explanation in terms of the possible worlds models of Stalnaker's semantics all hold that to explain is to provide causal information, where this notion is then understood as explicated in the text above (see, e.g., Lewis [1986]). And, as was seen, there is little hope that such information might enable us to dismiss some of the models as possible representations of Ann's belief state.

As shown in Douven and Romeijn's paper, (6.1) is of special interest because it provides a solution to van Fraassen's [1981] Judy Benjamin problem that fulfills all intuitive desiderata associated with the case. In particular, the Judy Benjamin problem describes a case in which, pre-analytically, the learning of a given conditional should have no effect on the learner's degree of belief for the antecedent of that conditional, just as in Example 6.1.1. And this is guaranteed by Adams conditioning applied in the way proposed by Douven and Romeijn, for we have the following as an instance of (6.1):

$$\mathrm{Pr}^*(\varphi) = \mathrm{Pr}(\varphi \mid \overline{\varphi})\,\mathrm{Pr}(\overline{\varphi}) \; + \; \mathrm{Pr}(\varphi \mid \varphi \wedge \psi)\,\mathrm{Pr}(\varphi)$$
$$= 0 \times \mathrm{Pr}(\overline{\varphi}) \; + \; 1 \times \mathrm{Pr}(\varphi)$$
$$= \mathrm{Pr}(\varphi).$$

It was previously believed that no Bayesian solution to the Judy Benjamin problem exists that has this property.[7]

However, this strength of the proposal is at the same time a drawback if the goal is to have an even moderately general Bayesian account of updating on conditionals. For even though it may be that often the learning of a conditional is irrelevant to the probability we assign to its antecedent – as in the Judy Benjamin case and in Example 6.1.1 – we know from Section 6.1 that this does not hold generally. Specifically, Bill's and Cheryl's responses in Examples 6.1.2 and 6.1.3, respectively, seem perfectly in order from an intuitive viewpoint. Hence, application of (6.1) would yield the wrong result in both cases.

Douven and Romeijn are aware of this problem and propose a general update rule for conditionals. The rule borrows from the belief revision literature the idea that propositions may be entrenched in our belief system to varying degrees. In Douven and Romeijn's proposal, these degrees of entrenchment are represented by weights and determine what will happen to our degrees of belief when we learn a conditional. Formally, where $\{\varphi_1, \varphi_2, \varphi_3, \ldots\}$ are the strongest consistent propositions in the algebra on which our degrees-of-belief function is defined, and where $w_i \in \mathbb{R}^+ \cup \{\omega\}$ is the weight assigned to proposition φ_i, the rule dictates that we minimize the following function:

---

[7] In particular, various so-called distance minimization rules, like the rule of relative entropy minimization already mentioned in note 2, give the wrong answer in the Judy Benjamin case. See on this Douven and Romeijn [2011]; also Joyce [1999:215 ff]. Douven and Romeijn [2011] present a distance minimization rule that does give the right answer in the Judy Benjamin case, but that rule has the same limitation as Adams conditioning (see below).

$$\mathrm{EE}(\mathrm{Pr}, \mathrm{Pr}^*) \;\; = \;\; \sum_i w_i \left(\sqrt{\mathrm{Pr}^*(\varphi_i)} - \sqrt{\mathrm{Pr}(\varphi_i)} \right)^2.$$

How learning a conditional affects our degrees of belief depends on the values of the weights that we assign to the φ_i's. The higher the weight assigned to a proposition – the stronger the proposition is epistemically entrenched, that is – the higher the cost (so to speak) incurred by changing the degree of belief for that proposition. In this way we can, for instance, make changing the degree of belief for the antecedent of a given conditional so costly that learning the conditional will not affect that degree of belief.

Douven and Romeijn's paper illustrates by means of numerical examples the great flexibility that the rule of EE minimization affords when it comes to modeling updates, whether on conditional or on non-conditional information. As Douven and Romeijn admit, however, they have nothing to say about where the weights their rule presupposes come from, nor about how they are related to a person's degrees of belief, nor about how they change over time (as one suspects they may do). This is a problem already in itself, but it is certainly a problem for our present purposes. For recall that we conceive of the current project as at least partly an empirical one. We would like to come up with a proposal that, for starters, gets the data from Examples 6.1.1–6.1.3 right, and that at a later stage may be subjected to more serious testing. And EE minimization manifestly is not such a proposal. Even if one can operationalize the relevant notion of weight – and it is by no means obvious that one can – then that is still of little help in the absence of a systematic account of how these weights change in light of new information one receives. Suppose we have determined both the weights and the degrees of belief a person presently assigns to the strongest consistent propositions in the algebra on which his or her degrees-of-belief function is defined. Further suppose that we are about to offer this person new conditional information. On this basis, and assuming the EE rule, can we predict how learning that information will impact his or her degrees of belief? Not in the absence of some story about how (if at all) that same learning event will influence the weights themselves. If, in that event, anything may happen to these weights, then anything may happen to the person's degrees of belief.

So, from an empirical point of view, the situation looks as follows: The thesis that updating on a conditional goes by conditionalizing on the corresponding material conditional makes clear, but also clearly false, predictions. That already follows from considering Examples 6.1.1 and 6.1.2; there is no point in subjecting this thesis to further empirical testing.

On the other hand, clear predictions are made neither by the thesis that updating on a conditional goes by conditionalizing on the corresponding Stalnaker conditional, nor by the thesis that such updating goes by imaging on that conditional; we would thus not know how to subject these to empirical testing, nor are they able to explain our intuitions about the examples from Section 6.1. The same holds for Douven and Romeijn's general rule of EE minimization. Until now, the only proposal that has verifiable consequences that are not obviously false is the variant of Adams conditioning proposed by Douven and Romeijn, but that rule, we saw, has only limited applicability. Moreover, it takes for granted, rather than attempts to explain, our intuitions about cases like those presented in the examples. The next section puts forward a model of updating on conditional information that is general, empirically verifiable, and supported by the examples considered so far.

6.3 Updating on conditionals as explanatory reasoning

Douven and Romeijn make no attempt to characterize the circumstances under which it would be reasonable to opt for their extension of Adams conditioning. The rule is explicitly said to apply if, *intuitively*, one's degree of belief for the antecedent of a conditional should not be affected by learning that conditional. To achieve a deeper understanding of what is involved in updating on conditionals, and to find out what fuels the intuitions assumed by Douven and Romeijn's rule, we start by contrasting Examples 6.1.1 and 6.1.2 (p. 152) with each other. Reflection on Example 6.1.2 strongly suggests that some explanatory reasoning is going on in this case. I submit that what makes Bill's response reasonable is that in light of (6.4), which he learned from Tom, Sue's having passed the exam would, if true, *explain* why she bought the skiing outfit; that makes her having passed the exam more credible. No such reasoning is going on, or would even seem to make sense, in Example 6.1.1. It is not as though Ann's learning (6.3) suddenly makes the antecedent of this sentence appear to be a good explanation for Ann's and Marian's not having sundowners at the Westcliff tomorrow. How could it, given that the latter is not an explanandum to begin with (it is not something known or believed to be the case)? Indeed, one would be hard pressed to designate anything in that example as an explanandum that the antecedent of (6.3) might be able to explain.

In a number of steps, I will try to make the suggestion look more plausible that explanation may figure in updating on conditionals, and will try to turn it into something worthy of the name "hypothesis." A first bit of additional support comes from considering what happens when we add a rival potential explanation to the story of Example 6.1.2:

Example 6.3.1 Suppose everything is as in Example 6.1.2, except that now Bill knows that Sue is going on a skiing vacation with some friends in five months. Then when Tom asserts (6.4), Bill does come to find it a bit more likely that Sue passed the exam, though to a lesser extent than in the original example. ◆

In this case, too, Bill's response seems utterly reasonable. That Sue passed the exam would still explain his earlier observation, and would presumably explain somewhat better why she bought the outfit now than does the hypothesis that, given that she will need a skiing outfit in five months anyway, Sue thought she might as well buy one right away. Still, the presence of this latter potential explanation, which in regard of explanatory goodness is not too far behind the former, mitigates the effect that learning (6.4) has on Bill's degree of belief for Sue's having passed the exam. By varying a bit the effect that learning (6.4) has on the explanatory status of that conditional's antecedent, we also vary a bit the expected effect this event has on Bill's degree of belief for the antecedent; this is a further indication that explanatory considerations can have a role in updates on conditionals.

Now consider again Example 6.1.3. At first blush, Cheryl's response might seem to have nothing to do with explanatory reasoning, and might rather be taken as an instance of a sort of probabilistic Modus Tollens. The argument for this claim would be along the following lines. We saw that Douven and Romeijn, as part of their adaptation of Bradley's Adams conditioning, assumed that learning a conditional leads the learner to set his or her degree of belief for the conditional's consequent given its antecedent equal to 1. Some might find this assumption too strong, but most would presumably agree that the designated conditional degree of belief will at least be *high* as a result of learning the conditional. For now, let us say that setting one's degree of belief for the consequent of a conditional given its antecedent to a value at least close to 1 is the first step in the process of updating on that conditional, whatever the further details of this process. Then next note the following:

Fact 6.3.1 Let $\Pr(\psi \mid \varphi) \approx 1$. Then $\Pr(\psi) \gtrsim \Pr(\varphi)$.[8]

---

[8] *Proof:* Suppose the condition holds. Then $\Pr(\varphi \wedge \psi) \approx \Pr(\varphi)$. So, given that $\Pr(\psi) \geqslant \Pr(\varphi \wedge \psi)$, it holds that $\Pr(\psi) \gtrsim \Pr(\varphi)$.

This might seem to be all we need to explain what is going on in Example 6.1.3. In particular – it might be said – upon learning (6.5), Cheryl sets her conditional degree of belief for Kevin's parents throwing a garden party given that Kevin passed the driving test to some value close to 1. But, given that in view of the spading it is evident to her that Kevin's parents probably will not give a garden party any time soon, she must, on account of Fact 6.3.1, make sure that her degree of belief for Kevin's having passed the test is low, too. This effectively means that she must lower her degree of belief for that proposition, given that – we said – her prior probability for Kevin's having passed the driving test was around .5 (and thus not low).

Still, a comparison with Example 6.1.1 indicates that this cannot be all there is to Example 6.1.3. For why is it that Cheryl's degree of belief for the antecedent of (6.5) goes down after learning the conditional while Ann's degree of belief for the antecedent of (6.3) stays the same after learning that conditional? Fact 6.3.1, which was invoked for explaining the former, applies quite generally, and thus also in the case of Example 6.1.1. Yet in that case we take it to imply that Ann will raise her degree of belief for the consequent of the conditional she learns rather than lower her degree of belief for its antecedent. It is hard to see how this difference between the two examples could be explained in purely probabilistic terms, given that, as far as the stories go, we are free to assume that the initial probabilities that appear relevant here (if any do) are all equal. That is to say, where Pr^A denotes Ann's degrees-of-belief function immediately before Ann's learning of (6.3), and Pr^C denotes Cheryl's degrees-of-belief function immediately before Cheryl's learning of (6.5), we may have all of the following: (i) $Pr^A(\text{rain}) = Pr^C(\text{pass})$; (ii) $Pr^A(\text{no sundowners}) = Pr^C(\text{garden party})$; (iii) $Pr^A(\text{no sundowners} \mid \text{rain}) = Pr^C(\text{garden party} \mid \text{pass})$; (iv) $Pr^A(\text{rain} \mid \text{no sundowners}) = Pr^C(\text{pass} \mid \text{garden party})$.

On the other hand, when we attend to the question of what explanatory reasoning might be going on in the two cases, we can discern a clear difference between them. In Example 6.1.1, we said, no such reasoning seems involved. But consider that, in Example 6.1.3, by learning (6.5), the negation of the antecedent of this conditional comes to be part of the best explanation for why Kevin's parents have now started spading their garden. Once Cheryl has learned the conditional, no explanation will appear even remotely satisfactory to her if it does not mention that Kevin failed the test. Just pointing at the fact that, say, Kevin's parents were tired of the rose beds and want to plant birch trees would for Cheryl still raise the question, "But why did they start spading *now*, given that they intend to throw a garden party if Kevin passed the test?" That Kevin's having failed would be part of the best explanation of something Cheryl knows to be the case makes that hypothesis more credible to her, and hence makes its negation – the antecedent of (6.5) – less credible, in line with our pretheoretical verdict about the case.[9]

The above proposal, while so far based on nothing but a handful of examples, finds theoretical backing in a recent discussion in the philosophy journals concerning the role of explanatory considerations. According to so-called explanationists, these considerations have confirmation-theoretic import. More exactly, in their view the fact that a hypothesis explains the available evidence better than do any rival hypotheses is itself evidence for that hypothesis, making that hypothesis acceptable (according to some authors), or at least highly credible (according to others), or more credible than its competitors (according to still others). A more general suggestion is that the credibilities assigned to competing hypotheses should reflect the explanatory statuses of those hypotheses, so that, all else being equal, one hypothesis should be more credible than another if the former is a better explanation of the data than the latter (whether or not the former is the best explanation). While it was traditionally thought that, however it is fleshed out exactly, the idea that explanation bears on confirmation is at odds with Bayesian confirmation theory, over the past years a number of authors have argued that explanation does play a role in our probabilistic reasoning, and that it does so, or at least may do so, to our benefit.[10] In fact, those authors have urged that explanatory considerations may come into play in probabilistic reasoning at various junctures and in a variety of ways.

The way that is most pertinent to the present topic concerns the heuristic value of explanation, as highlighted by Okasha [2000], McGrew [2003], and Lipton [2004, Ch. 7]. These authors suggest that explanatory considerations can serve as a heuristic to determine, even if only roughly, probabilities in cases where we would otherwise be clueless and could do no better than guessing. More specifically, their thought is that, where we are given a number of rival hypotheses, $H_1, \ldots, H_n$, but initially have no idea which priors to assign to each, finding that H_i is a better explanation

---

9 Note that the supposition that Kevin failed may be included in the best explanation of why his parents have started spading their garden, regardless of whether that supposition is true. It is generally acknowledged that being the best explanation does not require truth (and may therefore not be an unfailing mark of truth); see Douven [2002b] and [2011c, Sect. 3] for more on the relationship between best explanation and truth.

10 See, e.g., Okasha [2000], McGrew [2003], Lipton [2004, Ch. 7], Weisberg [2009], Douven [2013a], and Douven and Wenmackers [2015].

for the evidence at hand than H_j may, and often will, give us reason to assign a prior to H_i that is higher than the prior we assign to H_j.[11,12]

This suggestion is in the first instance meant to address the widely recognized fact that, standard Bayesian thinking to the contrary notwithstanding, we are not always able to assign a prior probability to every hypothesis that is relevant in a given context, nor can we always say how probable a particular piece of evidence is conditional on a given hypothesis – at least, we cannot always do so if what we say is intended to express more than a mere guess. In such situations, consideration of the explanatory power of a hypothesis may come to the rescue, or in any event may offer some help in figuring out – if only within certain bounds perhaps – what probability or probabilities to assign. But the idea that explanation has an epistemic role to play may have broader application. As Lipton [2004:108] notes, "explanatory considerations may be ... our way of handling certain aspects of inference that conditionalizing does not address." And while none of the above authors discuss the issue of updating on conditionals, it has emerged from the previous section that this issue may be another instance of an aspect of inference that is not addressed by conditionalization.

Just as the explanatory status of a hypothesis may go up due to things we learn, that status may also go down. This may happen for various reasons, for instance, because the explanatory status of a contrary hypothesis goes up – as in Example 6.1.3, where the negation of (6.5)'s antecedent comes to be part of the best explanation of Cheryl's evidence – or because one's earlier reasons for deeming a hypothesis to be a good explanation are undermined. In these terms, our examples suggest the following

---

[11] It might be thought that this proposal is inconsistent with the so-called Principle of Indifference, according to which we ought to assign each H_i the same prior, barring reasons to the contrary. But, first, explanationists may hold that explanatory considerations constitute precisely the "reasons to the contrary" the principle makes allowance for. Second, even if the proposal went against the Principle of Indifference, this would be of little significance, given that this principle is itself of doubtful standing; see, e.g., Gillies [2000, Ch. 3].

[12] For present purposes, it will do to rely on an informal understanding of the notion of one explanation being better than another. I also do not know of any satisfactory formal definition of this notion. Hintikka [1968] proposes that, given evidence E and competing hypotheses $H_1, \ldots, H_n$, hypothesis H_i is a better explanation of E than H_j iff $\Pr(E \mid H_i) > \Pr(E \mid H_j)$; in particular, the best explanation is the one which maximizes the likelihood of that evidence. But this proposal is useless if the evidence is already in, for if $\Pr(E) = 1$, then also $\Pr(E \mid H) = 1$, for all H such that $\Pr(H) > 0$. And typically the evidence *is* in when we invoke explanatory reasoning. More generally, the fact that probability is an intensional notion – sentences that express the same proposition ought to receive the same probability, according to probability theory – whereas explanation is hyperintensional – the way a proposition is presented to us may matter to its capacity to explain (cf. Douven [2005, Sect. 5]) – should make us skeptical of any attempt to define explanation in purely probabilistic terms.

hypothesis: If, upon learning a conditional, the explanatory status of its antecedent goes *up*, then this will lead to an *in*crease of the degree of belief for the antecedent. If, on the other hand, the antecedent's explanatory status goes *down* due to the learning event, then that will be accompanied by a *de*crease of the degree of belief for the antecedent. What is more, supposing some pretheoretically adequate measure of explanatory goodness, Examples 6.1.2 and 6.3.1 together suggest a further, quantitative hypothesis, namely, that the extent to which the explanatory status of a conditional's antecedent goes up (down) as a result of learning the conditional – how *much* better (worse) the antecedent comes to appear *qua* explanation – correlates with the extent to which the learner's degree of belief for the antecedent increases (decreases).[13]

Insofar as it is correct, the first hypothesis already shows that updating on conditionals is markedly different from updating on non-conditional information, at least for some conditionals. Moreover, if explanatory considerations may figure in some updates on conditionals, then that clearly backs those theorists who have been urging a rapprochement between Bayesian and explanatory reasoning. More generally, it would show the orthodox Bayesian doctrine to be seriously incomplete.

In the remainder of this chapter, I should like to consider the prospects for turning the "ifs" in the above qualitative hypothesis into "iffs." If the hypothesis can thus be strengthened, then it can be claimed that what underlies our intuition that, in Example 6.1.1, Ann's learning (6.3) should not affect her degree of belief for the antecedent of that sentence is the fact that this learning event does not alter the antecedent's explanatory status. It would also give an explication of the conditions under which the extension of Adams conditioning proposed by Douven and Romeijn applies, namely, whenever learning a conditional does not induce a change in the explanatory status of the conditional's antecedent. In other words, the question is whether or not the flowchart model depicted in Figure 6.2 could count as a general model of updating on conditionals. (That is to say, given that, as mentioned in Section 1.2, this book is concerned only with simple normal indicative conditionals, the question is whether the model of Figure 6.2 holds generally for *such* conditionals.)

---

[13] Hintikka's explication of the notion of best explanation, cited in note 12, naturally suggests a formal measure of explanatory goodness of hypothesis H in light of evidence E, to wit, $\Pr(E \mid H) - \Pr(E \mid \overline{H})$ or, more generally, $\Pr(E \mid H) - \sum_{i=1}^{n} \Pr(E \mid H_i)$, where the set of hypotheses $\{H, H_1, \ldots, H_n\}$ partitions logical space. See Schupbach [2011] and Douven and Schupbach [2015a] for other probabilistic measures of explanatory goodness. However, all these measures appear to face the same problem that we said Hintikka's proposal.

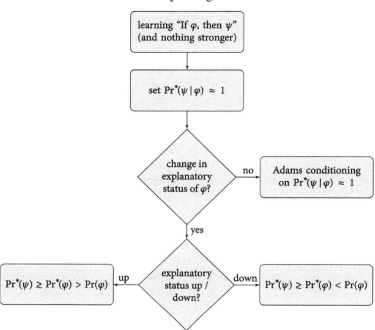

Figure 6.2 A flowchart representation of the model of updating on conditionals. Pr and Pr* are the degrees-of-belief functions before and after learning "If φ, then ψ," respectively.

Here is an example that immediately seems to suggest a negative answer:

Example 6.3.2 Two bags contain 100 balls each. Jimmy knows that one of the bags contains 90 white balls and 10 black balls, with half of the black balls having a yellow dot on them, while the other bag contains 10 white balls and 90 black balls, with all of the latter having a yellow dot on them. This is all Jimmy knows about the bags. Carol is now going to pick a ball from one of these bags. Jimmy is asked how likely he thinks it is that Carol is going to pick a black ball. He reckons that, given that it is equally likely that Carol will choose from the one bag as that she will choose from the other, the probability that the ball will be black is $(.5)(.1) + (.5)(.9) = .5$. After Carol has chosen a bag from which to pick a ball, Jimmy's friend Frank, who Jimmy knows to be privy to the content of each of the bags, tells Jimmy the following:

(6.6)   If Carol draws a black ball, it will have a yellow dot on it.

This causes Jimmy to raise his degree of belief that Carol is going to draw a black ball to .9.   ◆

After Jimmy has come to learn (6.6), he changes his degree of belief for its antecedent. Yet, it may be held, in this context learning (6.6) can hardly be taken to change the explanatory status of its antecedent. And so, it would appear, the example blocks the envisioned strengthening of our proposal. On closer inspection, however, this conclusion seems rash.

At the beginning of this book, it was seen that sometimes we use non-conditional sentences – like sentences (1.2a)–(1.2c) – to express conditional thoughts.[14] Conversely, we sometimes use conditional sentences without thereby expressing anything conditional. For instance, as remarked earlier, we use "If you're hungry, there are biscuits on the table" to indicate that there are biscuits on the table and that the addressee should feel free to take some. The above example shows that this non-conditional use of conditionals is not limited to such special conditionals. For while (6.6) would seem to be a perfectly ordinary conditional, given the details of the situation, and independently of the exact semantics of conditionals, (6.6) simply informs Jimmy that Carol is going to draw a ball from the bag with 90 black balls and 10 white balls. And that Carol is facing the designated bag is a proposition on which Jimmy can simply conditionalize. If he does, this should result in his believing to a degree of .9 that Carol is going to draw a black ball, precisely as happens in the example.

So, for the present, in the absence of any clear counterexamples, we may assume that the model of Figure 6.2 generally holds for the class of (simple normal indicative) conditionals. Just as important as the issue of generality is the fact that our model has clear empirical content, given that we know how to operationalize degrees of belief, and given that recent experimental studies on the role of explanation in reasoning show that also the notion of explanation can be operationalized.[15] One straightforward between-participants experiment suggested by the model asks one group of participants to rate the explanatory status of a proposition φ in the light of background knowledge provided by a vignette; asks a second group to rate that same status in an extension of the vignette in which a conditional "If φ, then ψ" has been learned, for some well-chosen proposition ψ; asks a third group to rate the probability of φ in the original vignette; and asks a fourth group to rate the probability of φ in the extended vignette. If this

---

[14] See also Bhatt and Pancheva [2006]. Lewis [1973a:4] makes the point for subjunctive conditionals.

[15] For experimental work on explanation, see, among others, Koehler [1991], Brem and Rips [2000], Lombrozo [2007], Koslowski et al. [2008], and Douven and Schupbach [2015a], [2015b].

is done for sufficiently many and sufficiently varied vignette–conditional pairs, the presence (or absence) of a correlation between the two variables would be evidence for (against) our model, and even for (against) a quantitative version of it. Naturally, the consequences of Fact 6.3.1, which have been incorporated in the flowchart representation of the model, provide further opportunities for empirical testing.

Even if it is general, the model presented here may still be only part of the story to be told about updating on conditionals, to be complemented by a more specific account of exactly how explanatory considerations guide the process of revising our degrees of belief. On the other hand, given that such explanatory considerations may lean heavily on our creativity and imagination, a very precise account of updating on conditionals may not be in the offing – let alone a rule which permits us to calculate, for any proposition and any conditional, what our degree of belief in the proposition should be after the learning of the conditional. Be this as it may, I would be content if the foregoing were at least a first step toward development of a comprehensive account and, as such, inspired further work about updating on conditional information, ideally from both philosophers and psychologists.

CHAPTER 7

Progress?

I am not under the illusion that I have been able to settle once and for all any of the questions that were listed at the beginning of this book. But nothing of that order was promised or could have reasonably been expected. At the same time, I do believe that some progress has been made in becoming clearer on a number of those questions.

Until very recently, the epistemology of conditionals was, for the most part, a tale of two theses: Stalnaker's Hypothesis (SH) and Adams' Thesis (AT). That the former is false and that the latter is true seemed to be the only two certainties in a sea of uncertainties and controversies. Neither "certainty" was backed by empirical evidence, and neither seemed to need such backing: the falsity of SH seemed to follow from indubitable formal results, and the truth of AT seemed a matter of course. It is more than ironic that, as we saw in Chapters 3 and 4, recent empirical results suggest that philosophers have gotten things wrong with respect to both claims: SH has been experimentally confirmed several times over,[1] and in one experiment AT was refuted (which is refutation enough).

More specifically, and as explained in Chapter 3, whereas the data apparently in favor of SH *might* betray a systematic error in how people judge the probabilities of conditionals, or in how they determine conditional probabilities, or in both, further empirical research was seen to support a more charitable interpretation of those data, one that seeks fault rather with an assumption underlying the formal results that had been thought to undermine SH. Still more specifically, the presented results on the generalized version of SH lend credibility to a thesis that thus far many had considered to be no more than an interesting theoretical possibility, to wit, that the interpretation of the conditional-forming operator may vary from one belief state to another. Thus, the answer to the question of what the probabilities of conditionals are may be as simple as was believed before

---

[1] Though see again the cautionary footnote 7 of Chapter 3.

Lewis presented his triviality results: probabilities of conditionals equal conditional probabilities.

In Chapter 4, it was seen that, while experimental studies showed AT to be false, these same studies showed there to be a high correlation between the degrees to which people judge conditionals to be acceptable and their conditional probabilities. On the other hand, when the empirical results were split out for different types of conditionals, the picture was messier, and it may become messier still if more types of conditionals are taken into account. So, whereas the issue of the probabilities of conditionals may be simpler than was generally believed, the issue of the degrees of acceptability of conditionals appears to be more complicated than was generally believed. But at least we now have an account of degrees of acceptability that rests on a solid footing.

In addition, we now have proposals about the categorical acceptability conditions of indicative and of concessive conditionals that were also seen to enjoy empirical support. Both proposals assign a critical role to the notion of evidential relevance, which thus far had been missing from the literature. Perhaps the presence of this notion in the designated accounts is enough already on its own to explain why we generally and strongly intuit that the assertion of a conditional conveys the existence of a link between its antecedent and consequent. However, nothing said in the foregoing preempts the question of whether the intuition has a deeper explanation, rooted perhaps in the semantics of conditionals – for instance, in the holding of an inferential connection between antecedent and consequent, as was suggested as a possibility – which might hold the real key to explaining why the notion of evidential support figures prominently in the acceptability conditions of conditionals.

Assuming the account of the categorical acceptability of conditionals defended in Chapter 4, Chapter 5 set out to investigate the question of which principles of conditional reasoning preserve acceptability and which do not. The main answer was given by a theorem proved here. It was shown to follow from this theorem that a number of principles generally deemed plausible are in fact invalid – in the sense of not guaranteeing the preservation of acceptability. However, we were able to explain away the seeming plausibility of some of the principles that were proven to be invalid. This was done by introducing the notion of degree of validity. It was hypothesized that people are more prone to mistake an invalid principle for a valid one, the higher the degree of validity of the principle. Two different ways of operationalizing the notion of degree of validity were proposed, each of which gives clear empirical content to the hypothesis. The hypothesis is ready to be tested, but in view of some methodological issues raised, testing it seems a task better left to seasoned experimentalists.

Finally, Chapter 6 offered a model of updating on conditionals that allows us to make predictions – mostly qualitative – about how learning a conditional will impact some of the learner's degrees of belief. The model presented there is simple and receives some initial empirical support from the fact that it is in agreement with our intuitions about a number of hypothetical cases. Naturally, it will have to prove its mettle in more extensive testing. To the extent that further data confirm the adequacy of the model, we have identified explanation as a key factor operative in the revision of our beliefs when we come to learn conditional information. And to the extent that orthodox Bayesians are reluctant to make room for this factor in their epistemology, that epistemology has been shown to be incomplete. Indeed, it was seen that the proposal dovetails nicely with recent calls for a more liberal Bayesian epistemology that acknowledges the epistemic relevance of explanatory reasoning.

On a more general level, I hope that this book helps make a case for combining formal work with empirical research on conditionals and, relatedly, for a systematic and sustained collaboration between philosophers and experimental psychologists. Such collaboration seems essential to me for conducting the studies on inferential principles and updating that were outlined in earlier chapters, but also in extending the work on probability and acceptability to important types of conditionals not covered here, most notably nested conditionals and counterfactuals. Still more generally, it was said that philosophers have of late become less enthusiastic about the purely intuition-driven approach that has dominated much of traditional philosophy. The work on AT reported in Chapter 4, which showed that an almost universally shared intuition about the acceptability of conditionals does not withstand empirical scrutiny, provides a reason, quite on its own, for taking a guarded attitude vis-à-vis the designated approach.

Most importantly, key questions pertaining to the semantics of conditionals are still wide open. But with regard to these questions, too, I believe that *some* progress has been made, in two respects. First, we had a critical look at the four different arguments that Bennett lists in his book as grounds for holding that conditionals do not express propositions, and we were able to discharge each of them. That came with a price tag: it must be admitted that *if* conditionals express propositions, then which propositions they express is relative to the speaker's (or thinker's) belief state. But it was mentioned that, in view of recent developments in the philosophy of language, this would not make the semantics of conditionals particularly eccentric. In short, when it comes to semantics of conditionals, there are more options on the table than has been believed by many since the publication of Lewis' triviality arguments.

Second, we have more to go on in choosing among the various options. The work so far undertaken on the epistemology of conditionals has led to a clearer grasp of the probabilities and the graded and categorical accept-ability conditions for conditionals as well as to a batch of new empirical data. Both may help us in our search for the proper semantics of condition-als. A search typically has a greater chance of success if one knows what one is looking for. And what we should be looking for is a semantics that can help explain why people tend to assign to conditionals probabilities that are equal to the probabilities they assign to these conditionals' consequents given their antecedents, that can help explain why people tend to deem a conditional acceptable only if the antecedent is evidence for the conse-quent, and why people seem to update on conditionals at least partly on the basis of explanatory considerations.

Appendices

Proof of Theorem 5.2.1

This appendix presents the proof of

Theorem 5.2.1 *All and only the following principles in Table 5.1 are valid: ANT, BR1, (the principal part of) CNC, MP, MOD, (the principal part of) RCE, RCEA, RCEC, (the principal part of) REF, WAND, and XOR.*

The proof will consist of two parts, the first part proving the validity of ANT, BR1, CNC, MP, MOD, RCE, RCEA, RCEC, REF, WAND, and XOR, and the second proving the invalidity of the remaining principles. Recall that the acceptability of conditionals is supposed to be governed by EST and that of non-conditional propositions by LT. Also recall that $\theta \geqslant .5$. Furthermore, CSO, RCEA, and RCEC have a conclusion to the effect that two conditionals are materially equivalent. EST is silent on the acceptability conditions of embedded conditionals, but, as stated in Section 5.2, it is natural to assume that it is acceptable that two conditionals are materially equivalent iff the acceptability of the one materially implies the acceptability of the other. As pointed out in the same section, analogous remarks apply to the negated conditional that occurs as a premise of CV, to the disjunctive conclusions of CEM, NR, and ROR, and to the conjunctive conclusions of CM and SDA. Finally, it will be assumed with Adams [1966], [1986] that conditionals with probability 0 antecedents have a corresponding conditional probability of 1.

Proof, part 1. ANT is valid in view of the fact that $\Pr(\varphi \wedge \varphi \wedge \psi) = \Pr(\varphi \wedge \psi)$. Both BR1 and MOD hold trivially on our proposal, given that their premises – of the form "If φ or not φ, then ψ" for BR1 and "If not φ, then φ" for MOD – are never acceptable. For BR1 this is straightforward. For MOD, suppose that $\Pr(\varphi) < 1$. Then $\Pr(\varphi \mid \overline{\varphi}) = 0$. Thus, "If not φ, then φ" is not acceptable in this case. Now suppose that $\Pr(\varphi) = 1$. Then, in view of the stipulation mentioned above, $\Pr(\varphi \mid \overline{\varphi}) = 1$, but we still do not have that $\Pr(\varphi \mid \overline{\varphi}) > \Pr(\varphi)$. So, in neither case is "If not φ, then φ" acceptable. CNC is valid provided we exclude conditionals with probability 0 antecedents. If $\Pr(\varphi) = 0$, then, in view of the same stipulation, $\Pr(\psi \mid \varphi) = \Pr(\overline{\psi} \mid \varphi) = 1$. And if $0 < \Pr(\psi) < 1$, then the evidential support condition will also be fulfilled for both "If φ, then ψ" and "If φ, then not ψ." Then $\bot$ should be acceptable, which cannot be right. However, if we exclude conditionals with probability 0 antecedents, the principle is valid, given that $\theta \geqslant .5$, which ensures that, if $\Pr(\varphi) \neq 0$, then at most one of $\Pr(\psi \mid \varphi)$ and $\Pr(\overline{\psi} \mid \varphi)$ can be greater than θ. Furthermore, on our proposal "If φ, then φ" comes out as acceptable provided $\Pr(\varphi) \neq 1$. (This also holds if $\Pr(\varphi) = 0$, supposing again the stipulation concerning conditional probabilities with probability 0 antecedents.) Hence, REF is valid. The principles RCE, RCEA, and RCEC all hold in virtue of the fact that probability theory respects logic and the further fact that together LT and EST make acceptability strictly a matter of probabilities, although RCE requires as a restriction that the probability of the consequent of the material and the indicative conditional be unequal to 1. After all, if $\vdash \varphi \supset \psi$, then $\Pr(\varphi \wedge \overline{\psi}) = 0$, so $\Pr(\varphi \wedge \psi) = \Pr(\varphi)$, and hence $\Pr(\psi \mid \varphi) = 1$, which exceeds θ and which also exceeds $\Pr(\psi)$, given the mentioned restriction. (This also presupposes the earlier stipulation.) RCEA and RCEC are unrestrictedly valid, given that probability theory does not distinguish between logically equivalent propositions.

The proofs that MP, XOR, and WAND are valid are slightly less straightforward. As for MP, note that "If not φ, then ψ" is acceptable only if $\Pr(\psi \mid \overline{\varphi}) > \theta$. But then $\overline{\varphi} \supset \psi$ is acceptable as well, in virtue of the fact that $\Pr(\varphi \vee \psi) \geqslant \Pr(\psi \mid \overline{\varphi})$. To see this, note that

$$\Pr(\varphi \vee \psi) \;=\; \frac{\Pr(\varphi \wedge \psi) + \Pr(\varphi \wedge \overline{\psi}) + \Pr(\overline{\varphi} \wedge \psi)}{\Pr(\varphi \wedge \psi) + \Pr(\varphi \wedge \overline{\psi}) + \Pr(\overline{\varphi} \wedge \psi) + \Pr(\overline{\varphi} + \overline{\psi})}$$

and

$$\Pr(\psi \mid \overline{\varphi}) \;=\; \frac{\Pr(\overline{\varphi} \wedge \psi)}{\Pr(\overline{\varphi} \wedge \psi) + \Pr(\overline{\varphi} \wedge \overline{\psi}))}.$$

To show that $\Pr(\varphi \vee \psi) \geqslant \Pr(\psi \mid \overline{\varphi})$, we use the following abbreviations: $\Pr(\varphi \wedge \psi) =: a$; $\Pr(\varphi \wedge \overline{\psi}) =: b$; $\Pr(\overline{\varphi} \wedge \psi) =: c$; and $\Pr(\overline{\varphi} \wedge \overline{\psi}) =: d$. Given these names, $\Pr(\varphi \vee \psi) = (a + b + c)/(a + b + c + d)$, and $\Pr(\psi \mid \overline{\varphi}) = c/(c + d)$. A little algebra tells us that

$$\Pr(\varphi \vee \psi) - \Pr(\psi \mid \overline{\varphi}) = \frac{a+b+c}{a+b+c+d} - \frac{c}{c+d}$$

$$= \frac{d(a+b)}{(c+d)(a+b+c+d)}.$$

And $d(a+b)/\big((c+d)(a+b+c+d)\big) \geqslant 0$. Hence, if $\Pr(\psi \mid \overline{\varphi}) > \theta$, then so is $\Pr(\varphi \vee \psi)$, and that is all we need for $\varphi \vee \psi$ to be acceptable.

To show that XOR is valid, we use the following abbreviations: $\Pr(\varphi \wedge \overline{\psi} \wedge \chi) =: a$; $\Pr(\varphi \wedge \overline{\psi} \wedge \overline{\chi}) =: b$; $\Pr(\overline{\varphi} \wedge \psi \wedge \chi) =: c$; $\Pr(\overline{\varphi} \wedge \psi \wedge \overline{\chi}) =: d$; $\Pr(\overline{\varphi} \wedge \overline{\psi} \wedge \chi) =: e$; and $\Pr(\overline{\varphi} \wedge \overline{\psi} \wedge \overline{\chi}) =: f$. (Note that, because $\vdash \overline{\varphi \wedge \psi}$, $\Pr(\varphi \wedge \psi \wedge \chi) = \Pr(\varphi \wedge \psi \wedge \overline{\chi}) = 0$.) Assume the premises are acceptable. So, in particular, $\Pr(\chi \mid \varphi) > \theta$, and thus $a/(a+b) > \theta$, which is equivalent to $a > \theta(a+b)$; and also $\Pr(\chi \mid \psi) > \theta$, and thus $c/(c+d) > \theta$ iff $c > \theta(c+d)$. Hence, $a+c > \theta(a+b) + \theta(c+d)$ iff $a+c > \theta(a+b+c+d)$ iff $(a+c)/(a+b+c+d) > \theta$ iff $\Pr(\chi \mid \varphi \vee \psi) > \theta$. As for the second part of the proof, note that $\Pr(\chi \mid \varphi) > \Pr(\chi)$ – which holds by assumption – iff $a/(a+b) > (a+c+e)/(a+b+c+d+e+f)$, which, with some algebra, can be seen to hold iff $ad + af > bc + be$. From this, it follows that $(\ast)$ $af - be > bc - ad$. Similarly, $\Pr(\chi \mid \psi) > \Pr(\chi)$ iff $c/(c+d) > (a+c+e)/(a+b+c+d+e+f)$, which again with some algebra can be seen to hold iff $bc + cf > ad + de$. From this, it follows that $(+)$ $bc - ad > de - cf$. And from $(\ast)$ and $(+)$, it follows that $af - be > de - cf$. Thus, if the premises are acceptable, then $af - be > de - cf$. To complete the proof, note that $\Pr(\chi \mid \varphi \vee \psi) > \Pr(\chi)$ iff $(a+c)(a+b+c+d) > (a+c+e)(a+b+c+d+e+f)$ iff $af + cf > be + de$ iff $af - be > de - cf$.

As for the validity of WAND, first note that without the stipulation concerning conditional probabilities with probability 0 antecedents, WAND would hold trivially, given that there are no models that make "If φ and not χ, then $\bot$" acceptable. However, given the said stipulation, there can be models that do make that conditional acceptable, to wit, models in which $\Pr(\varphi \wedge \overline{\chi}) = 0$, for then $\Pr(\bot \mid \varphi \wedge \overline{\chi}) = 1$. To see that WAND also holds given the stipulation, note that if $\Pr(\varphi \wedge \overline{\chi}) = 0$, then (i) $\Pr(\psi \wedge \chi \mid \varphi) = \Pr(\psi \mid \varphi)$. Given that, by the assumption that the premises are acceptable, (ii) $\Pr(\psi \mid \varphi) > \theta$ and (iii) $\Pr(\psi \mid \varphi) > \Pr(\psi)$, we have $\Pr(\psi \wedge \chi \mid \varphi) > \theta$ – by (i) and (ii) – and also $\Pr(\psi \wedge \chi \mid \varphi) > \Pr(\psi \wedge \chi)$, by (i) and (iii) and the fact that $\Pr(\psi \wedge \chi) \leqslant \Pr(\psi)$.

Proof, part 2. The proof that the remaining principles are invalid proceeds by constructing for each of these principles a schema and then showing how from that schema a counterexample to the principle can be derived for any value of $\theta \in [.5, 1)$. These schemas are basically truth tables with an assignment to each row in the table of either a constant or a variable, where the range of all the variables is $\mathbb{R}^+$. To avoid clutter, the presentation of the schemas will follow the notational convention that the values that are assigned to the various rows are assumed to be divided by the sum of all the values assigned in the schema; so, for example, in the first schema below, every occurrence of "n" is short for "$n/(2n + 3m)$" and every occurrence of "m" is short for "$m/(2n + 3m)$." Also, the principles BR2 and CN are invalid for the reasons mentioned in Section 5.4: there are simply no probability models that make their conclusion acceptable, but there do exist probability models that make their premise acceptable. The proof deals with the remaining principles in alphabetical order.

CC: It is already known from the paradoxes presented in Section 5.1 that CC is invalid. Depending on the value of θ, these paradoxes may require many propositions and multiple applications of CC. To see that for any admissible value of θ, a counterexample to CC can be obtained that requires only three propositions and one application of the principle, consider the class of probability models instantiating the following schema:

φ	ψ	χ	Pr	φ	ψ	χ	Pr
T	T	T	n	F	T	T	n
T	T	F	m	F	T	F	o
T	F	T	m	F	F	T	o
T	F	F	o	F	F	F	m

Note that, for any model in this class, $\Pr(\psi \wedge \chi \mid \varphi) = n/(n+2m)$, $\Pr(\psi \wedge \chi) = 2n/(2n + 3m)$, $\Pr(\psi \mid \varphi) = \Pr(\chi \mid \varphi) = (n + m)/(n + 2m)$, and $\Pr(\psi) = \Pr(\chi) = (2n + m)/(2n + 3m)$. Further note that

$$\frac{2n}{2n + 3m} - \frac{n}{n + 2m} = \frac{nm}{2n^2 + 6m^2 + 7nm},$$

which is positive given that n and m are positive. Thus, $\Pr(\psi \wedge \chi) > \Pr(\psi \wedge \chi \mid \varphi)$, and so "If φ, then both ψ and χ" is not acceptable on our proposal. At the same time, we have that

$$\frac{n + m}{n + 2m} - \frac{2n + m}{2n + 3m} = \frac{m^2}{2n^2 + 6m^2 + 7nm},$$

which is positive as well, given that n and m are positive. Thus, both $\Pr(\psi \mid \varphi) > \Pr(\psi)$ and $\Pr(\chi \mid \varphi) > \Pr(\chi)$. Finally, by taking n close enough to 1 and m close enough to 0, we can bring $\Pr(\psi \mid \varphi)$ and $\Pr(\chi \mid \varphi)$ as close to 1 as we want (and thus above θ whatever the exact value of θ is), for

$$\lim_{\substack{n \to 1 \\ m \to 0}} \frac{n+m}{n+2m} = 1, \qquad \lim_{\substack{n \to 1 \\ m \to 0}} \frac{2n+m}{2n+3m} = 1.$$

Consequently, we can make sure that both "If φ, then ψ" and "If φ, then χ" are acceptable according to our proposal, while "If φ, then both ψ and χ" is not acceptable.

CEM: To see that CEM is invalid, consider a probability distribution that assigns equal probability to the four instances of $\pm\varphi \wedge \pm\psi$. Then $\Pr(\psi \mid \varphi) = \Pr(\overline{\psi} \mid \varphi) = .5$. And whatever the exact value of θ, a probability of $.5$ will not be above θ.

CM: That acceptability is not closed under CM follows from a result proved in Douven [2007:155 f]. Specifically, it is shown there that probability models exist such that $\Pr(\psi \wedge \chi \mid \varphi) > \theta > \Pr(\psi \wedge \chi)$ yet $\Pr(\psi \mid \varphi) < \Pr(\psi)$ as well as $\Pr(\chi \mid \varphi) < \Pr(\chi)$.

CMon: Consider this schema:

φ	ψ	χ	Pr	φ	ψ	χ	Pr
T	T	T	k	F	T	T	0
T	T	F	1	F	T	F	0
T	F	T	1	F	F	T	0
T	F	F	$1/(3k)$	F	F	F	$1/(3k)$

In all models satisfying these constraints, $\Pr(\psi \mid \varphi) = \Pr(\chi \mid \varphi) = (k+1)/(k+1/(3k)+2)$ and $\Pr(\psi) = \Pr(\chi) = (k+1)/(k+2/(3k)+2)$. Thus, both $\Pr(\psi \mid \varphi) > \Pr(\psi)$ and $\Pr(\chi \mid \varphi) > \Pr(\chi)$, for

$$\frac{k+1}{k+\frac{1}{3k}+2} - \frac{k+1}{k+\frac{2}{3k}+2} = \frac{3k(1+k)}{\big(1+3k(2+k)\big)\big(2+3k(2+k)\big)}.$$

This is positive for $k > 0$. Also, by taking k large enough, we can bring $\Pr(\psi \mid \varphi)$ and $\Pr(\chi \mid \varphi)$ as close to 1 as we like, given that

$$\lim_{k \to \infty} \frac{k+1}{k+\frac{1}{3k}+2} = 1.$$

Finally, in these models it is *not* the case that $\Pr(\chi \mid \varphi \wedge \psi) > \Pr(\chi)$. For $\Pr(\chi \mid \varphi \wedge \psi) = k/(k+1)$, and

$$\frac{k+1}{k+\frac{2}{3k}+2} - \frac{k}{k+1} = \frac{k}{(1+k)\big(2+3k(2+k)\big)},$$

which is again positive for $k > 0$.

Contraposition: That Contraposition is invalid follows from two claims, namely, first, $\Pr(\overline{\varphi} \mid \overline{\psi}) > \Pr(\overline{\varphi})$ iff $\Pr(\psi \mid \varphi) > \Pr(\psi)$, and second, that there exist models such that not only $\Pr(\psi \mid \varphi) > \Pr(\psi)$ but also, for any admissible value of θ, $\Pr(\psi \mid \varphi) > \theta$ yet $\Pr(\overline{\varphi} \mid \overline{\psi}) < \theta$.

As for the first claim, let, for ease of notation, $\Pr(\varphi \wedge \psi) =: k$, $\Pr(\varphi \wedge \overline{\psi}) =: l$, $\Pr(\overline{\varphi} \wedge \psi) =: m$, and $\Pr(\overline{\varphi} \wedge \overline{\psi}) =: n$. Thus, the assumption that $\Pr(\psi \mid \varphi) > \Pr(\psi)$ amounts to the claim that $k/(k+l) > (k+m)/(k+l+m+n)$. Now, $k/(k+l) > (k+m)/(k+l+m+n)$ iff $k^2+kl+km+kn > k^2+kl+km+lm$ iff $kn > lm$ (recall here that $k, n > 0$) iff $kn+ln+mn+n^2 > lm+ln+mn+n^2$ iff $n(k+l+m+n) > (m+n)(n+l)$ iff $n/(l+n) > (m+n)/(k+l+m+n)$ iff $\Pr(\overline{\varphi} \mid \overline{\psi}) > \Pr(\overline{\varphi})$.

As for the second claim, consider the following set of constraints:

φ	ψ	Pr
T	T	$a^2 b$
T	F	ab
F	T	0
F	F	b

In each model satisfying these constraints, $\Pr(\psi \mid \varphi) = a^2 b/(a^2 b + ab)$ and $\Pr(\psi) = a^2 b/(a^2 b + ab + b)$. First, given that

$$\lim_{a \to \infty} \frac{a^2 b}{a^2 b + ab} = 1,$$

we can take $\Pr(\psi \mid \varphi)$ as close to 1 as we want, by choosing a large enough. Also, $\Pr(\psi \mid \varphi) > \Pr(\psi)$, given that $\Pr(\psi \mid \varphi) - \Pr(\psi) = a^2 b/(a^2 b + ab) - a^2 b/(a^2 b + ab + b) = a/\big((a+1)(a^2 + a + 1)\big)$, which is positive for all $a > 0$. On the other hand, $\Pr(\overline{\varphi} \mid \overline{\psi}) = b/(ab + b)$, and by taking a large enough, this can be brought as close to 0 as we want, given that

$$\lim_{a \to \infty} \frac{b}{ab + b} = 0.$$

So, by choosing a large enough, we can always create a model in which "If φ, then ψ" is acceptable but "If not ψ, then not φ" is not.

CS: To see that this principle is invalid, we consider the following schema:

φ	ψ	Pr
T	T	n
T	F	m
F	T	k
F	F	o

In all probability models satisfying this schema, $\Pr(\varphi \wedge \psi) = n/(n+m+k)$, which can be brought above θ by picking n large relative to $m+k$, whatever the exact value of θ. But however large we pick n, as long as we pick m and k both positive, it will hold that $\Pr(\psi \mid \varphi) \not> \Pr(\psi)$, so that "If φ, then ψ" is *not* acceptable. To see that given the above model, $\Pr(\psi \mid \varphi) \leqslant \Pr(\psi)$, note that $\Pr(\psi \mid \varphi) = n/(n+m)$ while $\Pr(\psi) = (n+k)/(n+m+k)$, and that hence

$$\Pr(\psi) - \Pr(\psi \mid \varphi) \;=\; \frac{n+k}{n+m+k} - \frac{n}{n+m} \;=\; \frac{mk}{(n+m)(n+m+k)}.$$

And this is positive for positive m and k.

CSO: Recall from Section 5.2 that we are interpreting CSO as implying that whenever "If φ, then ψ" and "If ψ, then φ" are both acceptable, the acceptability of "If φ, then χ" materially implies the acceptability of "If ψ, then χ," and vice versa. To show that, thus interpreted, CSO is invalid, we construct probability models in which "If φ, then ψ," "If ψ, then φ," and "If φ, then χ" are all acceptable, but "If ψ, then χ" is not. The models are instances of the following schema:

φ	ψ	χ	Pr	φ	ψ	χ	Pr
T	T	T	n	F	T	T	o
T	T	F	1	F	T	F	n
T	F	T	1	F	F	T	1
T	F	F	o	F	F	F	1

In these models, $\Pr(\psi \mid \varphi) = \Pr(\varphi \mid \psi) = \Pr(\chi \mid \varphi) = (n+1)/(n+2)$, which can be brought as close to 1 as we want, by picking n large enough. Moreover,

$$\Pr(\psi \mid \varphi) - \Pr(\psi) = \frac{n+1}{n+2} - \frac{2n+1}{2n+4} = \frac{1}{2n+4}.$$

Hence, $\Pr(\psi \mid \varphi) > \Pr(\psi)$. Thereby automatically $\Pr(\varphi \mid \psi) > \Pr(\varphi)$. Furthermore,

$$\Pr(\chi \mid \varphi) - \Pr(\chi) = \frac{n+1}{n+2} - \frac{n+2}{2n+4} = \frac{n}{2n+4},$$

which is positive for all admissible values of n, and so $\Pr(\chi \mid \varphi) > \Pr(\chi)$. However, $\Pr(\chi \mid \psi) < \Pr(\chi)$, for

$$\Pr(\chi) - \Pr(\chi \mid \psi) = \frac{n+2}{2n+4} - \frac{n}{2n+1} = \frac{1}{4n+2},$$

which is positive as well for all admissible values of n.

CT and Trans: The following schema can be used to show that both Cumulative Transitivity (CT) and Transitivity (Trans) are invalid:

φ	ψ	χ	Pr	φ	ψ	χ	Pr
T	T	T	n	F	T	T	n
T	T	F	2	F	T	F	0
T	F	T	0	F	F	T	n
T	F	F	1	F	F	F	5

In the models satisfying this schema, $\Pr(\psi \mid \varphi) = (n+2)/(n+3)$. This can be brought as close to 1 as we want (and thus above θ), by taking n large enough. Now, $\Pr(\psi) = (2n+2)/(3n+8)$. To see that $\Pr(\psi \mid \varphi) > \Pr(\psi)$, note that

$$\Pr(\psi \mid \varphi) - \Pr(\psi) = \frac{n+2}{n+3} - \frac{2n+2}{3n+8} = \frac{n^2 + 6n + 10}{(n+3)(3n+8)}.$$

This is positive for every admissible value of n. Also, $\Pr(\chi \mid \psi) = 2n/(2n+2)$. Again, this can be brought as close to 1 as we want. Moreover, $\Pr(\chi \mid \psi) > \Pr(\chi)$, for $\Pr(\chi) = 3n/(3n+8)$, and thus

$$\Pr(\chi \mid \psi) - \Pr(\chi) = \frac{2n}{2n+2} - \frac{3n}{3n+8} = \frac{5n}{(3n+8)(n+1)},$$

which is also positive for any admissible value of n. Furthermore, $\Pr(\chi \mid \varphi \wedge \psi) = n/(n+2)$. This too can be brought as close to 1 as we like. Besides, $\Pr(\chi \mid \varphi \wedge \psi) > \Pr(\chi)$, for

$$\Pr(\chi \mid \varphi \wedge \psi) - \Pr(\chi) = \frac{n}{n+2} - \frac{3n}{3n+8} = \frac{2n}{(3n+8)(n+2)},$$

which again is positive for all admissible values of n. Hence, the premises needed for an application of Trans as well as those needed for an application of CT can be satisfied by taking n large enough. However, $\Pr(\chi \mid \varphi) = n/(n + 3)$, and therefore it is *not* the case that $\Pr(\chi \mid \varphi) > \Pr(\chi)$. For

$$\Pr(\chi) - \Pr(\chi \mid \varphi) = \frac{3n}{3n + 8} - \frac{n}{n + 3} = \frac{n}{(3n + 8)(n + 3)}.$$

Clearly, this too is positive for all admissible values of n. As a result, given just a large enough value for n, "If φ, then ψ," "If ψ, then χ," as well as "If φ and ψ, then χ" are acceptable; yet "If φ, then χ" is not acceptable given any admissible value of n.[1]

CV: As mentioned in Section 5.2, we interpret "It is not the case that if φ, then not ψ" as requiring that the embedded conditional is *not* acceptable. Thus, for CV to be valid, it must be that if $\Pr(\chi \mid \varphi) > \theta$ and $\Pr(\chi \mid \varphi) > \Pr(\chi)$ and also either $\Pr(\overline{\psi} \mid \varphi) \leqslant \theta$ or $\Pr(\overline{\psi} \mid \varphi) \leqslant \Pr(\overline{\psi})$ (or both), then $\Pr(\chi \mid \varphi \wedge \psi) > \theta$ and $\Pr(\chi \mid \varphi \wedge \psi) > \Pr(\chi)$. To see that this does not generally hold, we consider the following schema, which will yield models such that $\Pr(\chi \mid \varphi) > \theta$, $\Pr(\chi \mid \varphi) > \Pr(\chi)$, $\Pr(\overline{\psi} \mid \varphi) \leqslant \Pr(\overline{\psi})$, and yet $\Pr(\chi \mid \varphi \wedge \psi) \leqslant \Pr(\chi)$:

φ	ψ	χ	Pr	φ	ψ	χ	Pr
T	T	T	1	F	T	T	0
T	T	F	k	F	T	F	0
T	F	T	m	F	F	T	1
T	F	F	0	F	F	F	m

To see that $\Pr(\chi \mid \varphi) > \Pr(\chi)$, note that $\Pr(\chi \mid \varphi) = (m + 1)/(k + m + 1)$ and that $\Pr(\chi) = (m + 2)/(k + 2m + 2)$. That the former is greater than the latter can be seen by considering that

$$\frac{m + 1}{k + m + 1} - \frac{m + 2}{k + 2m + 2} = \frac{m^2 - k + m}{(k + m + 1)(k + 2m + 2)}.$$

---

[1] See Douven [2011c] for an alternative proof of Trans. The proof given there does not carry over to a proof of CT. The principle labeled "CT" in that paper is not in Table 5.1 and has, to my knowledge, never been considered as a principle of conditional reasoning. It is the principle that whenever $\varphi \to \psi$ and $\psi \to \chi$, then $\varphi \wedge \psi \to \chi$. As follows from results in Douven [2011c], this principle is invalid in our sense as well. From results presented in the same paper and similar results presented in Roche [2012], it also follows that various weaker versions of Trans are invalid.

This is positive for any value of m that is large enough relative to k. Indeed, by picking m large enough, we can bring the difference between $\Pr(\chi \mid \varphi)$ and $\Pr(\chi)$ as close to .5 as we want, given that

$$\lim_{m \to \infty} \left[\frac{m+1}{k+m+1} - \frac{m+2}{k+2m+2} \right] = \frac{1}{2}.$$

Moreover, we can bring $\Pr(\chi \mid \varphi)$ as close to 1 as we want, also by picking m large enough:

$$\lim_{m \to \infty} \frac{m+1}{k+m+1} = 1.$$

At the same time, we have $\Pr(\overline{\psi} \mid \varphi) = m/(k+m+1)$ and $\Pr(\overline{\psi}) = (2m+1)/(k+2m+2)$. And to see that in our models it is *not* the case that the former is larger than the latter, but that in fact $\Pr(\overline{\psi}) > \Pr(\overline{\psi} \mid \varphi)$, note that

$$\frac{2m+1}{k+2m+2} - \frac{m}{k+m+1} = \frac{(k+1)(m+1)}{(k+m+1)(k+2m+2)}.$$

This is positive for all admissible values of k and m.

DEDUC: To see that DEDUC is invalid, consider this schema:

φ	ψ	χ	Pr	φ	ψ	χ	Pr
T	T	T	n	F	T	T	1
T	T	F	1	F	T	F	0
T	F	T	1	F	F	T	0
T	F	F	0	F	F	F	$2n$

In all probability models satisfying this schema, $\Pr(\chi \mid \varphi \wedge \psi) = n/(n+1)$, which can be brought as close to 1 as one likes, by taking n large enough. Furthermore, $\Pr(\chi) = (n+2)/(3n+3)$, which is smaller than $n/(n+1)$ for $n > 1$. Thus, by taking n large enough, we make "If φ and ψ, then χ" acceptable. However, $\Pr(\overline{\psi} \vee \chi \mid \varphi) = (n+1)/(n+2)$, which is smaller than $\Pr(\overline{\psi} \vee \chi) = (3n+2)/(3n+3)$, for

$$\Pr(\overline{\psi} \vee \chi) - \Pr(\overline{\psi} \vee \chi \mid \varphi) = \frac{3n+2}{3n+3} - \frac{n+1}{n+2} = \frac{2n+1}{(3n+3)(n+2)},$$

which is positive for any admissible value of n. Thus, "If φ, then either not ψ, or χ, or both" is not acceptable.

Modus Ponens: Consider the following schema to see that Modus Ponens is not valid either:

φ	ψ	Pr
T	T	n
T	F	n/m
F	T	0
F	F	1

In all models satisfying this schema, $\Pr(\varphi) = (n + n/m)/(n + n/m + 1)$, which can be brought as close to 1 as we like, by taking n large enough. Furthermore, $\Pr(\psi \mid \varphi) = n/(n + n/m)$, which can be brought as close to 1 as we like by taking m large enough relative to n. Moreover, given that $\Pr(\psi) = n/(n + n/m + 1)$, it obviously holds that $\Pr(\psi \mid \varphi) > \Pr(\psi)$. Still, we can always choose n and m such that both $\Pr(\varphi)$ and $\Pr(\psi \mid \varphi)$ are greater than θ while $\Pr(\psi)$ is not. To appreciate this, first note that

$$\Pr(\psi \mid \varphi) - \Pr(\varphi) = \frac{n}{n + \frac{n}{m}} - \frac{n + \frac{n}{m}}{n + \frac{n}{m} + 1} = \frac{m^2 - n - mn}{(m + 1)(m + n + mn)}.$$

Given that $m > 0$, we can make sure that $\Pr(\psi \mid \varphi) > \Pr(\psi)$ by picking n such that $n < m^2/(m + 1)$, which is compatible with our choosing m large relative to n (which is another constraint). To obtain our counter-model, then, we only have to make sure that $\Pr(\varphi) > \theta$ and $\Pr(\psi) \not> \theta$. (It will automatically hold that $\Pr(\psi \mid \varphi) > \theta$ and also that $\Pr(\psi \mid \varphi) > \Pr(\psi)$.) One way to ensure this starts by observing that

$$\Pr(\varphi) - \Pr(\psi) = \frac{n + \frac{n}{m}}{n + \frac{n}{m} + 1} - \frac{n}{n + \frac{n}{m} + 1} = \frac{n}{m + n + mn}.$$

Now set $\Pr(\varphi) = \theta + n/\big(2(m + n + mn)\big)$ while setting $\Pr(\psi) = \theta - n/\big(2(m + n + mn)\big)$, or equivalently

$$\Pr(\varphi) = \frac{2m\theta + 2n\theta + 2mn\theta + n}{2(m + n + mn)},$$

$$\Pr(\psi) = \frac{2m\theta + 2n\theta + 2mn\theta - n}{2(m + n + mn)}.$$

To obtain values for m and n as a function of θ, we solve the following for n:

$$\frac{2m\theta + 2n\theta + 2mn\theta + n}{2(m + n + mn)} = \frac{n + \frac{n}{m}}{n + \frac{n}{m} + 1},$$

$$\frac{2m\theta + 2n\theta + 2mn\theta - n}{2(m + n + mn)} = \frac{n}{n + \frac{n}{m} + 1}.$$

This yields that

$$n = \frac{2m\theta}{2m + 1 - 2\theta - 2m\theta}.$$

And this means that n will be the closer to $\theta/(1-\theta)$ the larger we choose m, for

$$\lim_{m \to \infty} \frac{2m\theta}{2m + 1 - 2\theta - 2m\theta} = \frac{\theta}{1 - \theta}.$$

By way of illustration, suppose $\theta = .9$, and choose $m = 100$. Then one easily verifies that $n = 9.375$, $\Pr(\varphi) = .904478$, $\Pr(\psi \mid \varphi) = .990099$, and $\Pr(\psi) = .895522$, from which it follows that both φ and "If φ, then ψ" are acceptable (given that also $\Pr(\psi \mid \varphi) > \Pr(\psi)$, which holds in any case), but ψ is not.

Modus Tollens: That this principle is not valid can be shown by means of the following schema:

φ	ψ	Pr
T	T	$m/\theta - m$
T	F	n
F	T	o
F	F	m

In all probability models satisfying this schema,

$$\Pr(\psi \mid \varphi) = \frac{\frac{m}{\theta} - m}{\frac{m}{\theta} - m + n};$$

and given that

$$\lim_{n \to o} \frac{\frac{m}{\theta} - m}{\frac{m}{\theta} - m + n} = 1,$$

we can bring this value as close to 1 as we want by taking n small enough. Also,

$$\Pr(\psi) \;=\; \frac{\frac{m}{\theta} - m}{\frac{m}{\theta} + n} \;<\; \frac{\frac{m}{\theta} - m}{\frac{m}{\theta} - m + n} \;=\; \Pr(\psi \mid \varphi),$$

given that $m > 0$. Furthermore,

$$\Pr(\overline{\psi}) \;=\; \frac{n + m}{\frac{m}{\theta} + n},$$

and this is larger than θ, given that

$$\frac{n + m}{\frac{m}{\theta} + n} - \theta \;=\; -\frac{n(\theta - 1)\theta}{m + n\theta},$$

which is positive. (Note that $\theta - 1$ is negative, because $\theta < 1$.) Hence, $\Pr(\overline{\psi}) > \theta$, for all admissible values of m and n. Finally, however,

$$\Pr(\overline{\varphi}) \;=\; \frac{m}{\frac{m}{\theta} + n},$$

and this is *smaller* than θ, for

$$\frac{m}{\frac{m}{\theta} + n} - \theta \;=\; -\frac{n\theta^2}{m + n\theta},$$

which is negative for all admissible values of m and n. Hence, in all these models, "If φ, then ψ" and $\overline{\psi}$ are acceptable, but $\overline{\varphi}$ is not.

NR and SA: The schema below shows that both NR and SA are invalid. SA is considered first, then NR.

φ	ψ	χ	Pr	φ	ψ	χ	Pr
T	T	T	1	F	T	T	0
T	T	F	m	F	T	F	1
T	F	T	1	F	F	T	0
T	F	F	0	F	F	F	m

In all probability models satisfying these constraints, $\Pr(\psi \mid \varphi) = (m + 1)/(m + 2)$, $\Pr(\psi) = (m + 2)/(2m + 3)$, and $\Pr(\psi \mid \varphi \wedge \chi) = 1/2$. First, by taking m large enough, we can bring $\Pr(\psi \mid \varphi)$ as close to 1 as we like. Second, $\Pr(\psi \mid \varphi) > \Pr(\psi)$, for

$$\Pr(\psi \mid \varphi) - \Pr(\psi) \;=\; \frac{m + 1}{m + 2} - \frac{m + 2}{2m + 3} \;=\; \frac{m^2 + m - 1}{2m^2 + 7m + 6},$$

which is positive for $m > \sqrt{5}/2 - 1/2$ (as well as for $m < -\sqrt{5}/2 - 1/2$, but such values for m are excluded). And third, $\Pr(\psi \mid \varphi \wedge \chi) < \Pr(\psi)$, for $1/2 - (m+2)/(2m+3) = -1/(4m+6)$, which is negative for any admissible value of m. So, for all large enough values of m, the above schema yields a model in which the premise of SA – "If φ, then ψ" – is acceptable but the conclusion – "If φ and χ, then ψ" – is not acceptable.

The conclusion of NR might still be made acceptable (in the sense that one of the disjuncts of that conclusion may be made acceptable) by making "If φ and not χ, then not ψ" acceptable. Note, however, that on all probability functions satisfying the above schema, $\Pr(\overline{\psi} \mid \varphi \wedge \overline{\chi}) = 0$. So, we neither have that $\Pr(\overline{\psi} \mid \varphi \wedge \overline{\chi}) > \theta$ nor that $\Pr(\overline{\psi} \mid \varphi \wedge \overline{\chi}) > \Pr(\overline{\psi})$.

OR: Consider the following set of constraints:

φ	ψ	χ	Pr	φ	ψ	χ	Pr
T	T	T	2	F	T	T	n
T	T	F	0	F	T	F	$1/n$
T	F	T	n	F	F	T	1
T	F	F	$1/n$	F	F	F	0

Given these constraints, $\Pr(\chi \mid \varphi) = \Pr(\chi \mid \psi) = (n + 2)/(n + 1/n + 2)$. Because

$$\lim_{n \to \infty} \frac{n + 2}{n + \frac{1}{n} + 2} = 1,$$

we can bring $\Pr(\chi \mid \varphi)$ and $\Pr(\chi \mid \psi)$ as close to 1 as we want, and thus above θ for any admissible value of θ. Furthermore, $\Pr(\chi) = (2n + 3)/(2n + 2/n + 3)$, and thereby $\Pr(\chi \mid \varphi) = \Pr(\chi \mid \psi) > \Pr(\chi)$, for

$$\frac{n + 2}{n + \frac{1}{n} + 2} - \frac{2n + 3}{2n + \frac{2}{n} + 3} = \frac{n}{(n + 1)^2 (n + 2(2n + 3))},$$

which is positive for any positive value of n. Thus, the acceptability conditions for both "If φ, then χ" and "If ψ, then χ" can be fulfilled. On the other hand, $\Pr(\chi \mid \varphi \vee \psi) = (2n + 2)/(2n + 2/n + 2)$. And this is smaller than $\Pr(\chi)$, for all positive n, given that

$$\frac{2n + 3}{2n + \frac{2}{n} + 3} - \frac{2n + 2}{2n + \frac{2}{n} + 2} = \frac{n}{(n^2 + n + 1)(n + 2(2n + 3))}.$$

Hence, the acceptability conditions for "If φ or ψ, then χ" are *not* fulfilled, for any value of $n > 0$. And so OR is not valid.

Or-to-if: That Or-to-if is invalid follows from this schema:

φ	ψ	Pr
T	T	$2n+1$
T	F	0
F	T	n
F	F	1

In all models satisfying this schema, $\Pr(\varphi \vee \psi) = (3n+1)/(3n+2)$. By taking n large enough, we can bring this probability as close to 1 as we want. Hence, we can ensure that $\Pr(\varphi \vee \psi) > \theta$, whatever the value of θ. On the other hand, $\Pr(\psi \mid \overline{\varphi}) = n/(n+1)$ and $\Pr(\psi) = (3n+1)/(3n+2)$. And

$$\Pr(\psi) - \Pr(\psi \mid \overline{\varphi}) \;=\; \frac{3n+1}{3n+2} - \frac{n}{n+1} \;=\; \frac{2n+1}{3n^2+5n+2},$$

which is positive as long as n is positive. So, $\Pr(\psi) > \Pr(\psi \mid \overline{\varphi})$, which means that at least one of the acceptability conditions of "If not φ, then ψ" is not fulfilled.

RCK: According to RCK, if $\varphi_1 \wedge \cdots \wedge \varphi_n$ entails ψ, then {"If χ, then φ_1," ..., "If χ, then φ_n"} entails "If χ, then ψ." To see that this cannot be generally valid, just take $\psi \equiv \top$. It holds necessarily that $\varphi_1 \wedge \cdots \wedge \varphi_n$ entails $\top$, yet even if for all $i \in \{1, \ldots, n\}$, "If χ, then φ_i" is acceptable (which can be), we will still not have that "If χ, then $\top$" is acceptable, given that $\Pr(\top) = 1$ so that we cannot have $\Pr(\top \mid \chi) > \Pr(\top)$. The case in which ψ is a tautology may be not so interesting, and one may wonder whether a version of RCK that requires ψ to be a contingent proposition *is* valid given our proposal. Not even that is so. Let φ_1 and φ_2 be contingent propositions, and consider the following: Trivially, $\varphi_1 \wedge \varphi_2$ entails itself. Now let "If χ, then φ_1" and "If χ, then φ_2" both be acceptable. Then, according to the restricted version of RCK we are considering, it should hold that "If χ, then φ_1 and φ_2" is acceptable as well. But we already know (from the proof that CC is invalid) that there are counter-models to this claim.

RCM: It is easy to see that RCM is invalid by simply setting $\chi \equiv \top$ and again observing that nothing can raise the probability of a tautology. Here too, however, one could consider a restriction of substitution instances of χ to contingent propositions. To see that, thus restricted, RCM is still invalid, consider the class of probability models satisfying this schema:

φ	ψ	χ	Pr	φ	ψ	χ	Pr
T	T	T	n	F	T	T	0
T	T	F	0	F	T	F	0
T	F	T	0	F	F	T	$2n$
T	F	F	1	F	F	F	1

The proposition that $\vdash \psi \supset \chi$ entails that $\Pr(\overline{\psi} \vee \chi) = 1$ and hence that $\Pr(\psi \wedge \overline{\chi}) = 0$. All models in the class we are considering satisfy this constraint. Also, in these models $\Pr(\psi \mid \varphi) = n/(n+1)$, which can be made as close to 1 as we want by taking n large enough. Besides, $\Pr(\psi) = n/(3n+2)$, which is evidently smaller than $n/(n+1)$ for $n > 1$. However, $\Pr(\chi \mid \varphi) = n/(n+1)$, and this is *smaller* than $\Pr(\chi) = 3n/(3n+2)$, for $3n/(3n+2) - n/(n+1) = n/(3n^2+5n+2)$, which is positive for $n > 0$. So, in none of the models we are considering is "If φ, then χ" acceptable.

ROR: Consider the family of probability models satisfying these constraints:

φ	ψ	χ	Pr	φ	ψ	χ	Pr
T	T	T	1	F	T	T	0
T	T	F	n	F	T	F	0
T	F	T	n	F	F	T	0
T	F	F	1	F	F	F	1

In all these models, $\Pr(\psi \vee \chi \mid \varphi) = (2n+1)/(2n+2) > (2n+1)/(2n+3) = \Pr(\psi \vee \chi)$. Also, by taking n large enough, we can bring the probability of $\Pr(\psi \vee \chi \mid \varphi)$ as close to 1 as we want. However, also in all these models, $\Pr(\psi \mid \varphi) = \Pr(\chi \mid \varphi) = (n+1)/(2n+2) = 1/2$, and that is *not* greater than θ, given that $\theta \in [.5, 1)$. Hence, ROR is not valid.

SDA: Consider the class of probability models satisfying these constraints:

φ	ψ	χ	Pr	φ	ψ	χ	Pr
T	T	T	0	F	T	T	n
T	T	F	1	F	T	F	1
T	F	T	n	F	F	T	0
T	F	F	2	F	F	F	1

In all models in this class, $\Pr(\chi \mid \varphi \vee \psi) = 2n/(2n+4)$. Note that this value can be brought as close to 1 as we want by taking n large enough.

Also, $\Pr(\chi) = 2n/(2n+5) < 2n/(2n+4) = \Pr(\chi \mid \varphi \vee \psi)$. Thus, we can always choose n such that the acceptability conditions for "If φ or ψ, then χ" are satisfied. However, we also have that $\Pr(\chi \mid \varphi) = n/(n+3)$. So

$$\Pr(\chi) - \Pr(\chi \mid \varphi) \;=\; \frac{2n}{2n+5} - \frac{n}{n+3} \;=\; \frac{n}{(2n+5)(n+3)},$$

which is positive, given that n is positive. As a result, φ is not evidence for χ. Thus, "If φ, then χ" is not acceptable in any of these models. And so SDA is not valid.

VCM: To see that VCM is invalid, consider the following schema:

φ	ψ	χ	Pr		φ	ψ	χ	Pr
T	T	T	n		F	T	T	1
T	T	F	m		F	T	F	0
T	F	T	0		F	F	T	n
T	F	F	0		F	F	F	0

In all models instantiating this schema, $\Pr(\psi \wedge \chi \mid \varphi) = n/(n+m)$, which can be brought as close to 1 as we like by taking n large enough relative to m. Furthermore, $\Pr(\psi \wedge \chi) = (n+1)/(2n+m+1)$, and $n/(n+m) > (n+1)/(2n+m+1)$ iff $2n^2 + nm + n > n^2 + nm + n + m$ iff $n^2 > m$, which again can be ensured by taking n large enough relative to m. However, $\Pr(\chi \mid \varphi \wedge \psi) < \Pr(\chi)$, given that $\Pr(\chi) - \Pr(\chi \mid \varphi \wedge \psi) = (2n+1)/(2n+m+1) - n/(n+m) = m(1+n)/\big((m+n)(1+m+2n)\big)$. And this is positive given our constraints on m and n.

Xor-to-if: Note that in all probability models satisfying the constraints

φ	ψ	Pr
T	T	n
T	F	0
F	T	m
F	F	n

$\Pr(\varphi \veebar \psi) = m/(m+2n)$, which can be brought as close to 1 as we want by taking m large enough relative to n. (Here, $\veebar$ symbolizes exclusive disjunction.) However, $\Pr(\psi) > \Pr(\psi \mid \overline{\varphi})$ iff $(m+n)/(m+2n) > m/(m+n)$ iff $m^2 + 2mn + n^2 > m^2 + 2mn$ iff $n \neq 0$. So, given any of these probability models, "Either φ or ψ (but not both)" is acceptable, yet "If not φ, then ψ" is not.

This completes the proof of Theorem 5.2.1.

APPENDIX B

Survey experiment materials

These sentences were used in the first stage of the survey experiment reported in Section 5.4.2:

- The UK recession was not as deep as was previously thought.
- Aggressive leopards are not afraid to enter human settlements.
- Next month's unemployment figures will shake up the US electoral landscape.
- Eating egg yolks increases artery wall thickness.
- The Taliban are a serious threat to stability in Afghanistan.
- American voters trust Democrats to protect Medicare.
- Fat around the internal organs is linked to diabetes in humans.
- The Greek government is under pressure from its population to win concessions from Europe.
- Chinese companies are plowing money into US assets at a record pace.
- In the Syrian conflict, the government is responsible for most of the deaths.

The following sentences were used in the second stage of the same experiment as well as in the control experiment:

- In the US, good education is not always within reach.
- The euro zone's economies are suffering from a severe economic downturn.
- A pandemic influenza could emerge from a number of different routes.
- Romney's tax plan would raise taxes on the middle class.
- The civil war in Syria is pushing Iraq closer to Iran.
- Alcohol misuse contributes to hypertension.
- People avoid expressing emotions at work.
- Stressful life events often precede episodes of depression.
- Dog breeders are required to have a license.
- Obama is holding a steady lead in Nevada.

Bibliography

Achinstein, P. [2001] *The Book of Evidence*, Oxford: Oxford University Press.

Adams, E. W. [1965] "The Logic of Conditionals," *Inquiry* 8: 166–197.

Adams, E. W. [1966] "Probability and the Logic of Conditionals," in J. Hintikka and P. Suppes (eds.) *Aspects of Inductive Logic*, Amsterdam: North-Holland, pp. 265–316.

Adams, E. W. [1975] *The Logic of Conditionals*, Dordrecht: Reidel.

Adams, E. W. [1986] "On the Logic of High Probability," *Journal of Philosophical Logic* 15: 255–279.

Adams, E. W. [1998] *A Primer of Probability Logic*, Stanford: CSLI Publications.

Adams, E. W. and Levine, H. P. [1975] "On the Uncertainties Transmitted from Premises to Conclusions in Deductive Inferences," *Synthese* 30: 429–460.

Adler, J. [2002] *Belief's Own Ethics*, Cambridge MA: MIT Press.

Anderson, A. R. [1951] "A Note on Subjunctive and Counterfactual Conditionals," *Analysis* 12: 35–38.

Appiah, A. [1985] *Assertion and Conditionals*, Cambridge: Cambridge University Press.

Arló-Costa, H. [2007] "The Logic of Conditionals," in E. N. Zalta (ed.) *Stanford Encyclopedia of Philosophy*, available at http://plato.stanford.edu/entries/logic-conditionals/.

Atlas, J. D. [2005] *Logic, Meaning, and Conversation*, Oxford: Oxford University Press.

Aust, F., Diedenhofen, B., Ullrich, S., and Musch, J. [2013] "Seriousness Checks Are Useful to Improve Data Validity in Online Research," *Behavior Research Methods* 45: 527–535.

Austin, J. L. [1956] "Ifs and Cans," *Proceedings of the British Academy* 42: 107–132.

Bamber, D. [2000] "Entailment with Near Surety of Scaled Assertions of High Conditional Probability," *Journal of Philosophical Logic* 29: 1–74.

Baratgin, J., Over, D. E., and Politzer, G. [2013] "Uncertainty and the de Finetti Tables," *Thinking and Reasoning* 19: 308–328.

Baratgin, J., Over, D. E., and Politzer, G. [2014] "New Psychological Paradigm for Conditionals: Its Philosophy and Psychology," *Mind and Language* 29: 73–84.

Barrouillet, P., Gauffroy, C., and Lecas, J.-F. [2008] "Mental Models and the Suppositional Account of Conditionals," *Psychological Review* 115: 760–771.

Barrouillet, P. and Lecas, J. F. [1999] "Mental Models in Conditional Reasoning and Working Memory," *Thinking and Reasoning* 5: 289–302.

Bennett, J. [1982] "Even If," *Linguistics and Philosophy* 5: 403–418.

Bennett, J. [2003] *A Philosophical Guide to Conditionals*, Oxford: Oxford University Press.

Benovsky, J. [2008] "The Bundle Theory and the Substratum Theory: Deadly Enemies or Twin Brothers?" *Philosophical Studies* 141: 175–190.

Bhatt, R. and Pancheva, R. [2006] "Conditionals," in M. Everaert and H. van Riemsdijk (eds.) *The Blackwell Companion to Syntax* (Vol. I), Oxford: Blackwell, pp. 638–687.

Blackburn, S. [1986] "How Can We Tell Whether a Commitment Has a Truth Condition?" in C. Travis (ed.) *Meaning and Interpretation*, Oxford: Blackwell, pp. 201–232.

Boutilier, C. and Goldszmidt, M. [1995] "On the Revision of Conditional Belief Sets," in Crocco, Fariñas del Cerro, and Herzig (eds.) [1995], pp. 267–300.

Bovens, L. and Hartmann, S. [2003] *Bayesian Epistemology*, Oxford: Oxford University Press.

Bradley, R. [2000] "A Preservation Condition for Conditionals," *Analysis* 60: 219–222.

Bradley, R. [2002] "Indicative Conditionals," *Erkenntnis* 56: 345–378.

Bradley, R. [2005] "Radical Probabilism and Bayesian Conditioning," *Philosophy of Science* 72: 342–364.

Braine, M. D. S. [1978] "On the Relation between the Natural Logic of Reasoning and Standard Logic," *Psychological Review* 85: 1–21.

Braine, M. D. S. and O'Brien, D. P [1991] "A Theory of *If*: Lexical Entry, Reasoning Program, and Pragmatic Principles," *Psychological Review* 98: 182–203.

Brem, S. and Rips, L. J. [2000] "Explanation and Evidence in Informal Argument," *Cognitive Science* 24: 573–604.

Burge, T. [1993] "Content Preservation," *Philosophical Review* 102: 457–488.

Burge, T. [1997] "Interlocution, Perception, and Memory," *Philosophical Studies* 86: 21–47.

Burgess, J. P. [1981] "Quick Completeness Proofs for Some Logics of Conditionals," *Notre Dame Journal of Formal Logic* 22: 76–84.

Burgess, J. P. [2004] Review of J. Bennett, *A Philosophical Guide to Conditionals*, *Bulletin of Symbolic Logic* 10: 565–570.

Byrne, R. M. J. and Johnson-Laird, P. N. [2010] "Conditionals and Possibilities," in M. Oaksford and N. Chater (eds.) *Cognition and Conditionals*, Oxford: Oxford University Press, pp. 55–68.

Callebaut, W. [1993] *Taking the Naturalistic Turn*, Chicago: University of Chicago Press.

Cantwell, J. [2008] "Indicative Conditionals: Factual or Epistemic?" *Studia Logica* 88: 157–194.

Carston, R. [2004] "Explicature and Semantics," in S. Davis and B. Gillon (eds.) *Semantics: A Reader*, Oxford: Oxford University Press, pp. 817–845.

Chalmers, D. and Hájek, A. [2007] "Ramsey + Moore = God," *Analysis* 67: 170–172.

Chandler, J. [2010] "The Lottery Paradox Generalized?" *British Journal for the Philosophy of Science* 61: 667–679.

Chisholm, R. M. [1964] "J. L. Austin's Philosophical Papers," *Mind* 73: 1–26.

Cialdea Mayer, M. and Pirri, F. [1993] "First Order Abduction via Tableau and Sequent Calculi," *Logic Journal of the IGPL* 1: 99–117.

Cialdea Mayer, M. and Pirri, F. [1995] "Propositional Abduction in Modal Logic," *Logic Journal of the IGPL* 3: 907–919.

Collins, J., Hall, E., and Paul, L. A. (eds.) [2004] *Causation and Counterfactuals*, Cambridge MA: MIT Press.

Cooper, W. S. [1978] *Foundations of Logico-linguistics*, Dordrecht: Reidel.

Cosmides, L. [1989] "The Logic of Social Exchange: Has Natural Selection Shaped How Humans Reason?" *Cognition* 31: 187–276.

Crocco, G., Fariñas del Cerro, L., and Herzig, A. (eds.) [1995] *Conditionals. From Philosophy to Computer Science*, Oxford: Oxford University Press.

Crupi, V., Fitelson, B., and Tentori, K. [2008] "Probability, Confirmation, and the Conjunction Fallacy," *Thinking and Reasoning* 14: 182–199.

Dancygier, B. [1998] *Conditionals and Predictions: Time, Knowledge and Causation in Conditional Constructions*, Cambridge: Cambridge University Press.

Davis, W. A. [1979] "Indicative and Subjunctive Conditionals," *Philosophical Review* 88: 544–564.

Declerck, R. and Reed, S. [2001] *Conditionals: A Comprehensive Empirical Analysis*, Berlin / New York: Mouton de Gruyter.

de Finetti, B. [1937] "La Prévision: Ses Lois Logiques, ses Sources Subjectives," *Annales de l'Institut Henri Poincaré* 7: 1–68.

De Neys, W., Schaeken, W., and d'Ydewalle, G. [2003] "Inference Suppression and Semantic Memory Retrieval: Every Counterexample Counts," *Memory and Cognition* 31: 581–595.

de Regt, H. W. and Dieks, D. [2005] "A Contextual Approach to Scientific Understanding," *Synthese* 144: 137–170.

DeRose, K. [1996] "Knowledge, Assertion, and Lotteries," *Australasian Journal of Philosophy* 74: 568–580.

DeRose, K. [2002] "Assertion, Knowledge, and Context," *Philosophical Review* 111: 167–203.

DeRose, K. [2010] "The Conditionals of Deliberation," *Mind* 119: 1–42.

DeRose, K. and Grandy, R. [1999] "Conditional Assertions and 'Biscuit' Conditionals," *Noûs* 33: 405–420.

Dessalles, J.-L. [2007] *Why We Talk*, Oxford: Oxford University Press.

Dietz, R. and Douven, I. [2010] "Ramsey's Test, Adams' Thesis, and Left-Nested Conditionals," *Review of Symbolic Logic* 3: 467–484.

Douven, I. [1999] "Inference to the Best Explanation Made Coherent," *Philosophy of Science* 66 (Supplement): S424–S435.

Douven, I. [2002a] "A New Solution to the Paradoxes of Rational Acceptability," *British Journal for the Philosophy of Science* 53: 391–410.

Douven, I. [2002b] "Testing Inference to the Best Explanation," *Synthese* 130: 355–377.

Douven, I. [2005] "A Principled Solution to Fitch's Paradox," *Erkenntnis* 62: 47–69.

Douven, I. [2006] "Assertion, Knowledge, and Rational Credibility," *Philosophical Review* 115: 449–485.

Douven, I. [2007] "Fitch's Paradox and Probabilistic Antirealism," *Studia Logica* 86: 149–182.

Douven, I. [2008a] "Underdetermination," in S. Psillos and M. Curd (eds.) *The Routledge Companion to the Philosophy of Science*, London: Routledge, pp. 292–301.

Douven, I. [2008b] "Kaufmann on the Probabilities of Conditionals," *Journal of Philosophical Logic* 37: 259–266.

Douven, I. [2008c] "The Evidential Support Theory of Conditionals," *Synthese* 164: 19–44.

Douven, I. [2009] "Assertion, Moore, and Bayes," *Philosophical Studies* 144: 361–375.

Douven, I. [2010] "The Pragmatics of Belief," *Journal of Pragmatics* 42: 35–47.

Douven, I. [2011a] "Indicative Conditionals," in L. Horsten and R. Pettigrew (eds.) *A Companion to Philosophical Logic*, London: Continuum Press, pp. 383–405.

Douven, I. [2011b] "Abduction," in E. N. Zalta (ed.) *Stanford Encyclopedia of Philosophy*, available at http://plato.stanford.edu/entries/abduction/.

Douven, I. [2011c] "Further Results on the Intransitivity of Evidential Support," *Review of Symbolic Logic* 4: 487–497.

Douven, I. [2012] "The Lottery Paradox and the Pragmatics of Belief," *Dialectica* 66: 351–373.

Douven, I. [2013a] "Inference to the Best Explanation, Dutch Books, and Inaccuracy Minimisation," *Philosophical Quarterly* 69: 428–444.

Douven, I. [2013b] "Putting the Pragmatics of Belief to Work," in A. Capone, F. Lo Piparo, and M. Carapezza (eds.) *Perspectives on Pragmatics and Philosophy*, Berlin: Springer, pp. 475–488.

Douven, I. [2013c] "The Lottery and Preface Paradoxes," in D. Pritchard (ed.) *Oxford Bibliographies Online: Philosophy*.

Douven, I. [2016a] "Inference to the Best Explanation: What Is It? And Why Should We Care?" in K. McCain and T. Poston (eds.) *Best Explanations: New Essays on Inference to the Best Explanation*, Oxford: Oxford University Press, in press.

Douven, I. [2016b] "How to Account for the Oddness of Missing-link Conditionals," *Synthese*, in press.

Douven, I. and Dietz, R. [2011] "A Puzzle about Stalnaker's Hypothesis," *Topoi* 30: 31–37.

Douven, I., Elqayam, S., Singmann, H., Over, D. E., and van Wijnbergen-Huitink, J. [2015] "Conditionals and Inferential Connections: A Hypothetical Inferential Theory," manuscript.

Douven, I. and Meijs, W. [2007] "Measuring Coherence," *Synthese* 156: 405–425.

Douven, I. and Romeijn, J. W. [2011] "A New Resolution of the Judy Benjamin Problem," *Mind* 120: 637–670.

Douven, I. and Schupbach, J. N. [2015a] "Probabilistic Alternatives to Bayesianism: The Case of Explanationism," *Frontiers in Psychology* 6, DOI=10.3389/fpsyg.2015.00459.

Douven, I. and Schupbach, J. N. [2015b] "The Role of Explanatory Considerations in Updating," *Cognition* 142: 299–311.

Douven, I. and Uffink, J. [2003] "The Preface Paradox Revisited," *Erkenntnis* 59: 389–420.

Douven, I. and Verbrugge, S. [2010] "The Adams Family," *Cognition* 117: 302–318.

Douven, I. and Verbrugge, S. [2012] "Indicatives, Concessives, and Evidential Support," *Thinking and Reasoning* 18: 480–499.

Douven, I. and Verbrugge, S. [2013] "The Probabilities of Conditionals Revisited," *Cognitive Science* 37: 711–730.

Douven, I. and Wenmackers, S. [2015] "Inference to the Best Explanation versus Bayes' Rule in a Social Setting," *British Journal for the Philosophy of Science*, in press

Douven, I. and Williamson, T. [2006] "Generalizing the Lottery Paradox," *British Journal for the Philosophy of Science* 57: 755–779.

Dudman, V. [1992] "Probability and Assertion," *Analysis* 52: 204–211.

Earman, J. [1992] *Bayes or Bust?*, Cambridge MA: MIT Press.

Edgington, D. [1992] "Validity, Uncertainty and Vagueness," *Analysis* 52: 193–204.

Edgington, D. [1995] "On Conditionals," *Mind* 104: 235–329.

Edgington, D. [1997a] "Vagueness by Degrees," in R. Keefe and P. Smith (eds.) *Vagueness: A Reader*, Cambridge MA: MIT Press, pp. 294–316.

Edgington, D. [1997b] "Commentary," in M. Woods, *Conditionals* (edited by D. Wiggins), Oxford: Oxford University Press, pp. 95–137.

Edgington, D. [2001] "Conditionals," in L. Goble (ed.) *The Blackwell Guide to Philosophical Logic*, Oxford: Blackwell, pp. 385–414.

Égré, P. and Cozic, M. [2011] "If-Clauses and Probability Operators," *Topoi* 30: 17–29.

Égré, P. and Cozic, M. [2014] "Conditionals," in M. Aloni and P. Dekker (eds.) *Handbook of Semantics*, Cambridge: Cambridge University Press, in press.

Elqayam, S. [2006] "The Collapse Illusion Effect: A Pragmatic–Semantic Illusion of Truth and Paradox," *Thinking and Reasoning* 12: 144–180.

Elqayam, S., Bonnefon, J.-F., and Over, D. E. (eds.) [2013] *Basic and Applied Perspectives for New Paradigm Psychology of Reasoning*, Special Issue of *Thinking and Reasoning* 19.

Elqayam, S. and Over, D. E. [2013] "New Paradigm Psychology of Reasoning," *Thinking and Reasoning* 19: 249–265.

Etlin, D. [2009] "The Problem of Noncounterfactual Conditionals," *Philosophy of Science* 76: 676–688.

Evans, J. St. B. T. [2002] "Logic and Human Reasoning: An Assessment of the Deduction Paradigm," *Psychological Bulletin* 128:978–996.

Evans, J. St. B. T., Handley, S. J., Neilens, H., and Over, D. E. [2007] "Thinking about Conditionals: A Study of Individual Differences," *Memory and Cognition* 35: 1759–1771.

Evans, J. St. B. T., Handley, S. J., and Over, D. E. [2003] "Conditionals and Conditional Probability," *Journal of Experimental Psychology: Learning, Memory, and Cognition* 29: 321–355.

Evans, J. St. B. T. and Over, D. E. [1996] *Rationality and Reasoning*, Hove: Psychology Press.

Evans, J. St. B. T. and Over, D. E. [2004] *If*, Oxford: Oxford University Press.

Evans, J. St. B. T., Over, D. E., and Handley, S. J. [2005] "Suppositions, Extensionality, and Conditionals: A Critique of the Mental Model Theory of Johnson-Laird and Byrne [2002]," *Psychological Review* 112: 1040–1052.

Evnine, S. [1999] "Believing Conjunctions," *Synthese* 118: 201–227.

Farrell, R. J. [1986] "Material Implication, Confirmation, and Counterfactuals," *Notre Dame Journal of Formal Logic* 20: 383–394.

Field, H. [2009] "What Is the Normative Role of Logic?" *Proceedings of the Aristotelian Society* (Supplementary Volume) 83: 251–268.

Fillenbaum, S. [1975] "If: Some Uses," *Psychological Research* 37: 245–260.

Fitelson, B. [1999] "The Plurality of Bayesian Measures of Confirmation and the Problem of Measure Sensitivity," *Philosophy of Science* 66: S362–S378.

Foley, R. [1979] "Justified Inconsistent Beliefs," *American Philosophical Quarterly* 16: 247–257.

Foley, R. [1992] "The Epistemology of Belief and the Epistemology of Degrees of Belief," *American Philosophical Quarterly* 29: 111–124.

Fricker, E. [1987] "The Epistemology of Testimony," *Proceedings of the Aristotelian Society* (Supplementary Volume) 61: 57–83.

Fricker, E. [1995] "Telling and Trusting: Reductionism and Anti-Reductionism in the Epistemology of Testimony," *Mind* 104: 393–411.

Fricker, E. [2006] "Testimony and Epistemic Autonomy," in J. Lackey and E. Sosa (eds.) *The Epistemology of Testimony*, Oxford: Oxford University Press, pp. 225–250.

Fugard, A., Pfeifer, N., Mayerhofer, B., and Kleiter, G. [2011] "How People Interpret Conditionals," *Journal of Experimental Psychology: Learning, Memory, and Cognition* 37: 635–648.

Gabbay, D. M. and Woods, J. [2005] *The Reach of Abduction*, Amsterdam: Elsevier.

Gärdenfors, P. [1975] "Qualitative Probability as an Intensional Logic," *Journal of Philosophical Logic* 4: 171–185.

Gärdenfors, P. [1982] "Imaging and Conditionalization," *Journal of Philosophy* 79: 747–760.

Gärdenfors, P. [1988] *Knowledge in Flux*, Cambridge MA: MIT Press.

Gärdenfors, P. [2000] *Conceptual Spaces*, Cambridge MA: MIT Press.

Gärdenfors, P. [2014] *The Geometry of Meaning*, Cambridge MA: MIT Press.

Gauffroy, C. and Barrouillet, P. [2009] "Heuristic and Analytic Processes in Mental Models for Conditionals: An Integrative Developmental Theory," *Developmental Review* 29: 249–282.

Geis, M. L. and Zwicky, A. [1971] "On Invited Inferences," *Linguistic Inquiry* 2: 561–565.

Geis, M. L. and Lycan, W. G. [1993] "Nonconditional Conditionals," *Philosophical Topics* 21: 35–56.

Gibbard, A. [1981] "Two Recent Theories of Conditionals," in Harper, Stalnaker, and Pearce (eds.) [1981], pp. 211–247.

Gilio, A. and Over, D. E. [2012] "The Psychology of Inferring Conditionals from Disjunctions: A Probabilistic Study," *Journal of Mathematical Psychology* 56: 118–131.

Gillies, A. [2004] "Epistemic Conditionals and Conditional Epistemics," *Noûs* 38: 585–616.

Gillies, D. [2000] *Philosophical Theories of Probability*, London: Routledge.

Girotto, V. and Johnson-Laird, P. N. [2004] "The Probability of Conditionals," *Psychologica* 47: 207–225.

Girotto, V. and Johnson-Laird, P. N. [2010] "Conditionals and Probability," in M. Oaksford and N. Chater (eds.) *Cognition and Conditionals*, Oxford: Oxford University Press, pp. 103–115.

Goodman, N. [1955] *Fact, Fiction, and Forecast*, Cambridge MA: Harvard University Press.

Green, M. S. [1998] "Direct Reference and Implicature," *Philosophical Studies* 91: 61–90.

Grice, H. P. [1989a] "Indicative Conditionals," in his *Studies in the Way of Words*, Cambridge MA: Harvard University Press, pp. 58–85.

Grice, H. P. [1989b] "Logic and Conversation," in his *Studies in the Way of Words*, Cambridge MA: Harvard University Press, pp. 22–40.

Hadjichristidis, C., Stevenson, R. J., Over, D. E., Sloman, S. A., Evans, J. St. B. T., and Feeney, A. [2001] "On the Evaluation of 'if p then q' Conditionals," in J. D. Moore and K. Stenning (eds.) *Proceedings of the 23rd Annual Meeting of the Cognitive Science Society*, Edinburgh, pp. 381–386.

Haegeman, L. [2003] "Conditional Clauses: External and Internal Syntax," *Mind and Language* 18: 317–339.

Haegeman, L. [2005] *The Syntax of Negation*, Cambridge: Cambridge University Press.

Hájek, A. [1989] "Probabilities of Conditionals – Revisited," *Journal of Philosophical Logic* 18: 423–428.

Hájek, A. [1994] "Triviality on the Cheap?" in E. Eells and B. Skyrms (eds.) *Probability and Conditionals*, Cambridge: Cambridge University Press, pp. 113–140.

Hájek, A. [2001] "Probability, Logic, and Probability Logic," in L. Goble (ed.) *The Blackwell Guide to Philosophical Logic*, Oxford: Blackwell, pp. 362–384.

Hájek, A. and Hall, N. [1994] "The Hypothesis of the Conditional Construal of Conditional Probability," in E. Eells and B. Skyrms (eds.) *Probability and Conditionals*, Cambridge: Cambridge University Press, pp. 31–46.

Hall, N. [1994] "Back in the CCCP," in E. Eells and B. Skyrms (eds.) *Probability and Conditionals*, Cambridge: Cambridge University Press, pp. 141–160.

Halpern, J. Y. [2003] *Reasoning about Uncertainty*, Cambridge MA: MIT Press.

Harper, W. L. [1976] "Ramsey Test Conditionals and Iterated Belief Change," in W. L. Harper and C. A. Hooker (eds.) *Foundations of Probability Theory, Statistical Inference, and Statistical Theories of Science* (Vol. I), Dordrecht: Reidel, pp. 117–135.

Harper, W. L. [1981] "A Sketch of Some Recent Developments in the Theory of Conditionals," in Harper, Stalnaker, and Pearce (eds.) [1981], pp. 3–38.

Harper, W. L., Stalnaker, R., and Pearce, G. (eds.) [1981] *Ifs: Conditionals, Belief, Decision, Chance, and Time*, Dordrecht: Reidel.

Hawthorne, J. and Makinson, D. [2007] "The Quantitative / Qualitative Watershed for Rules of Uncertain Inference," *Studia Logica* 86: 247–297.

Hertwig, R. and Gigerenzer, G. [1999] "The 'Conjunction Fallacy' Revisited: How Intelligent Inferences Look Like Reasoning Errors," *Journal of Behavioral Decision Making* 12: 275–305.

Heylen, J. and Horsten, L. [2006] "Strict Conditionals: A Negative Result," *Philosophical Quarterly* 56: 536–549.

Hintikka, J. [1968] "The Varieties of Information and Scientific Explanation," in B. van Rootselaar and J. F. Staal (eds.) *Logic, Methodology, and Philosophy of Science III*, Amsterdam: North-Holland, pp. 151–171.

Horn, L. [1989] *A Natural History of Negation*, Chicago: University of Chicago Press.

Horsten, L. and Douven, I. [2008] "Formal Methods in the Philosophy of Science," *Studia Logica* 89: 151–162.

Horwich, P. [1982] *Probability and Evidence*, Cambridge: Cambridge University Press.

Howson, C. [1984] "Bayesianism and Support by Novel Facts," *British Journal for the Philosophy of Science* 35: 245–251.

Howson, C. [1985] "Some Recent Objections to the Bayesian Theory of Support," *British Journal for the Philosophy of Science* 36: 305–309.

Howson, C. [2000] *Hume's Problem*, Oxford: Oxford University Press.

Howson, C. and Urbach, P. [1993] *Scientific Reasoning: The Bayesian Approach* (2nd edn.), La Salle IL: Open Court.

Hunter, D. [1996] "On the Relation between Categorical and Probabilistic Belief," *Noûs* 30: 75–98.

Jackson, F. [1979] "On Assertion and Indicative Conditionals," *Philosophical Review* 88: 565–589. (Reprinted, with postscript, in Jackson (ed.) [1991], pp. 111–135; the page references are to the reprint.)

Jackson, F. [1987] *Conditionals*, Oxford: Blackwell.

Jackson, F. (ed.) [1991] *Conditionals*, Oxford: Oxford University Press.

Jackson, F. [2006] "Indicative Conditionals Revisited," paper delivered at The Chinese University of Hong Kong, 27 March 2006, available at http://phil. arts.cuhk.edu.hk/phidept/TCIVP/jackson/indicative.pdf?mid=25-26.

Jeffrey, R. [2004] *Subjective Probability: The Real Thing*, Cambridge: Cambridge University Press.

Jennings, R. E. [1994] *The Genealogy of Disjunction*, Oxford: Oxford University Press.

Johnson-Laird, P. N. [1983] *Mental Models: Towards a Cognitive Science of Language, Inference, and Consciousness*, Cambridge MA: Harvard University Press.

Johnson-Laird, P. N. [1986] "Conditionals and Mental Models," in E. C. Traugott, A. ter Meulen, J. S. Reilly, and C. A. Ferguson (eds.) *On Conditionals*, Cambridge: Cambridge University Press, pp. 55–75.

Johnson-Laird, P. N. and Byrne, R. M. J. [2002] "Conditionals: A Theory of Meaning, Pragmatics, and Inference," *Psychological Review* 19: 646–678.

Joyce, J. M. [1998] "A Nonpragmatic Vindication of Probabilism," *Philosophy of Science* 65: 575–603.

Joyce, J. M. [1999] *The Foundations of Causal Decision Theory*, Cambridge: Cambridge University Press.

Kahneman, D. and Tversky, A. [1973] "On the Psychology of Prediction," *Psychological Review* 80: 237–251.

Kaplan, M. [1981] "A Bayesian Theory of Rational Acceptance," *Journal of Philosophy* 78: 305–330.

Kaplan, M. [1996] *Decision Theory as Philosophy*, Cambridge: Cambridge University Press.

Kaufmann, S. [2004] "Conditioning Against the Grain," *Journal of Philosophical Logic* 33: 583–606.

Kaufmann, S. [2005] "Conditional Predictions," *Linguistics and Philosophy* 28: 181–231.

Kemeny, J. [1955] "Fair Bets and Inductive Probabilities," *Journal of Symbolic Logic* 20: 263–273.

Kern-Isberner, G. [1999] "Postulates for Conditional Belief Revision," in T. Dean (ed.) *Proceedings of the Sixteenth International Joint Conference on Artificial Intelligence*, San Francisco: Morgan Kaufmann, pp. 186–191.

Kern-Isberner, G. [2001] *Conditionals in Nonmonotonic Reasoning and Belief Revision*, Berlin: Springer.

Khemlani, S., Orenes, I, and Johnson-Laird, P. N. [2012] "Negation: A Theory of its Meaning, Representation, and Use," *Journal of Cognitive Psychology* 24: 541–559.

Kleene, S. C. [1952] *Introduction to Metamathematics*, Amsterdam: North-Holland.

Klein, P. [1985] "The Virtues of Inconsistency," *Monist* 68: 105–135.

Kneale, W. and Kneale, M. [1962] *The Development of Logic*, London: Duckworth.

Koehler, D. J. [1991] "Explanation, Imagination, and Confidence in Judgment," *Psychological Bulletin* 110: 499–519.

Kölbel, M. [2000] "Edgington on Compounds of Conditionals," *Mind* 109: 97–108.

Koralus, P. and Mascarenhas, S. [2013] "The Erotetic Theory of Reasoning: Bridges Between Formal Semantics and the Psychology of Deductive Inference," *Philosophical Perspectives* 27: 312–365.

Koslowski, B., Marasia, J., Chelenza, M., and Dublin, R. [2008] "Information Becomes Evidence when an Explanation Can Incorporate It into a Causal Framework," *Cognitive Development* 23: 472–487.

Kratzer, A. [1986] "Conditionals," in A. M. Farley, P. Farley, and K. E. McCollough (eds.) *Papers from the Parasession on Pragmatics and Grammatical Theory*, Chicago: Chicago Linguistics Society, pp. 115–135.

Kratzer, A. [1991] "Conditionals," in A. von Stechow and D. Wunderlich (eds.) *Semantik: Ein internationales Handbuch zeitgenössischer Forschung/Semantics: An International Handbook of Contemporary Research*, Berlin: de Gruyter, pp. 651–656.

Kratzer, A. [2012] *Modals and Conditionals*, Oxford: Oxford University Press.

Kraus, S., Lehmann, D., and Magidor, M. [1990] "Nonmonotonic Reasoning, Preferential Models and Cumulative Logics," *Artificial Intelligence* 44: 167–207.

Krzyżanowska, K. H. [2012] "Ambiguous Conditionals," in P. Stalmaszczyk (ed.) *Philosophical and Formal Approaches to Linguistic Analysis*, Frankfurt: Ontos Verlag, pp. 315–332.

Krzyżanowska, K. H. [2013] "Belief Ascription and the Ramsey Test," *Synthese* 190: 21–36.

Krzyżanowska, K. H. [2015] *Between "If" and "Then,"* PhD dissertation, University of Groningen.

Krzyżanowska, K. H., Wenmackers, S., and Douven, I. [2013] "Conditionals, Inference, and Evidentiality," *Journal of Logic, Language, and Information* 22: 315–334.

Krzyżanowska, K. H., Wenmackers, S., and Douven, I. [2014] "Rethinking Gibbard's Riverboat Argument," *Studia Logica* 102: 771–792.

Kuipers, T. A. F. [2000] *From Instrumentalism to Constructive Realism*, Dordrecht: Kluwer.

Kulakova, E., Aichhorn, M., Schurz, M., Kronbichler, M., and Perner, J. [2013] "Processing Counterfactual and Hypothetical Conditionals: An fMRI Study," *Neuroimage* 72: 265–271.

Kyburg, H. [1961] *Probability and the Logic of Rational Belief*, Middletown CT: Wesleyan University Press.

Kyburg, H. [1970] "Conjunctivitis," in M. Swain (ed.) *Induction, Acceptance and Rational Belief*, Dordrecht: Reidel, pp. 55–82.

Kyburg, H. [1990] *Science and Reason*, Oxford: Oxford University Press.

Kyburg, H. [1997] "The Rule of Adjunction and Reasonable Inference," *Journal of Philosophy* 94: 109–125.

Kyburg, H. and Teng, C. M. [2001] *Uncertain Inference*, Cambridge: Cambridge University Press.

Lackey, J. [2007] "Norms of Assertion," *Noûs* 41: 594–626.

Lance, M. [1991] "Probabilistic Dependence among Conditionals," *Philosophical Review* 100: 269–276.

Lecas, J. F. and Barrouillet, P. [1999] "Understanding Conditional Rules in Childhood and Adolescence: A Mental Models Approach," *Current Psychology of Cognition* 18: 363–396.

Lehrer, K. [1975] "Induction, Rational Acceptance, and Minimally Inconsistent Sets," in G. Maxwell and R. M. Anderson (eds.) *Induction, Probability, and Confirmation* (Minnesota Studies in the Philosophy of Science, Vol. VI), Minneapolis: University of Minnesota Press, pp. 295–323.

Lehrer, K. [1990] *Theory of Knowledge*, London: Routledge.

Leitgeb, H. [2007] "Beliefs in Conditionals vs. Conditional Beliefs," *Topoi* 26: 115–132.

Levi, I. [1974] "On Indeterminate Probabilities," *Journal of Philosophy* 71: 391–418.

Levinson, S. [1983] *Pragmatics*, Cambridge: Cambridge University Press.

Lewis, D. K. [1973a] *Counterfactuals*, Oxford: Blackwell.

Lewis, D. K. [1973b] "Causation," *Journal of Philosophy* 70: 556–567.

Lewis, D. K. [1975] "Adverbs of Quantification," in E. L. Keenan (ed.) *Formal Semantics of Natural Language*, Cambridge: Cambridge University Press, pp. 3–15.

Lewis, D. K. [1976] "Probabilities of Conditionals and Conditional Probabilities," *Philosophical Review* 85: 297–315. (Reprinted, with postscript, in his *Philosophical Papers*, Vol. II, Oxford: Oxford University Press, 1986, pp. 133–156; the page references are to the reprint.)

Lewis, D. K. [1979] "Counterfactual Dependence and Time's Arrow," *Noûs* 13: 455–476. (Reprinted, with postscripts, in his *Philosophical Papers*, Vol. II, Oxford: Oxford University Press, 1986, pp. 32–66; the page reference is to the reprint.)

Lewis, D. K. [1981] "Ordering Semantics and Premise Semantics for Counterfactuals," *Journal of Philosophical Logic* 10: 217–234.

Lewis, D. K. [1986] "Causal Explanation," in his *Philosophical Papers* (Vol. II), Oxford: Oxford University Press, pp. 214–240.

Lindström, S. [1996] "The Ramsey Test and the Indexicality of Conditionals: A Proposed Resolution of Gärdenfors' Paradox," in A. Fuhrmann and H. Rott (eds.) *Logic, Action, and Information*, Berlin: W. de Gruyter, pp. 208–228.

Lindström, S. and Rabinowicz, W. [1995] "The Ramsey Test Revisited," in Crocco, Fariñas del Cerro, and Herzig (eds.) [1995], pp. 147–191.

Lipton, P. [2004] *Inference to the Best Explanation* (2nd edn.), London: Routledge.

Lombrozo, T. [2007] "Simplicity and Probability in Causal Explanation," *Cognitive Psychology* 55: 232–257.

Lowe, E. J. [1996] "Conditional Probability and Conditional Beliefs," *Mind* 105: 603–615.

Lycan, W. G. [2001] *Real Conditionals*, Oxford: Oxford University Press.

Lynch, M. P. [2009] *Truth as One and Many*, Oxford: Oxford University Press.

Machery, E., Mallon, R., Nichols, S., and Stich, S. P. [2004] "Semantics, Cross-Cultural Style," *Cognition* 92: 1–12.

MacFarlane, J. [2012] "Relativism," in D. Graff Fara and G. Russell (eds.) *The Routledge Companion to the Philosophy of Language*, New York: Routledge, pp. 132–142.

Mackie, J. L. [1973] *Truth, Probability and Paradox: Studies in Philosophical Logic*, Oxford: Oxford University Press.

Makinson, D. [1965] "The Paradox of the Preface," *Analysis* 25: 205–207.

Martin, D. [1998] "Mathematical Evidence," in H. G. Dales and G. Olivieri (eds.) *Truth in Mathematics*, Oxford: Oxford University Press, pp. 215–231.

Mates, B. [1953] *Stoic Logic*, Berkeley: University of California Press.

McDermott, M. [1996] "On the Truth Conditions of Certain 'If'-Sentences," *Philosophical Review* 105: 1–37.

McGee, V. [1985] "A Counterexample to Modus Ponens," *Journal of Philosophy* 82: 462–471.

McGee, V. [1989] "Conditional Probabilities and Compounds of Conditionals," *Philosophical Review* 98: 485–541.

McGrew, T. [2003] "Confirmation, Heuristics, and Explanatory Reasoning," *British Journal for the Philosophy of Science* 54: 553–567.

Mellor, D. H. [1993] "How to Believe a Conditional," *Journal of Philosophy* 90: 233–248.

Meyer, J.-J. and van der Hoek, W. [1995] *Epistemic Logic for AI and Computer Science*, Cambridge: Cambridge University Press.

Milne, P. [1991] "A Dilemma for Subjective Bayesians – and How to Resolve it," *Philosophical Studies* 62: 307–314.

Milne, P. [1997] "Bruno de Finetti and the Logic of Conditional Events," *British Journal for the Philosophy of Science* 48: 195–232.

Milne, P. [2012] "Indicative Conditionals, Conditional Probabilities, and the 'Defective Truth-Table': A Request for More Experiments," *Thinking and Reasoning* 18: 196–224.

Miyamoto, J. M., Lundell, J. W., and Tu, S. [1989] "Anomalous Conditional Judgments and Ramsey's Thought Experiment," in *Proceedings of the 11th Annual Conference of the Cognitive Science Society*, Hillsdale NJ: Erlbaum, pp. 212–220.

Moser, P. and Tlumac, J. [1985] "Two Paradoxes of Rational Acceptance," *Erkenntnis* 23: 127–141.

Moutier, S. and Houdé, O. [2003] "Judgement under Uncertainty and Conjunction Fallacy Inhibition Training," *Thinking and Reasoning* 9: 185–201.

Nelkin, D. [2000] "The Lottery Paradox, Knowledge, and Rationality," *Philosophical Review* 109: 373–409.

Nolan, D. [2003] "Defending a Possible-Worlds Account of Indicative Conditionals," *Philosophical Studies* 116: 215–269.

Nute, D. and Cross, C. B. [2001] "Conditional Logic," in D. M. Gabbay and F. Guenthner (eds.) *Handbook of Philosophical Logic*, Vol. 4 (2nd edn.), Dordrecht: Reidel, pp. 1–98.

Oaksford, M. and Chater, N. [2003] "Conditional Probability and the Cognitive Science of Conditional Reasoning," *Mind and Language* 18: 359–379.

Oaksford, M. and Chater, N. [2007] *Bayesian Rationality*, Oxford: Oxford University Press.

Oberauer, K., Weidenfeld, A., and Fischer, K. [2007] "What Makes Us Believe a Conditional? The Roles of Covariation and Causality," *Thinking and Reasoning* 13: 340–369.

Oberauer, K. and Wilhelm, O. [2003] "The Meaning(s) of Conditionals: Conditional Probabilities, Mental Models and Personal Utilities," *Journal of Experimental Psychology: Learning, Memory and Cognition* 29: 688–693.

Oddie, G. [2007] "Truthlikeness," in E. N. Zalta (ed.) *Stanford Encyclopedia of Philosophy*, available at http://plato.stanford.edu/entries/truthlikeness/.

Okasha, S. [2000] "Van Fraassen's Critique of Inference to the Best Explanation," *Studies in History and Philosophy of Science* 31: 691–710.

Olsen, N. S. [2014] *Making Ranking Theory Useful for Psychology of Reasoning*, PhD dissertation, University of Konstanz.

Olsson, E. J. [2005] *Against Coherence*, Oxford: Oxford University Press.

Oppenheimer, D. M., Meyvis, T., and Davidenko, N. [2009] "Instructional Manipulation Checks: Detecting Satisficing to Increase Statistical Power," *Journal of Experimental Social Psychology* 45: 867–872.

Over, D. E. [2009] "New Paradigm Psychology of Reasoning," *Thinking and Reasoning* 15: 431–438.

Over, D. E., Douven, I., and Verbrugge, S. [2013] "Scope Ambiguities and Conditionals," *Thinking and Reasoning* 19: 284–307.

Over, D. E. and Evans, J. St. B. T. [2003] "The Probability of Conditionals: The Psychological Evidence," *Mind and Language* 18: 340–358.

Over, D. E., Evans, J. St. B. T., and Elqayam, S. [2010] "Conditionals and Non-Constructive Reasoning," in M. Oaksford and N. Chater (eds.) *Cognition and Conditionals*, Oxford: Oxford University Press, pp. 135–151.

Over, D. E., Hadjichristidis, C., Evans, J. St. B. T., Handley, S. J., and Sloman, S. A. [2007] "The Probability of Causal Conditionals," *Cognitive Psychology* 54: 62–97.

Pfeifer, N. and Kleiter, G. D. [2010] "The Conditional in Mental Probability Logic," in M. Oaksford and N. Chater (eds.) *Cognition and Conditionals*, Oxford: Oxford University Press, pp. 153–173.

Politzer, G. and Bonnefon, J.-F. [2006] "Two Varieties of Conditionals and Two Kinds of Defeaters Help Reveal Two Fundamental Types of Reasoning," *Mind and Language* 21: 484–503.

Politzer, G. and Bourmaud, G. [2002] "Deductive Reasoning from Uncertain Premises," *British Journal of Psychology* 93: 345–381.

Politzer, G., Over, D. E., and Baratgin, J. [2010] "Betting on Conditionals," *Thinking and Reasoning* 16: 172–197.

Pollock, J. [1976] *Subjunctive Reasoning*, Dordrecht: Reidel.

Pollock, J. [1981] "A Refined Theory of Counterfactuals," *Journal of Philosophical Logic* 10: 239–266.

Pollock, J. [1990] *Nomic Probability and the Foundations of Induction*, Oxford: Oxford University Press.

Popper, K. R. and Miller, D. [1983] "A Proof of the Impossibility of Inductive Probability," *Nature* 302: 687–688.

Putnam, H. [1973] "Meaning and Reference," *Journal of Philosophy* 70: 699–711.

Quine, W. V. O. [1959] *Methods of Logic* (revised edn.), New York: Holt, Rinehart and Winston.

Quine, W. V. O. [1969] "Epistemology Naturalized," in his *Ontological Relativity and Other Essays*, New York: Columbia University Press, pp. 69–90.

Ramsey, F. P. [1926/1990] "Truth and Probability," in his *Philosophical Papers*, edited by D. H. Mellor, Cambridge: Cambridge University Press, 1990, pp. 52–94.

Ramsey, F. P. [1929/1990] "General Propositions and Causality," in his *Philosophical Papers*, edited by D. H. Mellor, Cambridge: Cambridge University Press, 1990, pp. 145–163.

Récanati, F. [2000] *Oratio Obliqua: An Essay on Metarepresentation*, Cambridge MA: MIT Press.

Récanati, F. [2003] "Embedded Implicatures," *Philosophical Perspectives* 17: 299–332.

Regier, T. [1996] *The Human Semantic Potential*, Cambridge MA: MIT Press.

Regier, T., Kay, P., and Khetarpal, N. [2007] "Color Naming Reflects Optimal Partitions of Color Space," *Proceedings of the National Academy of Sciences* 104: 1436–1441.

Reips, U.-D. [2002] "Standards for Internet-Based Experimenting," *Experimental Psychology* 49: 243–256.

Rieger, A. [2006] "A Simple Theory of Conditionals," *Analysis* 66: 233–240.

Rieger, A. [2013] "Conditionals Are Material: The Positive Arguments," *Synthese* 190: 3161–3174.

Roche, W. [2012] "Transitivity and Intransitivity in Evidential Support: Some Further Results," *Review of Symbolic Logic* 5: 259–268.

Rosenkrantz, R. D. [1992] "The Justification of Induction," *Philosophy of Science* 59: 527–539.

Rott, H. [1986] "Ifs, Though, and Because," *Erkenntnis* 25: 345–370.

Rott, H. [1989] "Conditionals and Theory Change: Revisions, Expansions, and Additions," *Synthese* 81: 91–113.

Ryan, S. [1996] "The Epistemic Virtues of Consistency," *Synthese* 109: 121–141.

Sanford, D. H. [1989] *If P, then Q*, London: Routledge.

Schupbach, J. N. [2011] "Comparing Probabilistic Measures of Explanatory Power," *Philosophy of Science* 78: 813–829.

Schurz, G. [1998] "Probabilistic Semantics for Delgrande's Conditional Logic and a Counterexample to his Default Logic," *Artificial Intelligence* 102: 81–95.

Schurz, G. and Thorn, P. D. [2012] "Reward versus Risk in Uncertain Inference: Theorems and Simulations," *Review of Symbolic Logic* 5: 574–612.

Segerberg, K. [1989] "Notes on Conditional Logic," *Studia Logica* 48: 157–168.

Sinnott-Armstrong, W., Moor, J., and Fogelin, R. [1986] "A Defense of Modus Ponens," *Journal of Philosophy* 82: 296–300.

Skorupski, J. [1989] *John Stuart Mill*, London: Routledge.

Skyrms, B. [1980] *Causal Necessity*, New Haven CT: Yale University Press.

Smith, M. [2010] "A Generalised Lottery Paradox for Infinite Probability Spaces," *British Journal for the Philosophy of Science* 61: 821–831.

Soames, S. [2003] *Philosophical Analysis in the Twentieth Century: The Age of Meaning* (Vol. II), Princeton: Princeton University Press.

Sobel, J. H. [1987] "Self-Doubts and Dutch Strategies," *Australasian Journal of Philosophy* 65: 56–81.

Sperber, D. and Wilson, D. [1986] *Relevance*, Oxford: Blackwell.

Spohn, W. [2013] "A Ranking-Theoretic Approach to Conditionals," *Cognitive Science* 37: 1074–1106.

Stalnaker, R. [1968] "A Theory of Conditionals," in N. Rescher (ed.) *Studies in Logical Theory*, Oxford: Blackwell, pp. 98–112.

Stalnaker, R. [1970] "Probability and Conditionals," *Philosophy of Science* 37: 64–80.

Stalnaker, R. [1975] "Indicative Conditionals," *Philosophia* 5: 269–286.

Stalnaker, R. [1976] "Letter to van Fraassen," in W. L. Harper and C. A. Hooker (eds.) *Foundations of Probability Theory, Statistical Inference, and Statistical Theories of Science* (Vol. I), Dordrecht: Reidel, pp. 302–306.

Stalnaker, R. [1984] *Inquiry*, Cambridge MA: MIT Press.

Stalnaker, R. and Jeffrey, R. [1994] "Conditionals as Random Variables," in E. Eells and B. Skyrms (eds.) *Probability and Conditionals*, Cambridge: Cambridge University Press, pp. 31–46.

Starr, W. B. [2014] "What 'If'?" *Philosophers' Imprint* 14: 1–27, available at `http://hdl.handle.net/2027/spo.3521354.0014.010`.

Swinburne, R. [2001] *Epistemic Justification*, Oxford: Oxford University Press.

Teller, P. [1973] "Conditionalization and Observation," *Synthese* 26: 218–258.

Tentori, K., Crupi, V., and Russo, S. [2013] "On the Determinants of the Conjunction Fallacy: Probability versus Inductive Confirmation," *Journal of Experimental Psychology: General* 142: 235–255.

Thorn, P. and Schurz, G. [2015] "Ampliative Inference under Varied Entropy Levels," *Journal of Applied Logic*, in press.

Tomasello, M. [2003] *Constructing a Language: A Usage-Based Theory of Language Acquisition*, Cambridge MA: Harvard University Press.

Tomasello, M. [2008] *Origins of Human Communication*, Cambridge MA: MIT Press.

Turri, J. [2011] "The Express Knowledge Account of Assertion," *Australasian Journal of Philosophy* 89: 37–45.

Tversky, A. and Kahneman, D. [1983] "Extension versus Intuitive Reasoning: The Conjunction Fallacy in Probability Judgment," *Psychological Review* 90: 293–315.

Unterhuber, M. [2013] *Possible Worlds Semantics for Indicative and Counterfactual Conditionals?*, Frankfurt: Ontos Verlag.

van Fraassen, B. C. [1976] "Probabilities of Conditionals," in W. L. Harper and C. A. Hooker (eds.) *Foundations of Probability Theory, Statistical*

Inference, and Statistical Theories of Science (Vol. I), Dordrecht: Reidel, pp. 261–301.

van Fraassen, B. C. [1981] "A Problem for Relative Information Minimizers in Probability Kinematics," *British Journal for the Philosophy of Science* 32: 375–379.

van Fraassen, B. C. [1988] "The Problem of Old Evidence," in D. F. Austin (ed.) *Philosophical Analysis*, Dordrecht: Reidel, pp. 153–165.

van Fraassen, B. C. [1989] *Laws and Symmetry*, Oxford: Oxford University Press.

van Wijnbergen-Huitink, J. [2008] *Modals, Conditionals and Compositionality*, PhD dissertation, Radboud University Nijmegen.

Verbrugge, S., Dieussaert, K., Schaeken, W., Smessaert, H., and Van Belle, W. [2007] "Pronounced Inferences: A Study on Inferential Conditionals," *Thinking and Reasoning* 13: 105–133.

von Fintel, K. [2011] "Conditionals," in K. von Heusinger, C. Maienborn, and P. Portner (eds.) *Semantics: An International Handbook of Meaning*, Berlin: de Gruyter, pp. 1515–1538.

von Fintel, K. [2012] "Subjunctive Conditionals," in G. Russell and D. Graff Fara (eds.) *The Routledge Companion to the Philosophy of Language*, New York: Routledge, pp. 466–477.

von Wright, G. H. [1957] *Logical Studies*, London: Routledge and Kegan Paul.

Wason, P. C. [1968] "Reasoning about a Rule," *Quarterly Journal of Experimental Psychology* 20: 273–281.

Wason, P. C. and Shapiro, D. [1971] "Natural and Contrived Experience in a Reasoning Problem," *Quarterly Journal of Experimental Psychology* 23: 63–71.

Weidenfeld, A., Oberauer, K., and Horning, R. [2005] "Causal and Non-Causal Conditionals: An Integrated Model of Interpretation and Reasoning," *Quarterly Journal of Experimental Psychology* 58: 1479–1513.

Weiner, M. [2005] "Must We Know What We Say?" *Philosophical Review* 114: 227–251.

Weintraub, R. [2001] "The Lottery: A Paradox Regained and Resolved," *Synthese* 129: 439–449.

Weisberg, J. [2009] "Locating IBE in the Bayesian Framework," *Synthese* 167: 125–143.

Williams, J. R. G. [2008] "Conversation and Conditionals," *Philosophical Studies* 138: 211–223.

Williamson, T. [1996] "Knowing and Asserting," *Philosophical Review* 105: 489–523.

Williamson, T. [2000] *Knowledge and Its Limits*, Oxford: Oxford University Press.

Williamson, T. [2009] "Conditionals and Actuality," *Erkenntnis* 70: 135–150.

Woods, M. [1997] *Conditionals* (edited by D. Wiggins), Oxford: Oxford University Press.

Wright, C. [1994] *Truth and Objectivity*, Cambridge MA: Harvard University Press.

Zhao, J., Shah, A., and Osherson, D. [2009] "On the Provenance of Judgments of Conditional Probability," *Cognition* 113: 26–36.

Index

Index

For EU product safety concerns, contact us at Calle de José Abascal, 56–1°,
28003 Madrid, Spain or eugpsr@cambridge.org.